Tales of the
NORSE GODS
AND
HEROES

TALES OF THE

NORSE GODS AND HEROES

Retold by

**BARBARA LEONIE
PICARD**

Illustrated by

KIDDELL-MONROE

London
OXFORD UNIVERSITY PRESS

Oxford University Press, Ely House, London W. 1

GLASGOW NEW YORK TORONTO MELBOURNE WELLINGTON
CAPE TOWN SALISBURY IBADAN NAIROBI DAR ES SALAAM LUSAKA ADDIS ABABA
BOMBAY CALCUTTA MADRAS KARACHI LAHORE DACCA
KUALA LUMPUR SINGAPORE HONG KONG TOKYO

First edition 1953
Reprinted 1958, 1961, 1967, 1970

0192745131

PRINTED IN GREAT BRITAIN
AT THE UNIVERSITY PRESS, OXFORD
BY VIVIAN RIDLER
PRINTER TO THE UNIVERSITY

For

CARLIE

Preface

In this book are some of the stories told by the Norsemen who lived in Scandinavia from about 2,000 to 1,000 years ago. We know them better, perhaps, as the Vikings, who sailed their ships along the coasts of Europe, plundering and laying waste, and, finally, settling and making their homes in France, in the Netherlands, in England, Ireland, and the Orkneys, and in bleak little Iceland. Even as far as Greenland they sailed, and to America, long before Columbus.

The people of the northlands were a nation of bold warriors and fine courageous women, who admired above all things strength in battle and bravery against great odds, and considered themselves disgraced for ever if they let a wrong to themselves or to their families go unavenged. They were a simple people, too, who enjoyed the simple things; good food and plenty of it, good ale to drink, and a crafty trick that could make them laugh.

In the first part of the book are the stories of their gods; gods who were even such as every Norseman longed to be, brave, dauntless warriors or cunning tricksters, with their lovely, loyal wives; for ever striving against the hated giants who were the pitiless northern snows and frosts, and the grim northern mountains.

In the second part are tales of some of the Norse heroes, tales such as the Norsemen loved to tell and listen to on the long winter evenings of the northern lands.

Svipdag and Menglod may be considered as a fairy story. It has all that a good fairy story needs: the brave young prince, the enchanted princess, and the wicked stepmother. And even if Svipdag's difficulties do solve themselves a little easily in the end, it is none the less a good tale for all that.

The story of Völund was carried by the Vikings into many lands. In England we know him as Wayland Smith who had his forge in a cave close to the White Horse in Berkshire.

Siegfried is the great hero of the German people. Many hundreds of years ago they were already telling how he fought with the dragon and owned a magic sword. The tale of his exploits travelled northwards into Scandinavia, where some details were lost and others added; and as Sigurd, Siegfried became the best-loved hero of the northlands, whose deeds were told and sung wherever men enjoyed a good tale or a fine song.

Ragnar Lodbrok really lived and was a Viking. Though little enough is known about his life, many stories grew up around his name, though most of them were no more than legends. Two of these legends are told here: his slaying of the dragon, and his marriage with Sigurd's daughter.

The last story in the book, *The Tale of Nornagest*, although itself a legend, touches history; for one of the characters in the story is King Olaf Tryggvason, who lived from about 969 to 1000 and converted Norway to the Christian faith. He is supposed to have been baptized by a hermit in the Scilly Isles while he was plundering along the English coast.

Some of the Norse names in the stories may seem a little difficult, both to spell and to pronounce; but at the end of the book there is a note on the pronunciation—it would be wise to read it before the stories—and also an alphabetical list of all names mentioned in the tales, with a note about each one. With the help of these, the difficulties should be much less.

Contents

PART ONE

Tales of the Norse Gods

I	The Beginning of All Things	1
II	The Building of the Citadel	9
III	The Mead of Poetry	15
IV	Idunn and the Golden Apples	25
V	Niord and Skadi	35
VI	Frey and Gerd	41
VII	The Lady of the Vanir	49
VIII	The Six Gifts	58
IX	The Theft of Miollnir	67
X	The Children of Loki	75
XI	Frigg and the Gift of Flax	82
XII	Geirröd and Agnar	87
XIII	Thor's Journey to Utgard	92
XIV	The Cauldron of Hymir	107
XV	Thor's Battle with the Giant Hrungnir	113
XVI	How Loki Outwitted a Giant	120
XVII	Odin and Rind	126
XVIII	The Death of Balder	133
XIX	How Loki was Cast Out by the Gods	140
XX	The End of All Things	150

ix

CONTENTS

PART TWO

Tales of the Norse Heroes

I   Svipdag and Menglod   155

II Völund the Smith   163

III The Story of the Volsungs   179

IV The Two Wives of Ragnar Lodbrok   288

V   The Tale of Nornagest   299

An Alphabetical List of Names mentioned in the Stories   305

A Note on Pronunciation   311

Part One

TALES OF THE NORSE GODS

I

The Beginning of All Things

THIS is the story the Norsemen told of how the world
began. In the very beginning of things there was only a vast
chasm, Ginnungagap, with, to the north of it, Niflheim, the
home of mist and darkness, and to the south, Muspellheim,
the home of burning fire.

When it touched the cold that rose from the chasm, the
damp mist from Niflheim turned to blocks of ice which fell
with a terrible sound into Ginnungagap; and as the fiery
sparks from Muspellheim fell upon these ice blocks they sent
up steam which turned to hoar-frost as it rose into the cold
air. And thus, with blocks of ice and with rime, the chasm
was slowly filled.

And out of the hoar-frost two figures took shape; one was a giant man, Ymir, the first of the ice-giants and the father of all evil creatures, and the other was the cow, Audumla. Ymir drank the milk of the cow and grew strong and flourished; while for her food, Audumla licked the blocks of ice for the salt that was in them. As the ice was melted by her warm tongue and her breath, at the end of the first day the hair of a head appeared. At the end of the second day the head and shoulders could be seen; and when the third day was passed, Buri the divine stepped forth from the ice. He was good and beautiful, and he was the father of all kindly creatures. And to him was born, by the means of magic spells, Borr, his mighty son.

Meanwhile, as Ymir slept, from the sweat that trickled from his body there sprang up another giant man and a giant-maiden; and from the soles of his feet came forth six-headed Thrudgelmir.

And there was strife between the good and evil beings, between the giants and Buri and his son Borr; and though the giants increased in numbers, they could in no way prevail, and for a long time the victory went neither to good nor to evil. But one day Borr took to wife a friendly giant-maiden named Bestla, and a son was born to them called Odin, who was very powerful, and mightier even than his father and his brothers.

And in time Odin led his brothers against the giants and slew Ymir, so that all the giants were afraid at the loss of their leader and would have fled away, but that they were drowned in the blood which poured from his wounds. Only two of them escaped, Bergelmir, son of six-headed Thrudgelmir, and his wife; and they fled to the very edge of space, where they made themselves a home and called it Iotunheim, the land of the giant people. And from them were descended all the frost and storm and mountain giants that later troubled the world.

Ymir's body was then rolled into the chasm and from it Odin created the universe. First, in the very centre, he formed Midgard, the world of men, from the flesh of the dead giant, and fenced it all about with his bushy eyebrows for a protection. From his bones Odin made the hills and mountains, from his teeth the stones and rocks, and from his curly hair the grass and trees and shrubs. And all around Midgard, like a sea, flowed Ymir's blood, and beyond this sea lay Iotunheim. Over all, as the sky, Odin set Ymir's skull, resting it upon the shoulders of four strong dwarfs, North, South, East, and West, that it might for ever remain in its place; and between Midgard and the hollow vault that was the sky, Odin scattered Ymir's brains as the softly drifting clouds.

Then, so that there should be light in this world that he had made, both by day and by night, Odin took sparks from Muspellheim and flung them across the sky for stars, and two larger sparks he set in two golden chariots to be the sun and the moon. In the chariot of the sun he placed a beautiful maiden to rule over the light of the day, while to a lovely youth he gave power over the moon. But they were not allowed to remain shining peacefully in the sky, for as soon as the giants spied them from far Iotunheim, they sent two great wolves, Skoll and Hati, to devour them, so that there might be darkness in the world once more. And that is why the sun and the moon are never still in their places, but must continually move across the sky, for ever flying from the hungry wolves.

When their first task of creation was accomplished, Odin and the other gods looked at the world which they had made, and they saw that creatures like maggots had bred in Ymir's

3

flesh, and crawled about above and below the earth. Some of these creatures were good and white and shining, and these the gods made into the elves of light, giving them the sunshine and the flowers and growing things to care for, and making them a home in Alfheim, between the earth and the sky. The other creatures were dark and misshapen, and of them the gods made the elves of darkness, to live for ever below the ground, mining gold and precious stones; and they became cunning workmen, skilled in all manner of crafts. But no one of them might ever come upon the earth except by night, for one ray of sunlight falling across his dark features would turn him to stone.

On a broad plain above the earth lay Asgard, where the gods lived. Here was their council chamber, and the great field where they met; and here, too, each had his own home, fair and bright. Bifrost, the rainbow, was the bridge between Asgard and Midgard, the earth, and along this three-coloured way would the gods walk to and fro.

At the will of Odin there came into being a great ash-tree, Yggdrasill, whose topmost branches overhung his halls. This tree had three roots, one in Midgard, another in Niflheim, and the third in Asgard itself. At each root there flowed a spring; that in Midgard was known as Mimir's well, where wisdom and understanding were stored under the care of the giant Mimir; and that in dark Niflheim as Hvergelmir, and beside this pool of Hvergelmir lived a dragon which gnawed night and day at the root of the tree, seeking ever to destroy it. But the spring that flowed by the root that was in Asgard was called the fountain of Urd, and on it swam two holy swans. This fountain was guarded by the Norns, three sisters who knew the past, the present, and the future, and each day they sprinkled the leaves of Yggdrasill with pure water from their well.

On the very top of Yggdrasill, above Odin's halls, brooded a mighty eagle with a hawk perched upon its head; and along the wide branches walked and browsed four stags and the goat Heidrun, who gave mead instead of milk for the gods to drink. A squirrel scurried up and down the tree, carrying tales and words of unfriendliness between the eagle and the dragon which lived by Hvergelmir, until they grew to hate each other.

In Midgard the flowers blossomed and the earth grew green and lovely, but there were as yet no men to enjoy this pleasant home that had been made for them. And then one day, as Odin walked along the seashore with Hönir, the bright god, his brother, and with Loki who ruled the fire, they saw two trees standing straight and tall. And Odin touched them and gave them spirit and human life; from Hönir they received sense and movement; while Loki laid his hands on them and gave them warmth and beauty and red blood to flow in their veins. And there on the seashore stood Ask and Embla, the first man and woman to be created; and from them were descended all other men and women.

The gods of the Norsemen were the Aesir and the Vanir. The Vanir were the gods of nature: Niord, the god of the shore and the shallow summer sea; and his son and daughter, Frey and Freyia, Frey who ruled over the elves of light and Freyia the goddess of love and beauty; and Aegir, the lord of the deep and stormy seas, with Ran his wife, who caught sailors in her net and drowned them. Aegir and Ran were not truly of the kindly Vanir, for they were cruel and more akin to the giants, but like the Vanir, they ruled over nature and were on good terms with all the other gods.

The Aesir were the gods who cared for men; Odin the Allfather, king of all the gods, wise and just and understanding; and Frigg, his queen, who presided over human marriages; Hönir, Odin's brother, the shining god, who lived among the Vanir; large, noisy Thor, the god of thunder, Odin's son, who always had a special corner in his heart for the peasants and the poor and the dispossessed; Tyr, the brave god of war; Balder and Höd, the twin sons of Odin and Frigg, Balder the god of daylight, who was the most beautiful of all the gods, and Höd who was blind and ruled over the hours of darkness; Hermod, Odin's messenger; and Heimdall, the divine watchman who kept guard over Bifrost, the bridge between Asgard and the world.

And lastly there was Loki, who was neither of the Aesir nor of the Vanir, nor yet of the giant race; crafty red-haired Loki, quick to laugh and quick to change his shape, the god of the fire that burns on the hearth, good and kindly when it wishes, but a merciless destroyer when it leaves its proper place. From the earliest days Odin and Loki had sworn an oath of brotherhood; and it was this which so often saved Loki in later times, when his cunning tricks so much displeased the other gods.

In Asgard Odin had three palaces; in one the gods met in council; and in another stood his throne, Hlidskialf, which served him as a watch-tower from where he might see all that passed not only in Asgard, but in Midgard and Iotunheim, and even in the depths of dark Niflheim, the home of mist, as well. Here would he sit with his two ravens perched upon his shoulders. Each day he sent these birds flying forth across the world and each evening they returned to tell him of the happenings of the day. At his feet would lie his two wolves who followed him like hounds wherever he went in Asgard, and at the feasting would eat the meat that was set before him; for the Allfather lived on mead alone, and no food passed his lips so long as he was among the gods, though when he travelled through Midgard, he lived like other men.

6

Odin's third palace was called Valhall and was set in the midst of a grove of trees whose leaves were gleaming gold. This palace had five hundred and forty doors, and its walls were made of glittering spears and its roof of golden shields. To this hall came all those warriors who had died in battle, when death had passed away from them as a dream, to feast and tell tales of their deeds as living men, and to test their fighting skill on one another with weapons and armour made of imperishable gold. For the Norsemen were great warriors, and they believed that when a battle raged, Odin would send out his warrior-maidens, the Valkyrs, to ride across the sky and fetch the slain to Valhall, where they would be with Odin himself, and feast upon the flesh of the boar Saehrimnir, which, though slaughtered and roasted each day, came back to life each night, and drink of the mead provided by the goat Heidrun. Thus every Norseman longed, when the time came, to die in battle; and his greatest fear was that he should suffer a straw-death, and die in bed, lying on his straw-stuffed mattress. For the spirits of all those who did not die fighting went down to dark Niflheim.

Odin never sought knowledge and wisdom, that he might use them to the good of both gods and men; and one day he went to Mimir's well, the fount of wisdom and understanding, which flowed by that root of the ash-tree Yggdrasill which grew in Midgard, and asked the giant Mimir to let him drink of the magic waters.

Mimir looked long at Odin before he answered, and then he said, 'Even the gods must pay for knowledge.'

'And what is the price of wisdom?' asked Odin.

'Give me one of your eyes as a pledge,' said Mimir.

Unhesitatingly, Odin plucked out one of his eyes and gave it to Mimir, and Mimir let him drink from the well, and straightway Odin was filled with the knowledge of all things

7

past and present, and even into the future could he look. And though his new knowledge gave him joy, it brought sorrow to him also, for he could now tell not only what was past, but also the grief that was to come. Yet he returned to Asgard to use his knowledge to help the other gods and those men who sought his aid.

And Mimir dropped Odin's eye into his well, and it lay there evermore, shining below the water, a proof of Odin's love of wisdom and his goodwill towards mankind.

II

The Building of the Citadel

WHEN Asgard was but newly built, the gods wished for
a strong citadel outside their walls that might withstand the
attacks of the unfriendly giants, should any of them chance
to cross the rainbow bridge Bifrost and reach even to Asgard;
and while they were considering the best way it might be
done, a stone-mason from Iotunheim came by and offered
them his help. From his smiles they saw him, though a giant,
to be no enemy, and they listened to his proposals.

'I can build you,' said the giant, 'a fortress that shall be
proof against any of your enemies, though all the mountain-
giants and all the frost-giants fall upon it as one man. And
this shall be done in no longer than three years. What say
you, Aesir and Vanir, shall I build your citadel for you?'

9

'If indeed your boast is true,' said Odin, 'your work would be much welcomed here. Yet tell us first, what reward will you claim when your task is done?'

'Give to me the sun and the moon from the sky, that they may serve as lamps to light my house, and give me Freyia of the Vanir for my wife, and I will think myself well paid.'

'Well paid would you be indeed,' exclaimed Niord, king of the Vanir, angrily. 'My daughter weds with no giant.'

And all the gods who were present murmured against the stranger's words, that they were presumptuous and over-bearing.

But Odin held up his hand for silence. 'Your demands are great,' he said, 'I wonder will your achievements match them. But even should they, it were a shame to take from the sky the sun and the moon and leave the world of men in darkness.'

The giant shrugged his shoulders. 'That is the payment which I ask, that and no other. If the price is too high, then must you do without your citadel. I care not.'

Odin considered a moment and then he said, 'This is a matter which cannot be decided lightly, it must be debated by the council of the gods.'

So he called the gods to his hall, and they gathered together; all save Thor who, as was often his custom, journeyed in the north, seeking adventure; and they talked long about the giant and his offer. 'It is true that we need a mighty fortress, and if this giant's words are not false, then he can build us what we want, far better than we ourselves could fashion it,' they said. 'But the reward he asks is too great, we cannot give to him the sun and the moon, and Freyia is not for any giant to wed.' And at last they decided, with regrets, that they must refuse the stranger's offer.

Then Loki, god of the firelight, spoke. 'It seems to me,' he said, 'that we should be fools to let this workman go without making him serve us, as well he can if what he boasts is true. He has said that in three years his task will be done, and our citadel standing strong and mighty. Let us say to him that if it is completed in the length of but one winter, we will give him the reward that he asks. Then, if he accepts our conditions, so shall we have our fortress, and so shall we keep the sun and the moon and lovely Freyia, for no builder, however skilled, could finish such a task alone in the space of but one winter.'

'I do not doubt,' said Niord, 'that he will refuse.'

'We can but make the offer,' said Loki. And the other gods agreed with him, and together they went to the giant and told him of their conditions.

'If the fortress is completed,' they said, 'before the first day of summer, and if you have worked alone, without anyone to help you, the sun and the moon and Freyia are yours. What say you to our offer?'

The giant considered, and then he said, 'If you will let me have with me my horse, to help drag the blocks of stone, then will I accept your conditions.'

The gods hesitated, and Odin said, 'If the work is done with the help of a horse, then it is not done alone.'

But Loki laughed. 'What is a horse, brother Odin, but a horse? It has no hands to build with. Let him have his horse to help him carry the stones, he will have work enough with the building to keep him labouring well into the summer.'

So, persuaded by Loki, the gods agreed, and the giant went to fetch his horse. On the first day of winter he returned, leading the horse, a great black stallion which he called Svadilfari, and he set to work at once; and before long it was apparent that the horse was worth two men. Svadilfari had no hands to build with, but all night long he dragged blocks of stone for the giant, and on into the short winter's day; and while the daylight lasted, the giant piled stone upon stone into the semblance of a fortress. And so the work went on apace, while the gods and goddesses watched anxiously, and none more anxiously than Freyia.

And when there were but three nights to go until the first day of summer, the citadel was completed, all but the gate and the gateposts, and Odin called the gods to council, that they might think how best to save the sun and the moon and keep Freyia out of Iotunheim; and they could see no way by which to do it.

'Let him who advised our bargain now find a means to evade it,' said Niord bitterly. 'Loki is ever wont to give us bad advice.'

And they all turned to where Loki sat and demanded that he should think of a trick whereby they might be saved from giving the giant his reward, and threatening him should he fail.

'I will find out a way, never fear,' said Loki. But they were angry with him and all spoke against him, so he rose and went quietly from the hall.

He went to a wood close to where the fortress towered high, and took the shape of a dainty-stepping grey mare; and that evening, when the stone-mason came by with his weary stallion dragging a huge block of stone, Loki left the shadow of the wood and whinnied. Svadilfari looked up and saw the mare and whinnied in reply, while the giant sought to urge him on with his load of rock. But when Svadilfari saw the mare turn as if to trot back into the wood, he broke the traces and galloped after. Away went Loki through the wood like the wind, with Svadilfari after him; and the giant, calling in vain to his horse, following them, but a long way behind.

All that night the giant roamed in the wood, seeking

Svadilfari; but in the morning he had to return alone to his work, dragging the huge blocks of stone himself and setting them in place. And by the first day of summer the work was still not completed, and the gate was yet lacking.

The gods were glad when they saw how the sun and the moon might remain in the sky to give light to men, and how Freyia would not have to go into Iotunheim, and how they had a fine impregnable fortress as well, all but the gate, and that they could build for themselves.

When the giant saw the smiles of the gods, he first grew angry; and then he grew suspicious, remembering the grey mare which had come out from the wood where he had never seen a horse before; and then he grew angrier still, crying to the gods that they had cheated him.

'How have we cheated you?' they asked. 'Prove it to us, and we will pay you all we owe.'

But he could in no way prove his words, and they laughed at him, while he stormed and raged and threatened them so greatly that they ordered him forth from Asgard with all speed. But he would not go, and vowed to be revenged.

At that moment Thor returned from his journeyings, and hearing the giant's shouts, came at once to see what a giant did in the home of the gods. When he heard the threats, he too grew angry, and became very mighty in his wrath. 'Insolent giant,' he thundered in his great voice, 'you shall pay dearly for those words.' And raising high the weapon he carried, he struck down the stone-mason and made an end of him.

Thus did the gods win a stronghold against their enemies and pay no price for it.

But to Loki, as a mare, was born an eight-legged foal, with all the strength of Svadilfari, his sire, and double the swiftness, because of his eight legs; and with all the grace of the grey mare that was the sly god of fire. And when Loki took again his own shape, he called the foal Sleipnir and gave him to Odin to be his horse; and of all horses brave Sleipnir was the best, and much beloved by the Allfather.

III

The Mead of Poetry

AMONG the Norsemen, the skalds, the poets who sang of the deeds of the gods and the heroes at the feasting, and who told tales of war and adventure during the long winter evenings when men were forced to stay at home, were held in high honour and thought to be inspired by the gods themselves. This is the story of the beginning of poetry.

When the world was very young, a dispute arose between the Aesir and the Vanir and they all met together to settle their differences, declaring that nevermore should there be anything but peace between them. And as a pledge of their everlasting friendship each one of them spat into a golden vessel, and from their spittle they fashioned a man and named

15

him Kvasir. This Kvasir was so wise that there was no question that he could not answer, and he went about upon the earth giving freely of his knowledge to all who asked of it, and he was greatly beloved.

But there were two of the elves of darkness, the dwarfs Fialar and Galar, whose best delight it ever was to do harm to others of kindlier disposition than themselves, and they looked at Kvasir and watched him and hated him for his goodness. So one day when Kvasir came by the cavern where they lived, they called to him, saying they had a question to put to him, and bade him stop and enter their home.

'Willingly shall I talk with you, good dwarfs,' said Kvasir, and stepped from the kindly light of the sun into their underground dwelling.

But it was no question that Fialar and Galar wished to ask him, for the moment that he came among them, they struck him down and killed him, rejoicing at their wickedness.

'That was well done, brother, was it not?' laughed Galar.

'It was indeed well done,' replied Fialar. 'And now let us take the blood of Kvasir and mix it with honey and make mead of it, for I am certain that the blood of such a one as Kvasir was would give great knowledge and wisdom to him who drank it, and the possession of such mead might serve us well one day.'

So the dwarfs caught Kvasir's blood in two vats and a cauldron and mixed it with honey, so that they had mead which had the power of giving to him who drank of it not only wisdom and understanding, but the gift of words by which to pass on that wisdom and understanding to other men in songs which would make glad their lives. Yet the dwarfs did not drink one drop of the mead themselves, for they cared nothing for knowledge or poetry; instead they

16

hid in their dark cavern the three vessels which held it, against a time when they might find it useful.

And the gods, watching from Asgard, saw how Kvasir no longer went about the world, helping men with his wisdom, and they asked concerning him; yet no one could tell them where he might be. But only Fialar and Galar laughed and said, 'His words were so wise, we have no doubt that as they rose to his lips they turned in his throat and choked him, and he lies dead somewhere.'

And time passed and the two evil dwarfs looked around for someone else whom they might harm, and their eyes fell upon Gilling, a giant who lived with his wife on the shores of the sea. So late one evening, when it was growing dusk and they might venture out without being turned to stone, they dragged an old boat down to the beach where Gilling walked and greeted him.

'Good day to you, friend Gilling,' said Fialar. 'We go fishing. Will you not come with us and share our catch? Our boat is large enough for three, even though one be a giant.'

And Gilling was glad and went with them, calling out to his wife that he would soon be home.

But the boat was old and leaky, and under the giant's weight, she slowly filled with water. 'Should we not turn back and row for the shore?' asked Gilling anxiously.

'It is nothing,' laughed the dwarfs. 'Surely Gilling is not afraid to wet his feet?'

And Gilling said no more, for fear of their mockery. But soon it became apparent that the boat was going to sink; and with a shriek of laughter, Fialar and Galar jumped overboard and swam easily for the shore. But as they had known, Gilling could not swim, and the boat sank and he was drowned, and the two dwarfs were well pleased.

'Now let us go and make an end of Gilling's wife,' said Galar; and they ran off to Gilling's house.

Outside the house there was a millstone lying. 'Take you the millstone and climb on to the roof,' said Fialar, 'and when she comes out through the door, drop it upon her head.'

So Galar climbed on to the roof and held the millstone above the doorway, and Fialar knocked upon the door. 'Open, open, goodwife,' he called, 'for I bring you sad tidings.'

Gilling's wife opened the door and let him in, and Fialar told her that her husband had been drowned. He made no great show of sorrow when he told her, but she was too grieved to notice, and wept unceasingly.

'Come, goodwife,' said Fialar, 'it will soon be dawn, and if you will go down to the beach with me I will point out to you the place where our boat sank and your husband died. It may ease your heart to see his cold sea-grave.'

He went to the door and opened it, and she came with him. At the threshold he leapt nimbly back, and as she stepped out through the doorway into the grey half-light, Galar dropped the millstone on her head, and she died in an instant.

Fialar laughed delightedly as Galar jumped down from the roof to him. 'It is a good thing done, brother,' he said. 'I had grown tired of her weeping.' And together they ran back to their cavern before the sun rose and caught them.

But Gilling had two sons named Suttung and Baugi, and when Suttung heard how his father and mother had died, he strode over to the cavern and caught the two dwarfs as they came forth at dusk. He carried them, one in each hand, to the seashore, and flung them out on to a rock which was covered by the water at high tide. 'There may you stay and drown,' he said. 'Swimming will not help you now, for if you reach the shore I shall be here, waiting for you, and back you will go into the water, as often as you try to escape me.'

Fialar and Galar were very much afraid, but in vain they pleaded for their lives. 'You had no pity on my father and my mother,' said Suttung. 'Why should I spare you?' And he waited on the shore for them to try to save themselves by swimming to the beach.

When they saw that no pleading could move him, the dwarfs grew silent and thoughtful. Then suddenly Galar whispered, 'Brother, why do we not offer him the mead we made from Kvasir's blood? It is our greatest treasure, surely it was kept for such a time as this?'

'That is well thought of, brother,' said Fialar.

So the dwarfs offered their precious mead to Suttung in exchange for their lives, and after a hesitation, Suttung accepted the price, and allowed Fialar and Galar to swim to the shore. 'It will go ill with you if you try to cheat me,' he warned them.

But the dwarfs did not cheat him. Thankful to have escaped drowning, they gave him the three vessels which held the mead, and Suttung carried them off to his home. Yet like the dwarfs, the giant cared nothing for wisdom or poetry, so he drank none of the mead, but hid the two vats and the cauldron in the very heart of a mountain close by his house, and set his daughter, Gunnlod, to guard it night and day.

Yet there is nothing so secret that rumour of it will not travel forth, and in time the gods learnt of the mead that had been brewed from Kvasir's blood and how it was sealed away in a mountain cavern, guarded by a giant-maid; and the gods thought, 'This mead should be ours, to give to whom we please, as inspiration.'

And Odin said, 'I will go to Iotunheim and fetch this mead for our use.' And he went from Asgard alone.

With a grey cloak about him, such as travellers wore, a wide-brimmed hat pulled well down over his one eye, and with a staff in his hand, Odin set off for Suttung's house. On the way he passed a field which belonged to Baugi, Suttung's brother. In this field Baugi's nine thralls were mowing hay, and Odin stood on the edge of the field and watched them at their work. They toiled slowly, for their scythes were blunt, so taking from his belt a hone, Odin called out to them and asked if they would care to have him whet their scythes. Eagerly they brought the scythes to him and Odin sharpened them upon his hone. When the thralls set to work again, they found that their scythes were sharper than they had ever been before. 'That hone is better than any in our master's house,' they said to each other. 'Why should we not have it for ourselves?' So they called out to Odin, where he yet stood, watching them, and asked if he would sell his hone to them.

'Willingly,' said Odin, and he named a price, and they agreed to it. But they immediately began to argue amongst themselves as to who should keep the hone when once they had bought it, and they fell to quarrelling.

'Let him who catches it keep it,' called Odin, and he threw the hone among them.

With eager shouts they rushed at it, each striving to be the first to pick it up, thrusting one another aside and striking each other with their keen scythes, and, in their greed, wounding one another so grievously that in a little while there lay nine dead thralls in a field of unmown hay. And Odin took up his hone and went on his way.

At dusk he came to Baugi's house and begged a night's lodging and a meal. As he sat among the servants he heard how the master of the house grumbled at the loss of his nine thralls who had slain each other while the hay was yet uncut;

and he rose and went and stood before Baugi and spoke quietly. 'I will bring in your hay for you,' he said, 'and that as fast as your nine men.'

Baugi looked at him carefully, and something in the stranger's air of quiet confidence made him believe his words, idle boasting though they would have sounded on any other lips. 'What is your name?' he asked.

'I am called Bolverk,' replied Odin.

'What wage do you ask?' said Baugi.

'No more than a draught of the mead which the dwarfs gave to Suttung your brother, when the hay harvest is gathered in.'

'The mead was given to my brother,' said Baugi, 'I cannot promise you what belongs to another. Nevertheless, when your work is done and my harvest is stored, I will go with you to Suttung and ask that he lets you drink of his mead. Will you chance his reply?'

'I will chance it,' answered Odin.

So Odin stayed and worked for Baugi until the end of the season, and he worked as fast as nine men and better. And when the harvest was all gathered in, he went to Baugi and said, 'My work for you is finished, let us now go to your brother, that I may have the wage I have earned.'

They went together to Suttung's house, and Baugi told his brother of the bargain he had made with the stranger and asked that Suttung might help him keep it. But Suttung was angry and refused, blaming Baugi for promising a reward that was not his own to give, and upbraiding him; so that Baugi left his brother's house ill pleased at the words that had been spoken to him.

Odin saw his frowns and said quietly, 'Why do you not take what he has so churlishly refused you? Yonder stands the mountain where the mead is hidden. Why do we not go there and see how we may enter in and reach Suttung's treasure?'

And because he was angry with his brother, Baugi agreed, and they went together to the mountain; and there Odin took from his belt an auger and handed it to Baugi. 'Bore me a hole through the rock that I may enter the mountain,' he said.

Baugi took the auger and looked long at Odin, and a suspicion came into his mind. 'Are you not of the Aesir?' he asked.

Odin laughed. 'There is no one called Bolverk among the Aesir. Hurry, Baugi, and bore me a hole through the mountain to Gunnlod's cavern.'

So Baugi bored long with the auger through the hard rock of the mountain, and at length he drew the auger out. 'There is your hole,' he said.

But Odin blew into the hole and his breath sent the chips of stone flying back into his face. 'You have bored deeply,' he said, 'but you have not yet bored through the mountain.'

'There is no cheating you,' thought Baugi, and he shrugged his shoulders and bored yet deeper into the rock. And at last he had bored a hole right through the mountain even into the cavern where the mead was hidden. 'I have done as you asked, Bolverk,' he said. 'Now enter the mountain if you can.'

Swiftly Odin changed himself into a snake and slipped into the opening; and as swiftly, Baugi struck at him with the auger, but missed him, and was angry.

Odin wriggled through the hole that Baugi had made and came at last to the cavern where Gunnlod guarded the two vats and the cauldron filled with the mead, and he stood before her in his own shape, shining and splendid, the king of all the gods.

And the lonely giant-maid looked up and saw him standing there, and watched him long and unsmilingly. She was lovely, but her eyes were dark with bitterness and her lips had forgotten how to laugh. 'Surely you are of the Aesir?' she said at last.

'I am of the Aesir, fair one,' replied Odin.

Gunnlod rose and her voice trembled. 'I have waited long in this cavern all alone,' she said. 'My father has forgotten me and cares not what becomes of me so long as his treasure is safe. It matters not to him that I live unwed and childless, with no home that I may call my own, if only his mead is untouched. But the gods have remembered me at last and sent me a husband from among themselves. They have sent me a husband and much joy.'

Odin shook his head. 'Small joy will you get of a husband from the gods,' he said gently, 'for I can stay with you no longer than three days. Yet because of those three days you will never be forgotten, always will you be honoured in the minds of men as Gunnlod, Odin's giant-wife, and the mother of his son. But the choice shall be yours, fair Gunnlod. Let it be as you wish.'

She looked at him long and knew that she loved him, and at length she smiled, for the first time in many months. 'I will be Odin's wife,' she said.

He took her hand. 'As a pledge of our love,' he said, 'let me drink of your father's mead.'

'You may drink,' she said, 'but no more than one draught from each of the three vessels, for fear of my father's wrath.' And she let Odin drink from the first vat. Odin took one draught, but in that draught he emptied the vat. On the second day she let him drink from the second vat, and he took one draught, but in that draught he emptied the second vat. On the third day she let him drink from the cauldron, and he took one draught, but in that draught he emptied the cauldron.

And on the morning of the fourth day, while Gunnlod still slept, Odin kissed her for the last time, without waking her, and turning himself once more into a snake, he wriggled through the hole that Baugi had bored in the rock. Once outside the mountain he changed himself into an eagle and flew back towards Asgard.

But Suttung had become suspicious after Baugi had asked him for a draught of mead as the price of Bolverk's hire, and from his house he had kept watch upon the mountain where the mead was hidden. So that when he saw a great eagle rise up and fly into the air, he guessed that a thief had been there, and he too took the shape of an eagle and set off in pursuit of Odin.

But the eagle that was Odin had a fair start and flew strongly, and reached Asgard safely. And when the gods saw it coming, they ran into the courtyard carrying a huge vat, and the eagle alighted on the rim of the vat and poured out the mead through its beak, so quickly that a few drops were spilled; and then took once more its rightful shape, and the gods welcomed back Odin amongst them again.

And from that day the gods kept the mead that was made from Kvasir's blood and gave it to those for whom they wished the gift of poetry, the true skalds and poets who gladden the lives of men. But the few little drops that Odin had spilled in his hasty flight from Suttung, these they left for any man to take; and that is why there will always be those who write bad verses and are a trial to their fellow men.

IV

Idunn and the Golden Apples

IN the cavern in the mountain, where the mead of Suttung
had been hidden, a child was born to Gunnlod, Odin's son
Bragi, the god of poetry and eloquence, greatest of all the
skalds. He quickly grew into a lovely youth and left his
mountain home to travel all about the earth, spreading music
far and wide.

One day as Bragi wandered, singing his sweet songs, he
met with Idunn, the daughter of old Ivaldi, who was one of
the dwarfs. Idunn was quite unlike her father and quite unlike
her brothers, who were hideous and excelled in all smith's
work, for she was fair and lovely to look upon and kindly

in her nature, and differed from the elves of darkness in that she might look upon the sun without being turned to stone. Sometimes her father would allow her to leave her dark underground home and walk abroad by daylight, among the flowers and the green trees, and it was on such a time that Bragi saw her and fell in love with her. Happy to escape for ever from her gloomy home and her brothers, she went joyously with Bragi, and they set off for Asgard, where they were well received.

To Idunn was given the charge of the golden apples that the gods and goddesses ate to preserve their immortal youth. For being descended partly from the divine Borr and partly from the giant-woman Bestla, the gods had not of themselves everlasting youth or immortality, but won them both by eating these golden apples.

One day, when Odin, Hönir, and Loki were travelling through the world, they reached a lonely valley where a herd of fine oxen grazed, and being weary and hungry they killed an ox and flayed it, and lighting a fire, they spitted the ox over the flames and sat down to wait until it should be roasted. But though they waited a great while, the meat remained uncooked, however high they piled the fire with wood and however brightly it burned.

'There is some power here that wishes ill to us, that is plain,' said Odin.

'There is no one here but ourselves,' said Hönir. 'We are quite alone; how should the mischief of an enemy touch us here?' And he and Odin flung more wood upon the fire in a vain attempt to cook their meal.

But Loki rose and walked a little way off and looked about him all around that desolate place where only the oxen grazed peacefully, and after a time he saw, perched unmoving on a tree close by, watching the Aesir with malevolent eyes, a huge eagle. Loki returned to the others. 'We are not alone,' he said with a little smile. 'See, in yonder tree, where the big eagle watches us.'

'Surely a bird would wish us no harm,' said Odin.

Loki laughed. 'An eagle is not always an eagle,' he said. 'You, my brother, have taken such a shape yourself before this day.'

'That is true,' replied Odin.

Hönir called out to the eagle, 'Is it you, great bird, who will not let our ox-flesh cook?'

And with a screech the eagle answered, 'It is I, strangers.'

'Come,' asked Odin, 'why should you bear us ill will?'

The eagle did not answer the question; instead it said, 'If you will share your meal with me, then will your meat cook.'

'You are welcome,' said Odin. 'Come and join us, and may what you say be true, for we are hungry.'

The eagle flew down from the tree, and alighting by the fire, fanned the flames with its wings, and though they rose no higher than before, in a short time the meat was roasted and ready to be eaten. 'I caused the fire to burn,' screeched the eagle, 'so mine should be the first portion.' And it took more than half the meat for itself, and tearing it with its strong beak, devoured it at once.

The Aesir were angered when they saw their meal eaten by another. 'You have left but little for us,' said Hönir. Yet the eagle cared not for his words and snatched at the meat that remained and tore a great piece from it.

Loki picked up a stick from the heap of firewood and struck at the eagle with it. 'Begone, wretched creature that would eat all our food,' he cried; and with a last screech the eagle rose into the air. But Loki found that he could in no way lift off the stick from the eagle's body, and in no way take his hands from the stick, so that he was raised up, high into the air, and carried away by the eagle's flight, hanging from the end of the stick with his feet brushing through the tree tops. In vain he called to the eagle to stop, for it paid no heed to his cries.

'You evil monster,' said Loki, 'you are no bird. Who are you?'

'I am Thiazi, the storm-giant,' replied the eagle, 'and it has long been my wish to harm the gods.'

'Release me,' said Loki, 'and I will pay whatever price you ask.'

'Do you promise that?' asked Thiazi.

'I promise,' said Loki.

'Then swear that you will put into my power Idunn and her golden apples,' demanded Thiazi.

'I will give you all the goddesses, if only you will set me down,' cried Loki.

'It is only Idunn that I want. Idunn and the golden apples, so that I too, like the gods, may have immortal youth.'

'You shall have them,' promised Loki; and the next moment he was falling to the ground. He picked himself up and walked back to where Odin and Hönir waited, anxiously.

'Who was it?' asked Odin.

'What befell you?' asked Hönir.

Loki shrugged his shoulders. 'How am I to know who it was? But whoever it was, he soon became afraid of the rash game that he was playing and let me go.' And that was all that he would tell them. But though he said nothing of it, he thought deeply on the promise that he could not break, and planned how he might keep his word.

One morning, when Bragi was absent, Loki went to the fair groves of Brunnak where Idunn dwelt and greeted her kindly. 'What think you of this, Idunn?' he asked. 'In a certain wood, a little way beyond Asgard, there stands an apple-tree and it bears fruit that seems to me to be as marvellous as yours.'

'That could not be, Loki,' exclaimed Idunn. 'There are no other apples like mine.'

'But I have seen them growing on a tree. They are smooth and cool and golden, just as yours are, though whether they have the same magic powers, I cannot tell. Yet why should they not, since their appearance is the same?'

'I cannot believe you, Loki. Surely this is some jest of yours?'

Loki laughed. 'Had I dreamt that you would doubt me, fair Idunn, I would have picked you an apple and brought it to you, that you might see for yourself.'

'I wish indeed that you had,' she said, 'for I should like above all things to judge these apples for myself.'

'Then come with me,' said Loki, 'and I will take you to the tree, and then you may tell me if I am not right.'

Idunn rose. 'I will go with you, Loki.'

'Bring your own apples,' he suggested, 'that you may match them with these others.'

So Idunn went from Asgard with Loki, bearing her precious casket of magic apples; and he led her into a dark wood, and there Thiazi, like an eagle, flew down and snatched her up and bore her away to his home in Iotunheim; Thrymheim it was called, a bleak, wintry fortress high up in the mountains where the wolves howled and the winds swept through the pines until their branches groaned. Here Idunn was kept imprisoned, and every day Thiazi went to her and threatened or besought her that she might give him her golden apples to eat; but Idunn only clasped the casket to her and refused.

And the days went by and all the gods save Loki wondered where Idunn might be. 'She will be with Bragi,' they said at first, 'wandering through the world, leaving gladness wherever they pass. Soon she will return.'

But time went on, and Idunn did not return; and the gods thought how she had never left them for so long before, without a taste of the golden apples. And they grew tired, with eyes that had lost a little of their brightness, and faces that had become lined. And at last Bragi returned from his journeying, alone. He was in despair when he heard of the disappearance of his wife; and the despair of the other gods and of the goddesses was equal to his own, for now they had no idea where Idunn might be.

Odin called the Aesir and the Vanir together in a council, and one by one the haggard, ageing gods told when they had last seen Idunn, hoping thereby to find some clue that might lead to her recovery. And one of them told how he had last seen her, laughing and holding her casket of apples, going from Asgard with Loki.

'Stand forth, Loki, and answer this. Tell us if those words are true.'

Loki stood before the other gods, alone in the middle of the hall. There were streaks of grey showing in his dark-red hair and his face was thinner, but his eyes were as bright and as scornful as ever, and his smile as mocking.

'Where is Idunn, Loki?'

Loki laughed a little. 'She is in Thrymheim with Thiazi the storm-giant, and her apples are there with her.'

In an instant there was a consternation in the council of the gods, all crying out against Loki who had betrayed Idunn to the giants, and not only Idunn, but the youth and strength of all the gods as well; while Bragi wept despairingly for his lost wife.

At last Odin called for silence and turned to Loki. 'You deserve no mercy from us,' he said, 'and the worst fate we can devise shall surely be yours unless you fetch Idunn back to us, with her golden apples. How say you, will you undertake to go to Thrymheim, or will you face our wrath?'

And after a while Loki said, 'I will go to Thrymheim, and maybe I shall prevail and return with Idunn and the apples. Yet I do not go because I fear your threats, but only because I am becoming a little weary of growing old and ugly, I who was reckoned amongst the most beautiful of all the gods.'

So Loki took the shape of a hawk with keen eyes and strong wings, and he flew northwards to Iotunheim, to the big stone halls of Thrymheim, with a high stone wall around. And there he waited until he saw Thiazi come forth, and noted that he looked no younger than he should have been, and thought to himself, 'It seems that Idunn has not been kindly with her apples. It is well.'

Then he flew over the wall, and spying out with his sharp eyes the room where Idunn sat, pale and weeping, her casket of apples still clasped in her arms, he flew in through the narrow window, and seeing she was alone, took his own shape. 'Cease your weeping, Idunn. It is I, Loki, come to visit you.'

She looked up, and in her joy at seeing one of the gods again, she sprang to her feet and ran to him, and then stopped, remembering that it had been he who had betrayed her to Thiazi. She backed away from him and held her casket even more closely to her. 'What do you here, Loki? Have you come to mock at me?'

Loki laughed. 'I have come to carry you home again. We have all grown weary for a sight of your smiles, and, I must admit, for the taste of your apples. Will you come with me, or would you rather stay here with Thiazi?'

KIDDELL-MONROE

Idunn wept. 'Take me away with you, Loki. Take me back to Asgard.'

He spoke magic runes over her, and in a moment she began to shrivel, and the casket with her, until she was no more than a nut lying on the floor. Quickly Loki became once again a hawk, and picking up the nut in his claws, he flew out through the window, and southwards towards Asgard. But Thiazi saw the hawk flying from Thrymheim, and suspected that one of the gods had come to rescue Idunn, so he changed himself into an eagle, as before, on that day when the Aesir had met him, and flew in pursuit of the hawk.

And steadily the great eagle gained upon the little hawk, until Asgard came in sight and Loki felt that he could fly no farther. But still he flew on, clutching the nut in his talons; and the gods saw him coming and raised a shout from the battlements. And they ran and piled wood before the walls of their home and set it alight so that the flames rose high. And the hawk that was Loki dropped down into the blaze as the eagle swooped upon him. But Loki was the god of fire, and came unscathed through the flames, with Idunn safely in his claws; while the eagle's wings were burnt. The gods ran forward to slay Thiazi, and in an instant he lay dead, and Loki stood there in his own shape; and while the others crowded round, he spoke magic runes over the little nut in his hand, and it became Idunn with her casket, and with a cry she ran to Bragi's arms.

As soon as the first greetings were over, Idunn gave to each of the gods and goddesses one of her apples; even to Loki, who in the joy was quite forgiven for his treachery; and at once they grew young and fair and straight again, with bright eyes and smiling lips. And there was great rejoicing in Asgard.

V

Niord and Skadi

WHEN she heard how her father had been killed by the
gods in Asgard, Skadi, the daughter of Thiazi the storm-
giant, tied on her snow shoes, slung her quiver of sharp
arrows over her shoulder, and taking up her bow, set off for
Asgard to avenge his death. Right into the hall of the gods
she came and challenged all who would to fight with her.

The gods watched her standing there, brave and angry,
in her cloak of fur and her flashing golden helmet that was
yet no brighter than her hair that hung down below it, one
giant-maiden against all the might of the gods, and their
hearts warmed towards her in admiration of her courage.

'What good think you it will do, Skadi, if you too die in Asgard as your father died?' asked Odin gently.

'My father must be avenged,' said Skadi. 'Or are all the gods too much afraid to fight against one giant-woman?'

'Thiazi was our enemy,' said Odin, 'but there is no one of us here who would willingly shed your blood. Go in peace, good Skadi.'

'My father must be avenged,' she repeated, 'and there is but I to avenge him. Since I heard that he was dead I have not smiled, my heart is cold and dulled with grief, and I think that I shall never laugh again.'

'We would call you our friend, Skadi, and not our enemy,' said Odin. 'We would see you living and happy, not dead at the gates of Asgard. Come, accept atonement for your father's death and be reconciled with us. Let us give you in recompense the best that we have to offer. Choose for yourself, Skadi, a husband from among the gods, and live in peace with him, no longer the daughter of the storm-giant, but one among the goddesses.'

Yet all Skadi would say was, 'My father must be avenged.'

But the gods sought to persuade her, saying, 'We should welcome you with honour, Skadi, and rejoice to have you as our friend.'

'Thiazi's eyes shall I take,' said Odin, 'and cast them up into the sky, two new stars in the heavens, in memory of him, to show that though our enemy, we ever held him in respect.'

A little appeased by his words, Skadi looked around her at all the gods assembled in the hall; wise and kindly Odin, great tawny-bearded Thor, smiling gentle Niord, handsome red-haired Loki who had been the cause of her father's death, Balder the young god of sunlight, the most beautiful of them all, with his fair white skin and his golden hair, and all the other gods before her. She looked at them all closely, thinking upon Odin's words, but ever her eyes returned to Balder, and at last she said, 'If I may have Balder for my husband, then I will forgive the wrong you did my father, and live in peace with you.'

'You may choose your husband for yourself, Skadi,' smiled Odin, 'but choose him by his feet alone, and abide by your choice.'

'There is no doubt but that Balder, being the most beautiful, will have the loveliest feet,' thought Skadi, 'and thus shall I know him instantly.' So aloud she said, 'To that I agree, but further demand that before I am to be your friend, you shall make me forget my grief, and laugh.'

'That will be a hard task,' said Odin, watching her pale unsmiling face.

'Not for me,' said Loki. And he rose from his place and going to Skadi set himself to make her laugh, with all the skill he had in jesting. And at his tricks and the tales he told, all the gods held their sides with laughing; but Skadi never even smiled, for she hated Loki who had caused her father's death, and she would have found it easier to laugh at the jests of any other of the gods.

But Loki's wit and cunning prevailed at last, and Skadi forgot her grief and anger and smiled a little, and then suddenly she laughed aloud.

'See,' said Loki, 'did I not promise that I should make you laugh?'

'No one could fail to laugh at your antics, when once you have set yourself to make him laugh,' said Skadi.

'And are we friends at last, fair Skadi?' asked Loki.

'We are friends,' she said. But in her heart she never forgave him for Thiazi's death, though his had not been the hand that slew the giant, and though she lived in peace and friendship with the gods from that day.

'Now must you choose a husband for yourself from among the gods,' said Odin. And Skadi's eyes were covered so that she could see no more than the ground before her, and Frigg led her down the length of the hall, past the gods as they sat on the bench along the wall, and Skadi carefully watched the feet of each as she passed him by.

Of some feet she found it easy to guess the owner; there were Odin's, hardened by his countless journeyings among men; and the huge feet below strong ankles that could belong to no one else than Thor; but she passed by them all, until she came to a pair of feet so white that the veins showed blue through the skin, with delicately arched insteps and shapely ankles, and she smiled to herself. 'These will be the feet of Balder,' she thought. But she said nothing until she had seen the feet of all the gods and found no others so beautiful. Then she returned to where he sat who owned the feet she thought to be the feet of Balder, and said, 'Surely you must be Balder, the god of the sun, and I will have you for my husband.' And she took away the cloth that covered her eyes and found that she stood before the kindly, smiling Niord, king of the Vanir; Niord who was lord of the winds and the waves as they broke on the shore, whose feet had never been hardened by the rocky mountain ways trodden by the other gods, for he walked but rarely save across the sandy beaches, among the little pools left by the tide, and his feet were fairer and whiter even than those of Balder who was otherwise the most beautiful of all the gods.

Skadi was disappointed at her choice, that she had been mistaken. But Niord was handsome and kindly, a husband such as would have pleased any maiden, and she resolved to be content, and smiled at him when he took her hand and pledged himself to her before all Asgard.

Niord had a palace on the seashore, Noatun, where the sea birds cried and the young seals gambolled and the wild swans which were sacred to him gathered. From here he ruled the sea around the coast, calming the waves called up by Aegir of the deeper ocean, and protecting the fishermen from cruel Ran and her nets. For him the sunlight rippled on the water in the little bays and creeks, and the wind played gently in and out his halls.

To this palace Niord brought Skadi, showing her all its delights, thinking that it would please her. And indeed, at first it seemed pleasant enough in contrast to her own bleak home of Thrymheim, but before many days had passed, Skadi hated it. She went to Niord and said, 'For many days I have not slept for the noise of the sea at night, and the crying of the sea birds by day fills me with melancholy. The winds that blow here are too gentle, so unlike the mountain tempests, and the little rippling waves seem puny and childish beside the memory of my own mountain torrents. Good Niord, I fear I cannot live with you much longer here, or, sleepless and homesick, I shall go out of my mind.'

'I am grieved that my home displeases you,' said Niord. 'You must not suffer on account of me.' He thought in silence for a moment, then went on, 'Let us spend a part of our time together here, and a part of our time at Thrymheim. In every twelve nights, let us pass nine at your own home and three here at Noatun. How will that please you, my Skadi?'

Overjoyed, Skadi hastened to make ready to return to Thrymheim, and Niord went with her, away to the bleak mountain fastness in Iotunheim, far, far to the north, where the magpies nested, that were Skadi's own birds. Nine days out of every twelve they spent in the stone home that had once been Thiazi's, while the wind raged down the mountains through the pines, and the snow lay close around. And Skadi stood in the courtyard with three magpies on her shoulder, watching the clouds hurtling across the leaden sky and laughing with delight at the wildness of it all; while Niord, wrapped in fur cloaks, huddled by the fire and thought of his pleasant home, so far away.

And at last Niord said to Skadi, 'I cannot sleep in Thrymheim for the howling of the wolves by night, and each day is colder than the last, and here there is no joy or comfort. Nine nights out of every twelve are too many for me to remain in this place.'

'And three nights out of every twelve are too many for me to pass in Noatun, where the sea birds scream, and three days out of every twelve are too many, while the sun shines dazzlingly on the water and blinds my eyes.'

'What then shall we do, my Skadi?'

Skadi shook her head, 'I know not, only that it seems we cannot live together happily.'

They talked long and made many proposals, only to reject them all; and at last it seemed to them that Skadi had been right, and they could in no way live together. So Niord and Skadi bade each other good-bye, and Niord went back to live in Noatun, where the wind played gently with the sunlit waves, and his wild swans flew about him when he walked abroad, beating the warm air with their white wings; and Skadi remained in Thrymheim with her chattering magpies that perched on the beams of her halls, where the wind howled as loudly by night as the wolves, while she listened to it in the darkness with fierce joy.

And thus each of them was happy once again, meeting only now and then, in Asgard, on days of festival.

VI

Frey and Gerd

FREY, the son of Niord, ruled over the elves of light in Alfheim, and sent gentle showers and warm sunshine to make the earth fruitful. His were the fields in harvest time which brought riches to men; and his the flowers which decked the land when the cold frost-giants of winter had been driven away by spring. He was young, and fair to look upon, and happy.

But one day he dared to sit on Hlidskialf, Odin's throne which stood in Odin's watch-tower, where none but the Allfather himself might sit. Frey sat upon the throne, looking all about him, across Asgard and Midgard and even into

Iotunheim, and fancying himself, in jest, to be the ruler of all things known; and he laughed with pleasure at his game.

But as he gazed out over Iotunheim, his eye lighted on the house of Gymir, one of the fierce mountain-giants; and while he watched, the door of the house opened, and Gerd, Gymir's daughter, came forth. She was the loveliest of all the giant-maidens, and the moment that he saw her, Frey knew that he could have no other bride. But he knew, too, that no maid of Gymir's line would consent to wed with one of the Vanir, their hated enemies.

He watched her as she crossed the courtyard from the house to her bower, followed by her serving-woman, carrying a distaff and white wool. And when she had gone from his sight and he could see her no more, still the memory of her as he had seen her remained in his mind to trouble him, and it was with a heavy heart that he left the watch-tower and returned to Alfheim, his own home.

'Fitly am I rewarded,' he thought bitterly, 'for my presumption in mounting Odin's throne, for now shall I have no peace or joy until Gerd is mine. And that can never be.'

Frey spoke not of his sorrow or his love to any of the other gods; but he could not hide his grievous longing, and he went among his companions with a mourning countenance, and cared no more for feasting and revelry. Nor did it concern him how things went on earth, whether the crops were good or poor, or whether the flowers blossomed or no.

Niord watched his son, how sick at heart he seemed, and he was sad that Frey spoke not to him of his secret sorrow. At last he sent for Skirnir, who was Frey's loyal servant and his friend.

'Skirnir,' said Niord, 'for days past have I watched my son troubled by some sorrow of which he will not speak. I would that you could find what ails him, that it might be remedied. Go now and see if you can move him to tell you what is amiss, for he loves you well, and may speak to you.'

Skirnir went to Frey where he sat in his wide hall alone, with downcast eyes, and spoke with him. 'Lord of the elves,' he said, 'giver of good things to the world, will you not tell me why it is that you sit thus alone and sorrowing? For perchance there might be some little thing that I, even I, your servant, could do to ease your heart.'

Frey looked up at him and sighed. 'Even by you, good Skirnir, could I not be comforted.'

'At least tell me why it is you grieve,' pleaded Skirnir, 'for you have ever trusted me.'

And after a while Frey answered him. 'In Iotunheim, in Gymir's house, there dwells a giant-maiden, Gerd, Gymir's daughter. I did but see her once as she stepped forth from her father's door, but it seemed to me in that one instant as though the sea itself and the very sky shone more brightly in the reflection of her beauty, so fair she is. But I am Frey of the Vanir, and she is Gymir's daughter, and he and his kin hate us for ever, so Gerd may never be mine.'

But Skirnir was brave and loved his master, and he determined that Frey should win Gerd and no more sit disconsolate. 'Lord of the elves,' he said, 'I will go to Iotunheim, to Gymir's house, and speak with Gerd and win her love for you. Give me for the journey Blodughofi, your horse that goes through fire and water and darkness and never falters, and your sword that slays whenever it strikes, and I will return with the maiden or with her promise, or I will never return again.'

Frey's face lightened a little with hope, and on earth a few flowers raised their drooping heads and a few green ears of corn grew ripe. 'If you will do this thing for me, good Skirnir, not only for the journey will I give to you my

sword, but for ever, a gift from Frey to his best-beloved
friend.'

He gave Skirnir eleven golden apples to carry with him,
and a golden ring, tokens of his love for Gerd; but Skirnir,
fearing lest gifts might not move her, secretly took a slip of
wood and carved it with magic runes, staining them with a
scarlet dye.

Then Skirnir girded on his master's sword and saddled and
bridled his master's horse. 'Come, brave Blodughofi,' he said,
'we must go a hard road together, and together we shall
come home at length, or in Iotunheim we both shall perish.'

Skirnir rode into Iotunheim, and a long and dreary way it
was; but at last the house of Gymir came in sight, tall and
wide, with a high wooden wall around it, and snarling hounds
at the gate.

A herdsman sat upon a little hillock close by, keeping
Gymir's flocks, and Skirnir greeted him and asked, 'Tell me,
herdsman who can see so far from the top of your hill, how
I may enter Gymir's house, for I would have speech with
Gerd.'

The herdsman laughed. 'Gymir's daughter is not for such
as you to speak with, stranger. You are rash, and indeed, I
think that you are out of your mind, that you would enter
Gymir's house. Ride back again the way that you came, or
soon you will be dead.'

'I shall perish when the time comes for me to perish,'
said Skirnir, 'and not before. And if it is today that I must
die, well then, it is today.' And he set Blodughofi at the wall
of Gymir's house, and the good steed galloped forward and
leapt right over the wooden paling, while the hounds howled
and snapped below.

In the house Gerd sat spinning with her serving-woman,
and there came a great noise from the courtyard without,

the hounds baying and a clattering of hoofs and a voice calling her. 'Go to the window,' said Gerd, 'and tell me what these sounds may mean, for they make the very walls of my father's house tremble and shake.'

The woman went to the window-place and drew aside the leather curtain that hung over it, and peeped out. 'In the courtyard a fair young stranger dismounts from a wondrous steed. He is like to no one that I have ever seen before in Iotunheim, and how he entered here I cannot tell.'

'Open the door,' said Gerd, 'bid him welcome and fill him a horn of mead, though I fear that one who comes so mightily can bode no good to us. I would that my father were home.'

So Skirnir entered Gymir's house and saw the lovely Gerd, and understood why Frey sat sorrowing all day. And Gerd laid down her distaff and looked at Skirnir closely, and questioned him. 'You are not one of the giant-people, stranger, and you are not one of the dwarfs, yet it is a mighty feat that you have performed today in entering my father's house. Are you of the elves or of the Vanir, or are you from Asgard, that you show no fear of Gymir's wrath?'

'I am not of the elves or the Vanir, nor of the Aesir, fair Gerd, yet have I come from Alfheim with love-gifts from great Frey. Here are eleven golden apples that he sends you, that you may listen to him kindly.' And Skirnir held out the apples to her.

But Gerd would not take them, and looked angrily at him. 'I accept no gifts from one of the hated Vanir. No tokens or words of love could ever pass between us. Go, tell that to your Frey.' And she picked up her distaff and went on with her spinning.

Skirnir held out the golden ring. 'Lest the apples might not please you, fair Gerd, my master sent you this ring, belonging to the gods.'

Gerd glanced at it scornfully. 'You may take it back to your master. What is gold to Gymir's daughter? My father has store of it enough. Farewell.' And she turned again to her spinning.

Then Skirnir drew Frey's bright sword, that slew whenever it struck. 'Though I am loath, fair Gerd, to harm one whom my master loves, yet shall I strike your beautiful head from your shoulders, if you will not be kind to him.'

The serving-woman cowered in a corner of the hall; but Gerd looked at him unafraid, her eyes hard and cold. 'I do not fear your sword, servant of Frey, nor yet your threatening words. But were my father here you would not speak so boldly, indeed, you would not speak at all, for he would have silenced your talking for ever.'

Skirnir sheathed the sword and took from his belt the slip of wood on which he had carved the magic runes. 'On a high hill,' he said, 'before the gates of Niflheim, sits the eagle who fans the winds with his wings. On that selfsame hill, wretched and alone, bound and tormented and mocked at of all, shall you pass your time in misery, if you refuse the true and faithful love of Frey. Your days shall be more anguish-laden than any you could dream of, food shall be hateful to you for that it prolongs your life, Odin the All-father shall be wroth with you for evermore, and Frey shall be your enemy, if his love you reject. Never a husband or a wooer shall you find, but dwell for ever lonely and hated of all, cursed by the gods and scorned by the giants, if for Frey you have no kindness. Magic runes have I written here to curse you with, fair Gerd. Very powerful they are, and this doom shall be yours unless you become Frey's bride.'

Gerd hid her face with her hands and shuddered, for she knew how mighty were the spells of the gods; and Skirnir watched her, waiting for her to speak; while the serving-woman wailed in the corner of the hall, her head covered by her skirt.

At last Gerd looked up. 'Though it would be a shame to me, and worse than death, to wed with one of the hated Vanir, yet do I fear your terrible runes, so that I must obey you.' She sighed. 'Drink one last horn of mead in my father's house, and then return to Frey and tell him that he has won Gymir's daughter for a wife, though heavy of heart she is, and consents not willingly.'

'Before I go,' said Skirnir, 'you must say where you will meet him, and when he may await you, and give me your word to be there.'

'There is a wide and silent forest, green and leafy, named Barrey, which I do not doubt is known to both of us. There will I meet Frey, nine nights from now.' And Gerd wept.

But Skirnir laughed for joy that he had served his master well, and mounting Blodughofi, he rode away from Iotun-heim.

Frey was standing before the gates of his house, awaiting him. He ran forward and caught at Blodughofi's bridle. 'Tell me, good Skirnir, had you any success?'

'In the forest of Barrey, nine nights from now, will Gerd await you, to be your bride.'

And Frey embraced his friend and said, 'The sword is yours, Skirnir, for never has anyone served me better. But, oh, how long will nine nights seem, until the time I can meet my Gerd!'

And when the ninth night was come, in sorrow Gerd went secretly from her father's house to the forest of Barrey, and there, with dread, she awaited the coming of Frey. 'Surely,' she thought, 'nowhere is there one more wretched than I, a giant-maid forced to wed with one of the hated Vanir.'

But then she looked up and saw Frey coming towards her, young and fair and bright, with sunlight in his golden hair even in the darkness; and she saw that he came as a lover, gentle and kind, and not as a conqueror, and she was unhappy no more.

And long they dwelt together in joy and peace.

VII

The Lady of the Vanir

BESIDES his son, Frey, Niord, king of the Vanir, had a daughter named Freyia, who, like her brother, was gay and happy and fond of the sunlight and the flowers. Freyia, the lady of the Vanir, was the loveliest of all the goddesses, and her home, Sessrumnir, was built on the wide space called Folkvangar. She was the goddess of love and beauty, and lovers prayed to her for joy and happiness and for the safety of their loved ones. When Freyia went abroad, she drove in a chariot drawn by cats, which were her favourite animals, while swallows flew about her, and cuckoos called their spring-like notes to welcome her, so that these two birds came to be held sacred in her honour.

Freyia was married to the god Od, and in his company she

49

found great joy, and would have been ever happy and con-
tented, had he been always with her. But Od was a great
wanderer, and it was his pleasure to leave Asgard often
and travel everywhere, seeing all there was to be seen, often
for many days on end. And in his absence Freyia sat alone
in Sessrumnir, bored and discontented, and sometimes weeping. Her tears were drops of red gold, not brine like mortal
tears, and they enriched the ground they touched. Sometimes Freyia would leave her home and wander through
the world, seeking for her husband; and often it was hard
to find him, so that she shed tears of loneliness and disappointment in many places; and that is why gold is dug from
the earth in many different lands. Yet when she found Od,
then there were no more tears, but only smiles and laughter,
as hand in hand they came home to Asgard together, the
swallows twittering about their heads, and the flowers
springing up where Freyia's feet had trodden.

One day when Od was away from home, Freyia, seeking
some consolation for his absence, wandered alone from
Sessrumnir through the fields, picking summer flowers for
her hair. Below a hill she came to a certain passageway which
led down beneath the earth to Svartalfheim, where the
dwarfs, the elves of darkness, lived and plied their trade as
smiths, mining the metals and precious stones from which
they made weapons and armour and jewellery surpassed by
none.

Curious, Freyia peeped into the passageway, staring into
the gloom, but nothing could she see; yet there came faintly
to her ears the sound of a distant hammering, the clink of
metal upon metal as the dwarfs went about their work.
Since Freyia knew how fine was the craftsmanship of the
dwarfs, and since she had nothing better to do in Od's
absence, she thought to herself, 'I will go into Svartalfheim

and see the dwarfs at work, it will while away the hours for me.' And she slipped into the dark passageway, which grew the lighter for her presence.

The farther Freyia went along the passage, the louder grew the sounds of hammering, while in the distance there appeared a glowing as of the furnace of a forge. Freyia walked towards this light, but on the way she passed an open doorway leading into a cave, and looking in, she saw four dwarfs sitting on the floor together, their heads bent close over some object which they were admiring.

'It is the finest thing that we have ever made,' said one of them.

'It is finer than any of our kinsmen could have wrought,' said another, 'and we do well to be proud of our skill.'

'It is fit for a goddess,' said a third dwarf.

'Indeed,' said the fourth, 'I do not doubt that any of the goddesses would be pleased to own it.'

Overcome by curiosity, Freyia slipped softly into the cave, trying to see, through the dim light, what it was that the four black dwarfs were looking at. Then one of them said, 'See, my brothers, is it not perfect?' And he held up above his head a necklace made of gold and gems, so bright that it lighted up the gloom of the cave and so beautiful that Freyia cried out in wonder at it. The four dwarfs heard her and leapt to their feet, turning around; and the one who held the necklace hid it behind his back. Suspiciously they stared at her.

'Who are you, stranger?' asked the first dwarf.

But before she had time to answer, the second exclaimed, 'Why, it is the lady of the Vanir, lovely Freyia herself, come to visit us. Are you not Freyia, fair one?'

'I am,' she said, never taking her eyes from the dwarf who held the necklace.

51

'We are honoured, brothers,' jeered the third dwarf, 'Freyia has paid us a visit. Hurry, fetch a stool that she may sit down.'

Two of them carried forward a wooden stool and placed it in the centre of the cave. The third dwarf made her a mocking bow, bending until his head touched the rocky floor. 'Be seated, fair guest,' he said.

But Freyia was still staring at the fourth dwarf, he who held the necklace hidden behind his back, and she noticed nothing else. 'What is that which you are holding?' she asked at last.

'A necklace we have made,' replied the fourth dwarf sullenly.

'Let me see it,' said Freyia.

'No.'

Freyia smiled and her voice was honey-sweet. 'Let me look at it,' she pleaded.

The fourth dwarf hesitated. 'What do you say, my brothers, shall she look at it?'

'What harm is there in looking?' laughed the third dwarf. 'By all means let her see it.'

The fourth dwarf held up the necklace and once again it lighted the cave, flashing like golden fire set with lesser lights of every hue. Freyia gazed at it, entranced.

'Look well on it, fair Freyia,' mocked the third dwarf, 'for it is not yours, and in Svartalfheim we keep what is our own.'

But Freyia never heard him; all else was forgotten as she stared in wonder on the necklace, a far lovelier jewel than any she possessed. At last she whispered, 'It is beautiful. Will you give it to me?'

Three of the dwarfs cried out indignantly, and the one who held the necklace hid it once again behind his back.

But the mocker held his sides with laughing and rocked upon his feet with mirth. 'Freyia wants our necklace,' he gasped. 'Freyia wants our necklace.'

'Give it to me,' begged Freyia. 'Good dwarfs, give your necklace to me.'

The dwarf who held it answered her. 'It is Brisinga-men, and we have made it with our own hands and laboured long at it. Brisinga-men is not to be given away to anyone who asks.'

'I will give you fair exchange for it,' said Freyia.

'What fair exchange could there be for Brisinga-men?'

'I will give to you all my other jewels, or the flowers that bloom where I have trodden, or the light that shines about my hair, or the spring-song of the cuckoo. Any of these or all of them, will I give you in payment for Brisinga-men.'

'What do we want with your jewels, we who have made Brisinga-men? What do we care for flowers, or the song of the cuckoo? And we have gold enough, and gems, in the heart of the earth, to shine for us, we do not need the brightness of your hair.' And all four of them laughed at her.

'Then tell me what price you will take for your necklace,' Freyia pleaded.

'It has no price,' said he who held it. 'It shall be ours to keep.'

'It is not for the Vanir to touch or to hold,' said another of the dwarfs.

But the mocking dwarf said nothing, and only watched her, his eyes alight with malice.

'I will pay any price you ask,' said Freyia.

'Brisinga-men has no price,' repeated the fourth dwarf sullenly.

But the dwarf who had mocked her whispered to the others so that she could not hear what he was saying, and

53

at his words they all stared at him, surprised, and then burst out into evil laughter, jumping up and down in their glee, so that Freyia once again caught sight of the necklace as the dwarf who held it stamped about in a dance of malignant delight.

'What price do you ask?' said Freyia again, fired by this latest glimpse of Brisinga-men.

The dwarfs turned to her and spoke together. 'She to whom we give Brisinga-men must willingly allow us to embrace her, that we may boast all through Svartalfheim that we have held the lady of the Vanir in our arms and kissed her.'

Freyia drew herself up, the necklace forgotten in her indignation, and her eyes flashed in anger. 'Black crawling vermin nourished by Ymir's rotting flesh, how dare you speak thus to a goddess?' And she turned and made to go from their cave.

But he who had mocked her called after her, 'Do not go without bidding good-bye to Brisinga-men, Lady Freyia. Look, see where Brisinga-men shines out in farewell for you.'

And Freyia turned and saw how all the dwarfs were holding up the necklace, high above their heads, their faces burning with mockery and malice, and their misshapen bodies shaking with mirth; and she paused and stared at the necklace, and hesitated. They shook it slowly from side to side, so that it glinted and sparkled. 'Look upon it well, fair Freyia, for you will never see it more.'

And Freyia looked, and in that moment she knew that there was nothing that she would not do to gain it, and goddess though she was, nothing which she would not suffer, that she might call it hers. 'I will pay your price,' she said.

They screeched with laughter, dancing about on the rocky floor of the cave and congratulating each other.

'Freyia will pay our price,' they screamed. 'The lady of the Vanir will buy our necklace.'

And Freyia waited, thinking only of the moment when she might snatch the necklace from their hands and run with it along the passageway, back to the daylight; while they ceased their mocking laughter and set to quarrelling among themselves as to which of them should kiss her first.

Brisinga-men remained Freyia's favourite jewel, and she wore it day and night, not even taking it off when she lay down to sleep. It was because he knew how much she valued it, that Loki made up his mind to steal the necklace in order to torment her, and he planned to go to Sessrumnir one night when Od was away on his wanderings and take it from around Freyia's neck while she slept.

Heimdall, the white one of the Aesir, the watchman of the gods, had a house beside Bifrost, the rainbow bridge that linked Asgard to the earth, and here he kept guard unceasingly to warn the gods of the approach of any of their giant enemies. Clad in white armour, mounted on his golden-maned horse, he rode back and forth across the rainbow bridge, ever wary. His teeth were of pure gold, so that his smiles flashed out like sunlight, and his hearing was so keen that he could catch the sound that grass made sprouting fresh and green, and the sound of the wool growing on the back of a sheep. His sight was so sharp that he could see a hundred leagues by night; and he needed less sleep than a bird.

One night, as he kept watch upon Bifrost, he saw a tiny fly flitting in through the window of Freyia's palace. 'What should a fly be doing, entering Sessrumnir by dark?' he wondered. 'It is by day such creatures are wont to be abroad.' And suspicious, he went closer, and watched carefully the doors and windows of Freyia's home.

Now, the fly was Loki who had taken the shape of so small a creature wishing to avoid Heimdall's keen eyes; and once inside Freyia's bedchamber, seeing her to be asleep, he took again his own form, and stealing quietly to the bed where Freyia lay, looked down upon Brisinga-men, glittering in the moonlight with a brighter radiance of its own. But the clasp of the necklace was beneath Freyia's neck on the side that she was lying, and he could not unfasten it without waking her.

Undaunted, Loki changed himself at once into a flea, and hopping on to the bed, he slipped below the coverlet and bit Freyia on the side that was uppermost. She stirred in her sleep and turned over, but did not wake up; and in a moment, Loki, once again himself, was standing beside the bed. He could now easily reach the clasp of the necklace; and very carefully, with gentle fingers, he unfastened it, and Brisinga-men was in his hands. Then quietly he stole from the room, and like a shadow went from Sessrumnir.

But Heimdall, who had never taken his eyes from Freyia's palace, saw him, and instantly he was upon him. Seeing Heimdall, Loki fled, faster than the wind; though fast as he was, Heimdall was yet faster and caught him up. But as Heimdall put out his hands to grasp hold of him, Loki, with a laugh, turned into a blue flame. Heimdall instantly became a cloud, damp and misty, and sought to engulf the flame and quench it, but Loki changed himself into a bear. 'Not so easily, Heimdall, do you conquer me,' he said, and began to lap up the dew of the cloud.

Then Heimdall also took upon himself the form of a bear, even greater than the other, and he and Loki fought together; two strong white bears, biting and scratching and rolling over and over upon the ground, until the night resounded with their snarling.

And when he saw that Heimdall was worsting him, Loki became a seal, wet and slippery, and slid from the grasp of the bear that was Heimdall. Then Heimdall took upon himself the shape of another seal, even mightier than the other, and once again the two gods fought, biting and barking angry taunts. All night they fought together, but before dawn Loki realized that he was beaten and Heimdall was the stronger. So like a flame he slipped from Heimdall's grasp and stood up as himself once more. 'You win, my friend,' he said, holding out Brisinga-men. 'Take the necklace back to Freyia if you will.'

And Heimdall became himself again and took the necklace from Loki. 'You are cunning, Loki,' he said, 'cunning and treacherous. But you are not cunning enough to deceive me, and you are too treacherous ever to be my friend.'

Loki shrugged his shoulders. 'That is as you think, white one. But it was a good fight for all that, even though I lost.' He smiled, 'And who knows, perhaps we shall fight again one day, and that time you may not be so fortunate.'

But Heimdall did not stay to answer him, for he was hurrying back to Sessrumnir with Brisinga-men, before Freyia awoke, so that she should not miss her necklace and be distressed.

VIII

The Six Gifts

THE wife of Thor, the mighty god of thunder, was golden-haired Sif, one of the loveliest of the goddesses. Her long hair fell about her feet, covering her like a cloak, and was her greatest treasure, the admiration of the gods, and the envy of all the other goddesses.

Sif was, indeed, so vain of her golden hair that Loki, in his love of mischief, thought one day how it would be a fine jest to cut it off. Accordingly, at a time when Thor was absent from Asgard, Loki stole one night to Thrudheim, his palace, and going to the room where Sif lay sleeping, he clipped off every golden tress without wakening her.

When Sif awoke in the morning and found her hair cut short, her distress was great, and nothing which the other goddesses might say could comfort her. She wept unceasingly, her head covered with a veil, until Thor came home, striding into Asgard, well pleased by the number of giants he had slain on his journeying, and shouting out a greeting to everyone he saw.

When he reached his palace and Sif ran not forth to welcome him, he was surprised, and went through his halls calling her. But no answer did he get until he found her weeping in a little room. 'What means this?' he cried. 'Why were you not beside the gate to greet me home? This is no way for a wife to welcome her husband.' But when he saw that she wept, his voice grew softer. 'What is amiss, my Sif?' he asked.

'You will not love me any longer when you know,' sobbed Sif. 'You will think me ugly and of no account.' And she took off the veil and showed him her cropped hair.

Furiously Thor shouted, 'Who has done this thing to you?'

'I know not, my dear lord, but I do fear it for the work of Loki. It is a jest such as he ever loves.'

'If it is Loki, he shall pay for it,' said Thor in a voice which thundered throughout Thrudheim, and snatching up his weapons, he hurried out to look for Loki, muttering threats as he went.

Loki saw him coming, frowning terribly and looking from side to side, as though he searched for someone. 'That scowl is the black cloud which comes before a thunderstorm,' thought Loki, and he made to slip quietly away. But Thor saw him go, and with a roar was after him and had caught him fast. 'Did you cut off Sif's hair?' he shouted.

'Why should I cut off Sif's hair?' asked Loki, trying in vain to free himself from Thor's mighty grip.

'I do not want to know why you should cut off Sif's hair, I have asked you did you cut it off, that is all I want to know. For if you did, then here is an end of your mischief, Loki, for I shall break your every bone and fling what is left of you, piece by piece, across the sky, beyond the very sun.'

'What good would that do to Sif?' asked wily Loki. 'Whether I cut off Sif's hair or another did, it is I, and I alone, who have the cunning and skill to find new hair for her. If you carry out your threats, friend Thor, you will always have a crop-haired wife.'

'Can you find new hair for her?' demanded Thor. 'As fine to the touch, as bright a gold, and as long as that which you destroyed?'

'I can do all that,' said Loki confidently.

'Then make haste and do it, and if you fail, there will be one god less in Asgard, I promise you. Go now and do as you boast.'

'Unhand me then,' said Loki, 'and I will show you what I can do.'

Reluctantly, Thor released him, and in a flash, Loki was gone. He went at once below the earth to Svartalfheim and sought out the two sons of Ivaldi, Idunn's brothers, who were famed amongst the dwarfs for their skill in all smith's work. He asked them if they could fashion for him fine golden threads, like hair, which, when placed upon Sif's head, would grow there, as would real hair; and they answered boastfully, 'We could do more for you than that, red Loki.'

And Loki thought to himself how it might soften the wrath of the other gods towards him if he took back to Asgard with him not only new hair for Sif, but a gift for the Allfather and a gift for Frey as well, and he smiled and said, 'Then fashion for me a ship that shall be the best of all ships and worthy of the gods, and a spear that will always find its mark and will disgrace not even such a warrior as Odin.'

'We shall do those things,' said Ivaldi's sons, and they set to work at once, with a great heaping of fuel on their furnace and a great blowing with their bellows and much hammering of metal; while Loki sat and watched them.

And after a time had passed, the sons of Ivaldi brought to Loki a cap of hair of finely-drawn-out threads of gold, as long as the height of a goddess. 'When this cap touches the head of Sif,' they told him, 'it will grow there as though it had ever done so.' And Loki took the hair from them and stowed it carefully away.

And they wrought with wood and metal, and after another space, they brought to him the ship Skidbladnir, with high-beaked prow and flashing shields along her sides. 'This ship,' they told him, 'will hold all the Aesir and all the Vanir, and no matter her course, she will have ever a favourable wind. Yet when there is no desire to sail in her, she may be folded up and carried in a wallet.' And Loki took the ship from them and folded her and put her in his wallet, and he smiled. 'That is a worthy gift for Frey,' he said.

And the sons of Ivaldi fashioned a shaft of strong ash-wood cut from Yggdrasill itself, and hammered red-hot iron and set it on the shaft, and brought to Loki the spear Gungnir. 'This spear,' they told him, 'can never miss its mark, and in the hands of Odin it will be a sure defence against all enemies.' And Loki took the spear and marvelled at it. 'You have done well,' he said. 'Your skill is indeed great.' He rose. 'And now farewell to you. I shall bear witness everywhere that the sons of Ivaldi are surely the finest smiths in all Svartalfheim.'

The two dwarfs grinned their broadest grins in pleasure,

that they had impressed a god with their craftsmanship, but before they could reply to Loki's words, a harsh voice spoke from the shadows around the doorway. 'That is a lie, Loki of Asgard, for the greatest smith in all Svartalfheim is my brother Sindri.'

'Who are you that boast so loudly?' asked Loki; while the two sons of Ivaldi protested furiously against the slight that was put upon them in their own forge.

A hideous dwarf came out from the shadows into the firelight. 'I am Brokk,' he said, 'and I can make good my boast, as you call it.'

'That can you not,' cried Ivaldi's sons, stamping their flat feet in rage.

'However skilled your brother,' said Loki, 'I warrant that he could not make three things to equal this hair, this ship, and this spear, which my friends here have made for me.'

Brokk laughed in scorn. 'He could not only match them, he could surpass them easily.'

'That could he not,' laughed Loki.

Brokk smiled maliciously and leant forward. 'Will you wager your head on it?' he asked.

'You are presumptuous,' said Loki, but he laughed again, good-humouredly. 'I will wager my head on it.'

Brokk rubbed his hands together and grinned. 'Your head against my head,' he said. 'My brother's skill against the skill of the sons of Ivaldi. They have made your three gifts for the gods, now shall Sindri make mine, and we will go together into Asgard and all the gods shall judge between us.'

'Tell Sindri to have a care,' said Loki, 'for with all his skill I do not doubt that he cannot fit his brother's head back on his brother's shoulders when once it is cut off. And off it will surely be before many hours are passed.'

The two sons of Ivaldi laughed with glee; but Brokk only smiled unpleasantly and went to seek his brother Sindri.

And after a time Loki followed him and listened outside the forge where Sindri worked, and heard how Brokk told his brother of the wager.

'If you will give me your help,' said Sindri, 'I will make for the gods three gifts that shall surpass by far those made by Ivaldi's sons.'

'I will give you all the help I can,' promised Brokk; and Sindri bade him pile the furnace high with wood and blow hard upon it with the bellows; and when the fire was red-hot he threw on it a pigskin. 'Do not cease to blow upon the fire,' he warned, 'or my work will be spoilt.' Then he went out from the smithy, and Brokk toiled at the bellows with all his might. And Loki smiled and turned himself into a gadfly and flew upon Brokk's hand and stung him. But the skin of the ugly dwarf was thick and tough, and he cared nothing for the sting.

Then Sindri returned and bade his brother cease blowing, and took from the fire the boar Gullinbursti, whose bristles were golden wires and shone like a lamp into every corner of the forge. Then he dropped a bar of gold into the furnace, and once more bidding Brokk cease not from blowing, he went from the smithy. Brokk worked the bellows with all his strength and Loki flew and bit him on the neck. But Brokk only shook his head a little, and ceased not in his blowing.

And when Sindri returned, he took from the fire with his tongs the golden arm-ring Draupnir. Then he laid a bar of iron in the furnace, and for the last time bidding Brokk blow without respite, he left the smithy. And Loki flew and settled on Brokk's forehead, and stung him so that the blood

63

ran down into his eyes and he could not see. Then Brokk ceased from his blowing long enough to wipe the blood away with his hand, and for that second only, the bellows fell flat.

When Sindri returned, he took from the fire the mighty battle-hammer Miollnir and dropped it hissing into a cauldron of cold water. But when he came to examine it closely, he found that it was shorter in the handle than he would have wished, because for a moment Brokk had ceased from blowing. 'Nevertheless, it is a mighty weapon,' said Sindri. He gave the three gifts to Brokk, and Brokk hurried with them to Asgard, going by night, when it was dark, that the sunlight might not fall upon him and turn him to stone.

And at an appointed time, all the gods gathered together to judge between the gifts made by Ivaldi's sons and those which Sindri had wrought; and first Loki handed over his three gifts, telling the virtue of each one.

As soon as he had the golden hair in his hands, Thor rose up and called out for Sif, and at the sound of his mighty voice, echoing through Asgard, she came hurrying from Thrudheim to the council hall, and Thor fitted the cap of hair upon her head, and immediately it grew there as though it were her own.

The gods were loud in their praise of Loki's first gift, declaring that now Sif was even more lovely than she had been before, and delightedly she ran back to Thrudheim that she might admire herself in her own silver mirror.

When Frey took hold of Skidbladnir, his ship, and saw how she would open out into a vessel large enough for all the gods and their steeds as well, he did indeed rejoice. And Odin found no fault at all in Gungnir as he held it in his hands and tested it. 'This is the most perfect weapon I have yet seen,' he said. And Loki smiled at the praise his gifts were having.

Then Brokk laid down his three gifts, giving first to Odin the golden arm-ring. 'This is Draupnir,' he said. 'Every ninth night eight rings of the same weight and form will fall from it, so that when the nights of but one year have passed, you may have filled a treasure store.'

'It is indeed a goodly gift,' said Odin, and placed the ring upon his arm.

Then Brokk gave Gullinbursti, the boar, to Frey. 'You may ride upon him, or he will draw your chariot for you,' he said. 'And you will never travel in the darkness when Gullinbursti carries you, for there will ever be the light from his bristles. And besides all this, he will go through water and through the air as easily as over the land.'

Frey took the boar and marvelled at it, saying, 'Indeed, I know not which of my two gifts pleases me more greatly, for they are both wondrous things.'

And then Brokk took the mighty battle-hammer and gave it into Thor's hands. 'This is Miollnir,' he said, 'and however far it is thrown, it will always return to your hand. And with your strength to wield it, it will ever be a sure protection for the gods.'

Overjoyed, Thor tossed the great hammer into the air as though it had been made of wood, and swung it round about his head until it seemed as though several skulls were in danger of being cracked, and Odin, smiling, bade him desist from his dangerous play.

And when the gods came to decide between those gifts made by the sons of Ivaldi and those which Sindri had fashioned, they found themselves unable to decide between the ring Draupnir and Gungnir the spear, or between Gullinbursti the boar and the ship Skidbladnir; but they all agreed that Thor's hammer was a greater prize than Sif's golden hair, for with its aid they might dwell secure in Asgard, well defended from the giants. And so Sindri was declared to be the winner, and Loki to have forfeited his head.

Brokk shouted with glee, but Loki laughed. 'Come and take me, Brokk,' he called. And instantly, like a flame going out, he had disappeared from the hall, and was away.

'Am I to be cheated of his head?' howled Brokk. 'Is there no justice among the gods?' And he appealed to Thor to bring Loki back to him, and willingly Thor went in pursuit, flourishing his hammer and shouting out to Loki. And after a short time he returned, dragging Loki with him, and flung him on the floor before the dwarf. With a dance of malicious triumph, Brokk took a knife from his belt. 'Now is your head mine, Loki,' he said, and took the fire-god by his red hair and brought the knife to his throat.

'Wait,' said Loki. 'My head is yours, but not any part of my neck, so take care that you touch not more than was in our wager.'

Brokk hesitated, and all the gods laughed at Loki's wit and cunning. 'Indeed, he speaks the truth, Brokk, his neck is not yours to harm.'

Brokk thought carefully and then released Loki sullenly. 'It is true,' he said, 'and so am I cheated. Yet since your head is mine, I may at least still your mocking tongue for a time.'

And he took an awl and thread from his belt and sewed Loki's lips together so that he could not speak; while the gods laughed long at the jest, and none more heartily than Thor, bent double in his mirth and slapping his thighs.

But it was not long before Loki had freed his lips and was as mocking and as scornful as ever he had been.

IX

The Theft of Miollnir

THOR's hammer, Miollnir, soon became one of the gods'
great treasures, counted amongst their most valued possessions as a sure defence against their giant enemies. So it was
with much distress that one morning Thor awoke to find
that it had gone from Thrudheim. He hurried forth at once
to look for Loki, thinking that maybe the god of fire had
played another of his tricks; but Loki was as surprised as
Thor himself to hear that Miollnir was vanished, and said
at once, 'I do not doubt that this is the work of the giants.
They will have stolen Miollnir away for their own safety.
I will go to Iotunheim and spy for you, and maybe I shall
find out where they have hidden it.'

So he changed himself into a hawk and flew northwards into Iotunheim, while Thor waited anxiously for his return. On and on flew Loki, but never a sign of Miollnir did he see, and at last he came to the barren lands of Thrym, the ruler of the frost-giants; and thinking to ask him if he had any knowledge of the hammer, he flew to where Thrym sat upon a little hillock close beside his great house, plaiting leashes out of gilded leather for the hounds that lay at his feet, and combing the manes of his horses.

Loki took his own shape, and the tall giant looked at him. 'Greetings, Thrym,' said Loki.

'Greetings, Loki from Asgard. What brings you here? How is it with the gods?'

Loki sighed. 'It goes but ill with the gods,' he said, 'for Thor has lost his hammer, and I do not doubt that it has been stolen. Can you give me tidings of it?'

Thrym threw back his head and laughed until the tears ran down his cheeks.

'Why do you laugh, my friend?' asked Loki.

And when Thrym could speak again he answered him, 'I laugh because Thor's hammer is hidden nine miles deep below the ground where Thor shall never find it. No, nor any of the gods.'

'Is there no other thing that would please you as mightily as does the hammer?' asked Loki. 'Some other thing which the gods could give to you in exchange for what they prize so highly?'

And Thrym thought, and then he said, 'I have heard much talk of the beauty of the lady of the Vanir, how of all the goddesses she is the fairest, and I have long wished for such a wife. Go you back and tell the gods that if they send me Freyia for my wife they may have Miollnir once again.'

'Small hope is there of getting Miollnir back, if Freyia is

to be the price,' thought Loki. But he said aloud, 'I will go to Asgard with your offer, Thrym, and maybe I shall return with an answer.' And in a moment he was once again a hawk and flying southwards towards Asgard.

Thor was waiting in the courtyard before his palace, pacing up and down and ever glancing with impatience at the sky for a sign of Loki; and as soon as he saw the black dot that was the hawk appear, he hurried forward, calling out, 'What news, Loki? Tell me quickly, what news of Miollnir?' long before Loki could have heard even his mighty shouts.

And when Loki came closer, Thor would not allow him time to take his own shape or even to alight upon the ground, before he was at his questioning, 'Tell me quickly, Loki, have you found where Miollnir is?'

'Miollnir is buried, nine miles below the earth, and only Thrym of the frost-giants knows where.'

'But did you not offer him other gifts in exchange? Did you not demand that he should tell you more?' Thor shook his fists in the air with impatience.

'Give me time to finish what I have to tell you,' said Loki. 'Keep silence for a moment.' And when Thor was quiet, he went on, 'Thrym will only give Miollnir back to us if we will send him Freyia as his bride.'

'Then why are we delaying?' demanded Thor. 'Come, let us away to Sessrumnir and tell Freyia of it, that I may have Miollnir back with no more loss of time.'

Loki alighted on the ground and became himself once more. 'Thor, Thor, where are you hurrying to? Do you suppose that Freyia will consent to marry with old Thrym, or that Od, her husband, will be pleased by the suggestion?'

Thor stopped and stared at Loki. 'I had not thought of that,' he said.

Loki laughed. 'For all that, there will be no harm in asking her. Come, Thor, let us go to Sessrumnir, but not at your pace.'

Together they went to Freyia's palace and found her there, though Od was, as so often, away wandering upon the earth. They told her of Thrym's offer, and immediately she flew into a great rage, so that the roof of her hall echoed with her indignation, and she even tore Brisingamen, her necklace, from around her neck, and flung it on the floor. 'How dare one of the giant race offer for my hand as though I were not among the highest of the Vanir? How dare he speak such words to you? And how dare you hear them? And having heard them, how dare you repeat them to me?'

Thor wished himself a long way off, but Loki waited. smiling quietly, until she stopped for breath, and then he said, 'It were best that this matter be put before the council. and debated by all the gods—yes, and the goddesses—so that you may speak to all of us, Freyia, and make your refusal known.'

So Odin called the gods and goddesses to his council hall, and they discussed how they might win back Miollnir and yet keep Freyia for themselves; but no way could they find to do this.

And then at last Heimdall, the watchman, spoke, 'Since Miollnir is Thor's own weapon, and none knows so well how to use it, it seems to me most fitting that Thor himself should go to the home of Thrym and fetch his hammer back.'

With a shout Thor interrupted him. 'It is easy for you to speak, Heimdall, from your post upon Bifrost. But if I go to Thrym's house—though I am strong, as you all know well—I shall be but one against many, and lacking my best weapon. Willingly would I go alone into the house of Thrym had I any hope of success, but without Miollnir I fear that I should perish.'

'I had not intended, Thor, that you should go as a warrior,' said Heimdall. 'But if Freyia would lend you a robe and a cloak, and a veil to cover your head, Thrym would think that it was Freyia herself come for the wedding feast, and would give Miollnir into your hands, and so might you obtain a victory, even against so many.'

Thor jumped up, shouting in his anger so that the very roof beams shook. 'Shall I, Thor of the Aesir, put on woman's garb and go as a bride to Iotunheim? Why, ever after would all the gods and goddesses, yes, and all the giants too, laugh at me for an unmanly coward.'

'The giants could not laugh, Thor,' said Heimdall, 'when you had smashed their skulls for them.'

But Thor would hear no more of the suggestion, and grew angrier with each moment, though all the gods sought to persuade him to assent to Heimdall's plan.

At last Loki said, 'Perhaps, Thor, you would prefer that the giants should leave Iotunheim in their numbers and come against Asgard, knowing that we lack Miollnir to keep them off.'

Thor fell silent for a moment, thinking. 'Come, Thor,' said Loki, 'the safety of all Asgard depends on you. And if you will go to Thrym, decked as a bride, I will go with you as your handmaiden.'

And at last Thor consented, saying, 'Since it is for the safety of all Asgard, I will go. Though if any laughs at me for it afterwards, he will not laugh long.'

So, still grumbling and protesting, Thor suffered his huge tawny beard to be shaved off. 'It will grow all the thicker and the mightier for it after,' said Loki encouragingly. Then he was dressed in a fine robe, reaching to his feet, with a girdle hung with keys, and a long cloak over it; and above all, a thick veil to cover his head. And Freyia, thankful indeed that it was not she who was to go to Iotunheim, herself hung Brisinga-men around his neck, loath though she was to part with it for any time.

Then, when Loki had been dressed in a plain kirtle and a cloak, with a veil to hide his red hair, the two of them climbed into Thor's chariot which was drawn by two strong goats, and away they sped towards Iotunheim, sparks flying from the hoofs of the goats, such speed they made.

When Thrym saw the chariot coming across the barren plain before his home, and spied by the glinting that one of the figures in it wore Freyia's necklace, he leapt up and shouted to his servants to make ready his halls to receive his bride. 'Great wealth have I,' he said, 'many herds of jet-black oxen with gilded horns, great coffers of jewels, and bags of gold, and rich am I accounted among the giants. Yet rich not only among the giants, but among the gods as well, shall I be counted now, since Freyia has come into Iotunheim to be my wife.'

While his servants strewed fresh rushes on the floor, and set up the benches and tables, Thrym went out from his house to welcome Thor and Loki. He took Thor by the hand and led him to the high seat at the end of the hall, thinking, 'How big and strong her hand is, and how tall a maiden is this Freyia, a fit wife indeed for a giant lord.'

The servants hurried in with food and drink, roasted ox-flesh, salmon, huge loaves, beer and mead; and sweetmeats for the women. Thor, by himself, ate one whole ox and eight large salmon, hurrying great mouthfuls of food under his veil; and when he was offered one of the dainty cakes that had been prepared for the bride, he ate not one, but all of them, and drank three vats of beer. Such an appetite was unrivalled, even by the giant-women, and Thrym wondered greatly at it. 'Indeed,' he said, 'never have I seen a bride who ate more than the lady of the Vanir, or who could drink more deeply than fair Freyia. Is such the custom of the goddesses?'

And Loki, who stood behind Thor's chair, leant his head forward and whispered into Thrym's huge ear, 'For eight nights has my mistress fasted, so greatly has she longed to come to your house.' And Thrym was well pleased at the words.

'I am glad that she has longed to see me,' he said, 'for I too have longed to look upon her face,' and he moved aside a little the veil that covered Thor's head. But when he saw Thor's eyes flash angrily at him, he let fall the veil and cried out, startled, 'Her eyes burn like fire! Why should the eyes of Freyia burn thus?'

And again Loki leant forward and whispered in his ear, 'Her eyes are bright and burning with weariness, since for eight nights she has not slept, so greatly has she longed to come to your house.' And Thrym was once more well pleased by his words.

Then Thrym's sister came forward and stood before Thor and asked, 'Fair Freyia, wife of my brother, will you not give to me a gift, as is the bridal custom? A golden ring from your white arm, or a brooch?'

But before Thor could reply to her, Thrym called out, 'A moment, sister. A gift have I for my bride and I will give it to her now.' He turned to his men. 'Bring in the hammer of Thor that was to be the marriage price.'

And his servants carried in Miollnir, and Thrym took it from them and laid it across Thor's knees. 'There, my fair bride, is my marriage gift. You may send it back to Asgard, if you will. Do I not keep well my promises?'

And Thor's right hand closed around Miollnir's handle, and in his heart he rejoiced to feel it in his grip again. Then rising, he swung the hammer above his head, and felled Thrym to the ground. At once there was an uproar in the hall, as the giants sought to escape the fury that had come among them; but Thor went about, striking down to the left and to the right, and no one escaped from him that day. Of all Thrym's household, there was no one left alive.

And that was how Thor won back his hammer, Miollnir, out of Iotunheim.

X

The Children of Loki

THE gentle goddess Sigyn was Loki's wife, and they dwelt together in Asgard, and much sorrow did Loki cause her by his mischief against the gods, for she ever feared their wrath upon him.

One day he tired of Asgard. 'I will go into Iotunheim and find myself a home among the giants, and take to myself a giant-wife, for the gods have grown tedious to me,' he said. And forthwith he left Asgard and travelled into Iotunheim, caring naught for Sigyn's tears. In Iotunheim he met with Angrboda, a grim-faced giant-woman, and smiling at the contrast which she offered to the lovely goddesses of Asgard, he took her to be his wife, and lived with her in a cave in the heart of a dark wood.

There in the wood were three monstrous children born to Angrboda and Loki; Fenris-Wolf, Iormungand, and Hel. Fenris-Wolf was a huge grey wolf with gaping jaws and sharp white teeth, who grew with speed to an enormous size. Iormungand was a serpent, hideous and scaly and ever-increasing in length. And Hel was a giant-maiden; one half of her face and half of her body were fair and comely, but all down the other side, from head to toes, her flesh was cold and livid, as might be the flesh of a corpse, and her eyes were dark and deep and pitiless, and no man might look on them without shuddering.

Time passed, and in their home in the wood, Loki's three children grew, so that at last Odin saw them from his throne that was set in his watch-tower, Hlidskialf, and because there was nothing hid from him, he knew that they would live to cause great sorrow to the gods. And he sighed, and tried what he could to prevent that sorrow. He sent to the wood, to Loki's home, and had his three terrible children brought to Asgard, and he pondered long over what he might best do with them.

Then to Hel he said, 'The abode of happiness is no place for you, nor will it ever be. Therefore begone to lowest Niflheim, and be queen there of all those dead who do not die in battle.' And in the depths of cold and misty Niflheim, he had a palace built for her, with high walls and a strong gate, and there she ruled over the spirits of the dead, all save those who entered Valhall.

And to Iormungand he said, 'The home of the gods, where love and kindness dwell, is no place for you. Therefore begone for ever from Asgard into the deep sea.' And he lifted up the serpent and cast him into the sea which flowed all around Midgard. And there Iormungand grew and flourished, until in time he encircled the whole world, and so remained, his tail between his teeth; and thus was he called the Midgard-Serpent.

But to Fenris-Wolf the Allfather said, 'Since much may be achieved by gentleness, and even savage natures may be tamed, remain you with us in Asgard, and in time you may come to be our friend.'

So Fenris-Wolf remained in Asgard and grew mightier and fiercer with each day, until, of all the gods, only Tyr, the brave god of war, dared go near to feed him. And at last the gods saw that Fenris-Wolf never would be tamed; and Odin, knowing that in the end he was to cause them great destruction, ordered that he was to be bound in chains, that he might do no harm until the appointed day which even the father of the gods himself could not prevent.

So the gods made a strong fetter which they called Laeding, stronger than any ten of them could have broken, all dragging on it at once; and they took this chain to Fenris-Wolf and said to him, 'See, here is a chain which we have made to test your strength. Let us bind it about you to see if you can break it, for your strength seems to us to be most wonderful.'

'You may bind me with your chain,' said Fenris-Wolf, 'and I will give you good proof of my strength, I promise you.'

They bound him, and he stretched himself, and Laeding burst asunder, and all the gods pretended great admiration, and praised Fenris-Wolf, though in their hearts they were troubled.

Then the gods made a second chain, stronger even than the first, and called it Dromi. This chain they took to Fenris-Wolf, saying, 'See, here is a fetter even greater than the last. Let us see you break it also.'

And Fenris-Wolf looked at the huge links of the chain

77

and said, 'Come, bind me, and I will show you my strength yet again.'

They bound him, and he stretched himself once, he stretched himself twice, and the chain broke apart, and he was free again. And all the gods hid the frustration of their hopes and were loud in their praise of the strength of the wolf.

And it became a saying among the Norsemen, 'To get free out of Laeding' or 'To dash out of Dromi', when anything that was most hard was attempted and achieved.

After their second failure to bind Fenris-Wolf, the gods all met together to discuss what they might next do, and Odin sent for Skirnir who was Frey's servant and his friend, and bade him go to Svartalfheim and ask the dwarfs to make for him with sorcery a chain which no strength might break. So Skirnir went to Svartalfheim, below the earth, and asked the most skilled of all the dwarfs if they could make such a thing for the gods.

'We can indeed,' they answered him, 'though it will not be easy, and the task will take us many days.'

So they forged for him a chain which they called Gleipnir, made of six things which have no being: the roots of a rock, the beard of a woman, the sinews of a bear, the spittle of a bird, the breath of a fish, and the sound of a cat's footsteps. And when the chain was made they gave it into Skirnir's hands, and he marvelled at it, that it was so slender and smooth and like a silken thread to the touch, and yet had such strength in it.

Skirnir returned to Asgard with Gleipnir and was eagerly welcomed by the gods, who immediately went to Fenris-Wolf and bade him go with them to an island set in the midst of a lake, saying that they had yet another chain with which to test his strength.

Willingly Fenris-Wolf went with them, for he had grown greatly since the last time they had tried to bind him, and he had no doubt that he would succeed yet once again in breaking any fetter they brought to test him with. But when he saw Gleipnir, how thin and weak it seemed, he grew suspicious lest there were sorcery in it, and he would not suffer himself to be bound.

And when the gods would have persuaded him, he said, 'I do not trust your chain, it is too slight. If you must bind me with it, then let one of you, as a pledge of good faith, put his right hand into my mouth while the bonds are being made fast.'

And the gods looked at one another, and no one spoke; for there was not one of them there who would willingly have lost his right hand. But when a little while had passed, Tyr went forward and laid his hand between the jaws of the wolf.

Then the gods bound Fenris-Wolf with Gleipnir, and when he was well and truly fast, they bade him loose himself, and the great beast stretched and strove against the chain. But the more strongly that he struggled, the firmer grew Gleipnir; until at last he saw that the gods had tricked him, and that he never would be freed. And the gods rejoiced that he was bound at last, and their danger past for a time; but with a growl like thunder, Fenris-Wolf closed his mighty jaws and bit off Tyr's right hand at the wrist.

Then the gods chained Fenris-Wolf to a rock, that he might remain there until the end of all things came.

And in time Loki grew weary of the cave in the dark wood where he dwelt with Angrboda, and he came out of Iotunheim and returned to his home in Asgard; at which Sigyn rejoiced greatly, to have him with her once again, for she loved him well.

KIDDELL-MONROE

XI

Frigg and the Gift of Flax

FRIGG's palace in Asgard was named Fensalir, and there she
lived, attended by the other goddesses and honoured as their
queen. Among those who served her were golden-haired
Fulla, her handmaiden, who kept the casket which held
Frigg's jewels, and fastened on her golden shoes; Hlin, who
went forth into the world of men to care for those whom
Frigg would keep under her protection; Gna, her messenger,
who rode the swift horse Hofvarpnir; Syn, her doorkeeper,
who kept from Fensalir all those whom Frigg did not wish
to have enter her halls; and Eir, who was skilled in the use
of herbs and simples, and taught their properties to the
women of the northlands.

But Frigg did not always remain in Fensalir, for often she went to Midgard and concerned herself with the lives of men and women, to help them and answer their prayers.

A certain poor peasant once lived with his wife in a little house in a valley. Each day he would go to pasture his few sheep on the mountain which overlooked the valley, and always would he take his cross-bow with him, for sometimes he had the luck to shoot one of the wild mountain goats and carry it home for his wife to cook.

One day he saw such a goat, finer and larger than any he had seen before, and leaving his sheep to graze, he climbed towards the boulder where it stood. But as he came close enough to shoot at it, it suddenly leapt away, higher up the mountain, and then stood once again upon a rock too far away for his arrows to reach. He climbed yet higher in pursuit of it, but it was ever the same, and when he was close to the goat, the animal fled, and at last it vanished altogether from his sight. And when the man looked about him, he saw that in his eagerness to kill the goat, he had climbed to the very top of the mountain, where before him rose up a huge gleaming glacier. Then he noticed that there was an opening in this glacier, as it might have been a door. Boldly the peasant went inside, wondering what he would see there, and immediately he found himself in a cave of shining ice, glittering with a thousand gems.

In the centre of the cave stood a fair and gracious lady, robed in shining white, with a bunch of little blue flowers in her hand; Frigg herself, with all around her, her attendants crowned with mountain blossoms, and smiling.

Awed, the peasant fell upon his knees, guessing her to be a goddess. Kindly she welcomed him, and offered him a gift to take away with him. 'Anything that is in this cavern you may have and take back to your home,' she said.

His wondering eyes saw all the glittering gems in the ice, all the gold and jewels worn by the goddess and her maidens, and he considered the riches that any one of them might mean to him and his wife, poor as they were; yet ever his eyes went back to the bunch of little blue flowers, bluer than the sky, as blue as her own lovely eyes, which Frigg held in her hand. And at last, though he knew not why, the man said, 'If you would give to me the flowers which you hold in your hand, goddess, that is all the blessing I would ask of you.'

And Frigg smiled, well pleased by his request. 'They are yours,' she said, 'and so long as they are fresh and flourish, so long shall you live and prosper, but when they wither and fade, so will you sink and die. Take them, and with them the bag of seed that I shall give you. Sow it on the land that is your own, and take good care of the plants that grow from it.' And she held out to him the bunch of little blue flowers. He rose and went to her and took it from her hand, then, dazzled by the brightness of her face, he closed his eyes; and when he opened them again, a moment later, he was alone on the mountain top, a bunch of strange blue flowers in his hand, and at his feet a leathern bag of seeds.

Marvelling, he returned home and told his wife of all that had befallen him, and showed her the flowers and the bag of seed. Angrily she upbraided him, saying, 'Why did you not ask for a ring of gold or a jewel that we could have sold? Little enough is the comfort we shall get from a bunch of flowers and a few seeds.'

But the man said nothing to her angry words, he only put his blue flowers in a safe place; and the next day, before he went to the mountain with his sheep, he dug the little plot of land that was his, and planted the seeds which Frigg had given him.

And in time green shoots appeared above the earth, and he tended them and kept the ground free from weeds, until the shoots grew into tall plants with little leaves and tiny flower buds. And then one day the peasant saw that the flowers were opening in the sun, and they were the same blue flowers as those in the bunch which Frigg had given him; and he was pleased, for the little field of blue reminded him of a memory that he would ever treasure, how he had seen and spoken with great Frigg herself.

But his wife said in scorn, 'Your flowers may look very pretty, but what use are they to us? Why, they are not even fodder for the sheep.'

In time the blue petals in the field dropped and the man sighed; but the seed heads ripened and grew heavy, and he smiled to hear the sound which they made when the wind passed through them, rippling them as though they had been a sea. Then the leaves and stems faded and lost their green freshness, and when they were yellowed for two-thirds of their length, one morning, when the peasant and his wife arose at dawn, they saw Frigg, smiling and kindly, standing with her maidens beside their little field.

'You have tended well the seeds I gave you,' she said. 'And now have I come to show you what you must do with the flax, that it may bring you prosperity.'

And she showed them how to pull up the flax plants and steep them in water until their fibres loosened, and after, how to dry them in the sun and beat them with a wooden mallet and comb them to tear apart the strands. And then she showed the peasant's wife how to spin a thread from them, strong and smooth, and weave with it as though it had been wool; and when the task was finished, the woman had a length of linen, the first that she had ever seen. Then with a blessing on them both, Frigg went away.

The peasant sold the linen for a good price, and from the seeds that he had saved from his plants, he sowed more flax the following year, so that again he had linen to sell. And in time he and his wife grew rich, with good food to eat and a large house to live in, wide fields of bright-flowered flax and a store-room filled with bales of linen; and their children grew up happily, in plenty, and learnt from their parents the secret Frigg had taught them.

And in all these years the little blue flowers in the bunch which Frigg had given to the peasant in the glacier on the mountain retained their freshness and did not fade, as she had promised. And though in time the woman died, after a long and happy life, the man lived on, to see his grandchildren grow up, and after them his great-grandchildren, all in much prosperity.

But one morning, when he looked at the bunch of blue flax-flowers, he saw that they were beginning to droop and fade, and he knew that the time had come for him to die, and he was content. 'But I would see yet once again great Frigg, before I die, that I may thank her for my happy life,' he said to himself. And bidding farewell to his family, he set off up the mountain to seek her.

He was an old man and the climb was hard, but he did not falter, and at last he stood on the very top before the great glacier. Once again he saw the door of ice, and once again he stepped in boldly; and there, as before, were Frigg and her maidens, smiling and kindly.

'You are welcome,' said Frigg, 'we have awaited you. Come and dwell with us for ever in peace and joy.' And the door of ice closed behind the old man, and he was never seen again by his friends. But his flax fields flourished for the good of his family for many generations.

XII

Geirröd and Agnar

ODIN and Frigg concerned themselves much with the welfare of Geirröd and Agnar, the two young sons of King Hraudung; and seeing one day from the watch-tower of Hlidskialf how a sudden autumn storm arose when the two boys were out alone in their little boat, they caused the boat to reach an island off the coast, where the boys might safely come to land. Here Geirröd and Agnar found no one living save an old man and his wife in a little house, who welcomed them kindly, and bade them stay until the wind dropped and they might launch their boat for home once more.

Now, the old man and woman were really Odin and Frigg who had taken mortal shape to help the boys, and, having a fancy to keep near them for a little longer, they caused the

87

winter storms to set in around the coast, so that the boys could not sail out in their little boat for the danger. So during all the winter months, the two boys remained on the island, kindly treated and cared for by the old man and his wife.

Geirröd, the younger son, became Odin's favourite, and Odin taught him much of the use of arms; and on the long winter evenings as they sat before the fire, told him stories of battle-glory, which the boy heard with eagerness. But the shy, dreamy Agnar was more dear to Frigg, and he spent much time at her side, learning greatly from her of wisdom and courage and gentleness towards his fellow men.

When the spring came, and the harsh winds dropped and the sea grew calm, Odin and Frigg bade farewell to the two boys and watched them row towards the coast. Then, well pleased with their two fosterlings, they returned to Asgard.

But not both the boys reached home, for when the little boat touched the coast of their father's land, Geirröd, ever the quicker, jumped out first, and as he turned to his brother, a sudden wicked thought came into his head, and taking the oars from the boat, he pushed her out to sea with Agnar still aboard. A breeze sprang up which blew her far from the shore, and with no oars to row for land, Agnar and the boat were soon lost to sight.

Then Geirröd returned to his father and told how Agnar had been drowned in a sudden squall, and how he himself had only been saved by the kindness of an old man and his wife living on a little island, where he had passed the winter; and his story was believed by King Hraudung, who saw no reason why his son should be lying.

When some years had passed, Odin and Frigg sat together in Hlidskialf and again they thought on Geirröd and Agnar and looked down on them. 'See,' said Odin, 'my Geirröd is now a great king, while your Agnar is no more than a thrall in the halls that should be his.'

And Frigg saw that it was even so, and Agnar, unknown to his brother, had not drowned, but was among the servants in Geirröd's house. Yet she said, 'It is better by far to be a thrall and kindly-hearted, than a great king and miserly.'

'What mean you by that?' asked Odin.

'It is said,' replied Frigg, 'that King Geirröd is so mean that if too many guests come to his house unbidden, he tortures some to scare away the others.'

'That,' said Odin, 'cannot be the truth. When he was a boy, my Geirröd was ever brave and noble, he would not stoop to such shameful deeds.'

'I warrant you that if you went to Geirröd's halls, you would find it even as I say,' declared Frigg.

'That can I not believe,' said Odin. 'Nevertheless, I will go and prove you wrong.'

So Odin went down to Midgard, clad in a dark-blue cloak with a wide-brimmed hat, and set off for King Geirröd's house. But as soon as he was gone from Asgard, Frigg sent her handmaiden, Fulla, with a warning to King Geirröd, that there was an evil sorcerer even then on his way to harm him, and bade him beware of any stranger at whom his dogs did not bark.

Now, Geirröd was not truly inhospitable, in this Frigg had lied, for she wished to see him punished for his crime against his brother, but when he heard that he was in danger from an evil sorcerer, he ordered his servants to bind and bring to him any stranger whom his watch-dogs failed to attack.

And when Odin, in his dark-blue cloak, came up to Geirröd's gate, the dogs, knowing him to be divine, uttered no sound and slunk away, as though they were afraid. So the servants took Odin and led him before their master, saying, 'Here is a stranger, lord, whom the dogs dared not attack.'

Geirröd looked long at Odin, and then asked his name. 'I am called Grimnir,' Odin replied.

'You are an evil sorcerer, come here to work me ill,' said Geirröd.

'That is untrue,' answered Odin. And though Geirröd questioned him long and searchingly, he would say no more than that.

So Geirröd had him bound to a pillar in his great hall, between two fires piled high with wood, that in the pain of the scorching he might speak concerning himself; and for eight nights he left him bound. And on the ninth evening, while King Geirröd feasted, Agnar the thrall, who should have been a king, stole unnoticed to where the stranger suffered, and in pity, gave him a horn full of ale to drink, whispering that he thought it a shame that the king should treat him thus without a cause.

Later that evening, in the midst of the feasting, Odin suddenly raised his voice in a loud chant, throwing back his head against the pillar, the firelight shining on him, as his words rang through the hall, so that all who were present fell silent to hear him. In his song Odin told of the beginning of the world, and of the gods and their homes in Asgard, and of the great ash-tree Yggdrasill. He told the names of the Valkyrs who chose the slain warriors from the battle-field, and he told all the names of Odin, which he took when he went about the earth, and Grimnir was one among them. Then he cried out, 'Hail to you, King Agnar, for you alone shall rule your father's lands, and this boon I give to you as a reward for the drink you offered me. But you, King Geirröd, shall perish, even on your own sword.'

Geirröd, who with all the others had been listening to Odin's chant in wonder, now grew angry at his words, and drew his sword, meaning to hew down the stranger who dared to insult him in his own house. But Odin called out in a mighty voice, 'Hear me, all you who are here tonight, for I am Odin and this is the truth that I have spoken.'

When he heard these words and saw the great light that shone about the stranger's head, and knew that he was indeed Odin, King Geirröd rose up hurriedly to take him from the fire. But he forgot the sword that lay across his knees, and it slipped to the ground, point uppermost; and in his haste Geirröd stumbled and fell upon his own sword, and it pierced him through the heart, even as Odin had foretold.

Then Odin called forth Agnar the thrall, and having named him for the rightful king, he disappeared from sight, being seen no more in those halls. But Agnar ruled long and justly, and was ever kind to strangers.

XIII

Thor's Journey to Utgard

IN company with Loki, and not alone as was more usual for
him, Thor once set out for Iotunheim to seek adventure. He
took with him Miollnir, his great hammer, and his belt that
increased his strength twofold, and he and Loki travelled
in his chariot that was drawn by his two goats.

Towards evening they came to the home of a poor farmer
who offered them shelter for the night, not knowing who
they might be. But he had not in his house enough meat to
feed two guests, and ashamed by his poverty, he apologized
for the meagre fare which was all that he could give to the
strangers.

Thor smiled. 'There is a remedy for that, good farmer,'

he said. And unharnessing his goats from the chariot, he slew them both. 'There lies meat enough for us all,' he said. 'Flay them and bid your good wife busy herself with the cooking, and so shall there be an ample meal for two hungry travellers and for you and your family besides.'

So helped by his son, Thialfi, the farmer flayed the goats, and his wife prepared the goat-flesh for their supper.

'Lay the hides away from the fire, lest they are burnt,' warned Thor. 'And then, as we eat, let us cast on to them the bones of the goats, taking care that none are broken.'

Soon a fine supper was ready, and they all sat down to eat. There was goats' meat in plenty, well roasted, and new-baked bread; and while the bones were picked clean and tossed aside on to the goatskins and the ale cups were re-filled time after time from the vat, the meal passed with much mirth and enjoyment. Thor with his huge tawny beard and his great appetite made the rafters ring with his mighty laughter at red-haired Loki's sly jesting, until the farmer and his wife thought that never had they entertained two more pleasing guests.

The youth Thialfi, his head a little heavy from the ale that he had drunk, holding a thigh-bone of one of the goats, looked at it longingly and wished that he might break it to eat the marrow, and wondered why his father's loud-laughing guest should take so much care to have the bones kept whole. He sighed at the thought of wasting a marrow such as was not come by every day in a house where there was poverty; and then he looked up to see that the hand-some, red-haired other stranger was watching him with a little smile, from his seat beside the fire.

'And why not, lad?' asked Loki quietly. 'What is there against it? The marrow in that bone would be well worth eating.'

Thialfi blushed that his thoughts had been guessed aright, and he looked away. But a few moments later he raised his eyes again and saw that Loki was still watching him, and it seemed to him that Loki's smile was now a little touched with scorn. 'Am I a child, that I should be afraid to disobey a foolish order?' thought Thialfi, and with a quick glance to see that no one else was watching him, he took up his knife and split the bone and ate the marrow out of it. And from the hearth he heard Loki laugh, very quietly.

In the morning, Thor rose up before any of the others were awake, and taking Miollnir, he touched the goat-hides and the bones lightly with the hammer, and immediately the goats stood up, alive and whole. But then Thor saw that one of them was lame in a hind leg. His angry shouts roused the others. 'Someone has broken a bone of my goat,' he said, and his voice thundered through the little house, as he swung his hammer above his head.

'It is Thor. It is Thor himself, and could be no other,' cried the farmer to his wife. And trembling and fearful, he and his family knelt before Thor and implored his pardon for whatever wrong they might have done. And no one of them was more afraid than young Thialfi.

But Loki stood calmly by the ashes of the hearth and smiled to himself at the uproar.

'Take all that we have, great one, but spare us,' pleaded the farmer. 'It is little enough that I have to offer you, for I am a poor man. Yet will I give you the best that I have in recompense. Take my son Thialfi to be your servant. Though young, he is strong, and no man can run as fast as he. He will serve you faithfully. Only spare us all, I beg of you.'

At their terror and their distress, Thor's anger cooled and he laid Miollnir by. 'I will take your son,' he said, 'and

94

may I find him as loyal and as willing as you declare him to be.' And at his words there was joy in the little house once more.

Leaving his goats and his chariot in the care of the farmer and his wife, Thor continued on his way to Iotunheim, striding off with great steps, with Loki at his side, and followed by Thialfi bearing food for the journey.

After a time they crossed the sea into Iotunheim, and went on eastwards through the giants' land, and when night fell they had not yet found anywhere to shelter. But going on a little way in the darkness, they saw before them the shape of a large building with an entrance at one end, very wide and high. Going through this entrance, they found themselves in a hall, and receiving no answer to their calls, they lay down in the darkness and were soon asleep.

But at about midnight they were all three awakened by a great shaking of the earth, and the walls of the house trembled as though they might at any moment fall. Thor jumped up and cried out to his companions, and together they groped around in the darkness of the hall until they came upon a smaller room leading from it, and here they remained, Thor sitting in the doorway with Miollnir held across his knees. The earth had by this time ceased to tremble, but soon there came a noise as of thunder close by, and this continued unbroken until the dawn.

When it was light, Thor went out from the house and saw, lying on the ground near by, an enormous man, and it was this giant's snoring that had sounded as though it were a thunderstorm, and his lying down to rest that had caused the earth to shake. Thor girded on his belt that increased his strength twofold, and gripping Miollnir tightly, he went over to the giant; but as he approached, the huge man awoke and sat up and looked at him.

'Who are you, large stranger?' asked Thor.

'I am called Skrymir,' answered the giant, 'and I have no need to ask your name, for I do not doubt from your appearance that you are Thor himself. Am I not right?'

'I am indeed Thor of the Aesir.'

Skrymir yawned and stretched his arms. 'Good morning to you, Thor,' he said. And then he caught sight of his glove, lying a little way off. 'Why, Thor,' he said, 'what have you been doing with my glove?' And he put out his hand to pick it up, and Thor saw that it was no less than the giant's glove which, in the darkness, he and the others had taken for a house; and as for the little room where they had hidden from the earthquake, it had been the thumb of the glove.

'Whither are you bound, my friend?' asked Skrymir.

'We go to the fortress which is called Utgard,' replied Thor.

Skrymir was silent for a moment, then he asked, 'Since you seem to be journeying even in the same direction as I myself, will you not give me your company along the way, Thor, and you too, red-haired Loki?'

'Willingly,' said the two gods.

So first they settled down to eat their morning meal, Thor and his companions from the bag which Thialfi had carried, and the giant from his own huge sack. And after they had eaten, Skrymir proposed that the others should give him their food to carry as well as his own, and they dropped their bag into the sack and he tied up the sack and slung it over his back, and they all set off together.

At evening they reached a grove of great oak-trees, and here Skrymir suggested that they might shelter for the night, and on the others' assenting, he flung down his sack of food, saying, 'I am tired and I would sleep. Let you share out the food, Thor.' And with that he lay down and was soon snoring like a thunderstorm.

Thor took the sack. 'Even if you have no wish to eat, good Skrymir,' he said, 'we others are hungry.' And he made to open the sack and take out the food. But try as he might, he could find no way to loosen the knots of the thongs with which it was tied; and after a time he became mightily angered at the waste of labour, and taking up Miollnir, he went to where Skrymir lay, and swinging the hammer, smote him on the head. Skrymir rolled over and opened his eyes and asked sleepily, 'What is the matter, Thor? It seems to me as though a leaf has fallen on my head and woken me, or was it you who wakened me to tell me you had eaten and were about to go to rest?'

And Thor was ashamed that his great blow had seemed no more to the giant than the fall of an oak-leaf, and he said, 'We have indeed eaten and are about to lie down to sleep. Good night to you, Skrymir.'

Supperless, Thor and Loki lay down under another tree with Thialfi close by, and none too happy in their minds at the thought of their travelling companion, they fell asleep, for they were tired.

At midnight Thor was awakened by the sound of Skrymir's mighty snoring, and could not go to sleep again by reason of the noise. He bore it for as long as he could, and then arose, and taking Miollnir, went again to where the giant lay, and struck him upon the head an even greater blow than the last that he had dealt him, and Miollnir sank deep into the giant's brow.

But Skrymir only awoke and opened his eyes and said, 'Why, are you there, Thor? An acorn must have dropped from the oak-tree and woken me. It is dark, surely it is not yet time to rise?'

And Thor, ashamed that such a mighty stroke had seemed no more to Skrymir than an acorn fallen from a bough, said, 'It is no later than midnight, Skrymir. There is yet time for us to sleep.'

But Thor slept no more that night. Instead he lay and wondered how he might destroy a giant so powerful that even Miollnir seemed a harmless weapon against him. 'For,' he thought, 'it were best that such a one, who may yet prove an enemy to Asgard, however well disposed he now may be, should not be allowed to escape.' And a little before dawn, hearing from his snores that Skrymir was still sound asleep, Thor once more took up Miollnir and went to where the giant lay. And then, with all his strength, he crashed his mighty hammer down upon the giant's upturned temple, and he saw it sink in, even to the haft.

But Skrymir only sat up and passed his hand across his cheek and said, 'The birds must be nesting in this tree, for I thought I felt a twig fall upon my head.'

And Thor was silent, angry and ashamed that the strongest of the gods had proved so puny in power against one who came from Iotunheim.

Skrymir rose and said, 'Our ways must part here, Thor and red-haired Loki, for I must go north towards the hills, and to the east lies the fortress which is called Utgard, where you wish to go. But before we part, let me give to you a word of good advice. I have marked how you three have whispered among yourselves that I am tall and broad and that my strength is great, but in Utgard there are others taller and broader and mightier in strength by far than I. Therefore it were well if, when you come to Utgard and meet its lord, you do not boast of your small prowess.' He paused and laughed. 'Best would it be, little Thor, if you went not on to Utgard, but turned back here. Yet if go there you must, take care that you heed well what I have said. Farewell.' Then, picking up his sack of food, Skrymir slung it over his shoulder and strode away towards the hills. And Thor and Loki and the farmer's son were not sorry to see him go.

'What say you,' asked Thor, 'do we pay heed to his words and go back, or do we go on, as we had intended?'

Loki, ever ready for an adventure, smiled. 'We go on,' he said, 'for I am hungry, and that Skrymir has taken all our food with him.'

So they went on together, and at midday they came to a plain on which stood a huge fortress, so high that they had to stretch their necks and bend their heads backwards to see the top of it. When they came up to this fortress, they found that it had a massive gate of iron bars which was locked fast. But so tall and wide was the gate, that Thor and his companions were easily able to slip in between the bars and so come into the courtyard. The house door being open, they went into the great hall, and it was indeed a vast room, with a bench running along each side, and on the benches many giants sitting at meat. And at the end of the hall, on the high seat, sat the lord of Utgard himself.

Thor and Loki went boldly up to him and greeted him. He looked them up and down and smiled in scorn. 'It seems, from what I have heard of his appearance, that you must be Thor from Asgard,' he said. 'But, oh, what a tiny weakling seems this great Thor of whom I have heard so much. Come now, strangers, are you skilled at any feats? For no one who is not greater than his fellows at some one thing or another sits down to eat in Utgard. What say you, have you any craft or skill?'

And while Thor hesitated, remembering how small his strength had seemed beside the might of Skrymir, Loki spoke. 'I am hungry,' he said, 'and I have waited long for this morning's meal. I will warrant that there is no one here who can eat more quickly than I, when once good food is set before me.'

The lord of Utgard laughed. 'We shall soon try you, red-haired Loki,' he said, 'to see whether you boast without good reason.' And he called down the hall to one of his servants who was named Logi, that he should match himself against his master's guest, to see who could eat more quickly.

A great trough filled high with roasted meat was carried in and set down in the hall; and Loki threw off his cloak and tossed back his flaming hair, and sat at one end of the trough, with the giant Logi at the other; and at a sign from the lord of Utgard, they both began to eat at once. And each of them ate as fast as he was able, so that they both came face to face in the middle of the trough and all the meat was gone. Loki looked up. 'What think you of that for an appetite?' he asked.

But the lord of Utgard pointed to the trough and said, 'It was not ill done, but see, my servant can do better.' And Loki saw that the giant had eaten not only all the meat off the bones, but the bones and his half of the trough as well.

And all the giants in the great hall laughed, and none so loudly as their lord. And Thor frowned in anger and red-dened in shame that the gods had been worsted yet again by those from Iotunheim. But Loki only shrugged his shoulders and said, 'Nevertheless, it was a good meal, and I enjoyed it greatly.'

Then the lord of Utgard turned again to Thor and said, 'Come, Thor, what of your other companion? In what does he excel?' He pointed to Thialfi. 'That youth there, is there anything at which he is more accomplished than any other man?'

'I have never yet been beaten by any other man when the

fleetness of my foot was in the question,' said Thialfi. 'Match me against any of your runners, and I will undertake to win a race on any course you choose.'

The lord of Utgard smiled. 'You must indeed run swiftly if that is so,' he said. 'But let us go out to the courtyard and see you prove your words.'

They all went forth from the house to the huge courtyard, which was as wide as any field, and there the lord of Utgard called out a youth named Hugi and bade him run against Thialfi. 'Let them run three times,' he said.

So they ran together once across the courtyard from end to end. And when Hugi reached the farther wall, he was so far ahead of Thialfi that he turned back and ran a little way to meet him.

'That was well run, Thialfi,' said the lord of Utgard. 'I think that never has there come here a man who could run so fast as you. Yet do you not run fast enough to beat my Hugi.'

They ran a second time, and when Hugi reached the farther wall, Thialfi was little more than half-way along the course.

'You run well, Thialfi,' said the lord of Utgard, 'but I do not think that you will win this race.'

And Thialfi and the giant lad ran a third time; and when Hugi had reached the farther wall, Thialfi was not yet half-way across the courtyard. And a great cheer went up from the men of Utgard, for Hugi the winner.

'The sport has made me thirsty,' laughed their lord. 'Come, let us go back into the house and drink. And perhaps there is some small thing at which you, great Thor, are skilled, that you may prove yourself to us of Utgard?'

'I can drink with anyone,' said Thor, 'and drink more deeply.'

'Well said,' laughed the lord of Utgard. And he called to

his serving-boy to bring his drinking horn. 'If this horn is drained in one draught,' he said, 'it is considered that the drinker drinks well, and well enough if it is drained in two. But no one here is so poor a drinker that he cannot drain the horn in three.'

Thor looked at the horn and thought that though long, it was not so very large, and he was thirsty. 'I shall drink it all off easily in one draught,' he said to himself, and raised the horn to his lips. But though he drank deeply and until his breath failed him, when he came to look into the horn, it seemed as though there were yet a great deal within to be drunk.

'If anyone had told me,' said the lord of Utgard, 'that great Thor could not empty my horn in one draught, I should have called him a liar. But now have I seen it with my own eyes. Yet have I no doubt that a second draught will empty it.'

Thor did not answer him, instead he put the horn to his lips again and drank an even mightier draught than the first. But when he had to pause for breath, and he looked into the horn, it seemed as though he had drunk but very little.

'Come, Thor,' said the lord of Utgard, 'you may be reckoned a mighty drinker among the Aesir, but not so here. Yet surely you will not fail to empty my horn at a third attempt?'

Then Thor grew very angry and he determined to succeed, and he drank for a third time with all his might. But when he paused and looked into the horn once more, though the drink was certainly less, still was there much left to be finished. And Thor handed back the horn to the serving-boy and would not drink again, while the lord of Utgard laughed.

'It seems that you are no mighty drinker when judged by our men,' he said. 'But tell me what else you can do.'

'Such draughts would not be considered mean in Asgard,'

said Thor, 'and there, too, is my strength considered great enough. Try me with some feat of strength, and I will not fail in that.'

'There is a little thing which our youths here find much sport in doing,' said the lord of Utgard, 'and it is such a little thing that I should not dare to suggest that the great Thor should try it, had I not seen for myself that he is less mighty than I had ever supposed him to be.'

'What thing is this?' asked Thor, frowning.

'No more than to lift up my cat from the floor,' said the lord of Utgard. And as he spoke there came into the hall a large grey cat.

Thor looked at it. 'That were easily done,' he said. 'It is but a cat, though it is large.' And he went to it and put his hands below it and made to pick it up. But the cat arched itself as he raised it, and the higher he raised it, the higher grew the arch of its back, so that he could in no way lift it up. And at last, after he had put forth all his strength, he had been able to do no more than raise one of the cat's paws from the ground.

The lord of Utgard said scoffingly, 'That matter has gone as I fancied it would, and Thor is proved to be a very little man beside our youths, that he cannot lift up a cat from the floor.'

Thor was greatly angered, and he cried out, 'Now have you made me wrathful with your gibes, and when I am filled with rage, then is my strength increased. Come, let any of you who will, step forth and wrestle with me, and I will show him that my strength is not to be despised.'

But no one answered his challenge, and the giants all sat in their places and laughed at him.

'Indeed,' said the lord of Utgard, 'it appears that there is no one here who would not consider it a disgrace to match himself against one so weak as you have proved yourself to be. But lest you should call us cowards when you tell this tale back home in Asgard, I shall send for Elli, my old nurse, and she will fight with you.'

And immediately there came into the hall a tottering old woman. 'There stands Elli,' laughed the lord of Utgard. 'Let us see the great Thor prove himself her equal.'

But Thor would not. 'Shall I wrestle with a woman, and she an old crone who has seen many years pass by? I, Thor of the Aesir, the strongest of the gods? Why, I should be shamed for evermore that I put forth my strength against a creature so feeble and defenceless.'

'She has thrown many a good man before today,' said the lord of Utgard. 'And if you hold back, all we here shall think that you are afraid of an old woman.'

Stung by his taunts, Thor went forward and took hold of the old nurse, but the harder that he gripped her, the firmer she stood; and when, in her turn, she took a grasp of him, he rocked upon his feet. And try as he might, with all his god's strength, Thor was unable to keep his stand, and he fell down upon one knee.

Then the lord of Utgard called to bid the game to cease, and Thor arose, discomforted at his disgrace, that he had been unable to withstand the petty strength of one old woman. But the lord of Utgard said, 'Evening is upon us, let us to the feasting, and I warrant that you who are from Asgard will not find our cheer unworthy of your notice.' And he led Thor and Loki to seats close by his own; and much of that night they all spent in eating and drinking the good food and ale that were set before them; so that for a while the two gods forgot how they had shown themselves to be of little account in Utgard.

The next day, after the morning meal, Thor and Loki and

young Thialfi set off from Utgard early, and the lord of the
fortress went a little distance with them to speed them on
their way. When they came to the place where they were to
part, the lord of Utgard asked Thor with a smile, 'How
think you that your journey to Utgard has fallen out? Are
you content with it?'

And Thor frowned and said, 'Truly, I have gained naught
but shame and dishonour from my journey to your home.'

But the lord of Utgard shook his head. 'Indeed you have
not, great Thor,' he said. 'Now that we have left Utgard
many steps behind, I will tell you the truth. If I have the
power to keep you out, never again shall you set foot within
my fortress. And I will say this also to you, that had I known
how great was your strength, I would not have permitted
you to enter there even this once. For you must know that
it was I whom you met on your way and knew as Skrymir,
and I had prepared against your coming to my fortress certain enchantments. The first was when you would have
unloosed my sack which held the food. I had fastened it
with iron and a spell, so that no one might undo it. And when
you struck me those three blows as I slept, the first and least
of them would have been enough to kill me, had it reached
its mark. But I had put a mountain between myself and you,
even that mountain which you see yonder, and your great
hammer struck deep into the rock. If you look, you may
see how it has cleft it in three places. So also was it sorcery
in my fortress. He against whom you, Loki, did contend, my
servant Logi, he is wild-fire which can burn the trough and
the bones no less easily than it can devour the meat from
them. And when you, Thialfi, matched yourself in speed
against my Hugi, it could not have been that you should win,
for Hugi is thought, and what can run more quickly? And
the horn, great Thor, was also an illusion, for when you

drank from my horn, though you seemed to have drunk but little, then it was indeed a marvel to us at Utgard, for the other end of the horn was out in the sea, so how could you empty it? When you reach the sea on your journey home, mark well how the tide-line has dropped lower. And when you tried to lift up my cat, Thor, that too was a wonder, for it was no cat, but the Midgard-Serpent, which lies coiled about the earth. When we saw you raise up one of the cat's paws from the ground, then did we tremble indeed at your might. And that you should withstand in the wrestling with old Elli, my nurse, and sink no farther than upon one knee, that was truly marvellous, for she is no other than old age, and who can resist old age?' After a moment the lord of Utgard went on, 'Now must we part, Thor and red-haired Loki, and I am glad that it is so. And I may tell you before we part, that if ever you come again to Utgard, I shall, with all the wiles and sorcery I know, defend myself and my fortress against you. Yet I trust that we may never meet again, great Thor, for you are very mighty.'

When Thor heard how he had been tricked, he grasped Miollnir and flourished it above his head, very wrathful; but in that instant the lord of Utgard vanished, and was nowhere in sight. 'Let us go back to the fortress and cast it down, stone by stone,' thundered Thor. But when they looked, there before them was the plain whereon had stood the fortress, but Utgard was no longer there, and the wide land was empty.

So Thor and his companions returned the way that they had come, and Thor was very angered; though Loki smiled and shrugged his shoulders, caring little. And when they came to the sea, they saw that it was even as the lord of Utgard had told them, and the waters had diminished with Thor's mighty draughts, and thus were formed the ebb-tides.

XIV

The Cauldron of Hymir

AEGIR, the god of the deep ocean, once went to Asgard for a feasting, and so pleased was he at his entertainment, that he invited all the gods to feast with him, in his palace below the waves, at harvest time. 'But,' he said, 'I fear that the cheer which I can offer you may not be as splendid as your own, for though there is no lack of good meat in my house, I have but a small cauldron for the brewing of mead. Yet perchance you may overlook this, if the food is plentiful.'

The gods laughed, and agreed to drink but little when they went to Aegir's feast; all save Thor, who said, 'Good meat is nothing to me, when I cannot drink my fill. You should find yourself a larger cauldron, Aegir.'

'But where am I to find a cauldron large enough to brew

mead for all the gods?' asked Aegir. 'Had I a goat like your Heidrun, who gave mead instead of milk, then would all be well, or had I the cauldron of old Hymir the giant, then would I have one great enough to satisfy the thirst of all the Aesir and the Vanir, even had each one of them Thor's appetite for drink.'

'If the cauldron of Hymir is all you want to make your feast worthwhile attending,' said Thor, 'then shall you have it, and in good time for the brewing.'

'How shall that be, Thor?'

'Why,' laughed Thor, 'I shall fetch it for you myself.' He looked around at the other gods. 'Which of you will come with me?'

'If my one hand is any help to you, then I will go with you,' said Tyr.

'Well spoken, Tyr, I could wish for no better companion. I warrant we shall have an adventure worthy of us both.'

So, taking Miollnir and his belt and gloves which gave him greater strength, Thor set out for Iotunheim with Tyr, and after a long journey they came to Hymir's house, set near the cold sea in a barren, rocky place, where Hymir's cattle grazed on the sparse grass.

Thor knocked loudly on the gate, but Hymir was out hunting, and in the house were only Hymir's wife and his nine hundred-headed mother. The old giant woman looked at them with her twice nine hundred eyes, and cared not for what she saw, and muttering with all her nine hundred mouths, she returned to her place by the fire. But Hymir's wife received them kindly, and gave them mead to drink; and when she heard her husband's footsteps in the courtyard, she hid them behind a row of cooking vessels which hung from a beam that was slung between two pillars. 'Wait there until I have told him of your coming,' she whispered, 'for my husband has often slain an unexpected guest with but one glance of his fiery eyes.'

When Hymir came in, the icicles rattling on his beard and hanging from his bushy eyebrows, his wife told him that they had two guests from Asgard who were even then hidden behind the cooking pots; and at her words the giant cast such a baleful glance in their direction that the beam split open and the brazen vessels fell to the floor with a great clatter, and all of them were broken save the largest cauldron; and Thor and Tyr stepped forth.

Hymir looked at them. 'You are not welcome,' he grumbled, 'since you come from Asgard, but it shall not be said of Hymir that he turned away a guest.' And he ordered his servants to slaughter three oxen for their supper.

His mighty appetite sharpened by the long journey to Hymir's house, Thor ate, by himself, two of the roasted oxen, leaving but one for the others. Hymir frowned greatly when he saw this and said, 'Tomorrow, if you sup in my house, let it be on what I have caught from the sea in the morning.'

'Willingly,' said Thor. 'For I shall welcome a day's fishing with you, Hymir.'

So the next morning, when Hymir dragged his boat down to the shore, Thor went with him and stood waiting. 'You are too small a person to go in my great boat,' taunted Hymir. 'Wait you on the beach until I return with my catch, for I go fishing for whales.'

'And I,' retorted Thor, 'go fishing for something larger than a whale.'

'Then you will need bait, little Thor. Go, find some first,' jeered Hymir.

Thor went straightway to where Hymir's oxen grazed, and choosing out the largest of the herd, he slew it and cut off its head, and returned to the shore. 'You are not a guest whom many would welcome,' said Hymir in anger, when he saw that his finest ox was dead.

But Thor only answered, 'Now that I have bait, will you take me fishing with you?'

Hymir laughed. 'You would no doubt be frozen in a very little while if you rowed out as far from land into the icy sea as I am wont to do.' And he pushed the boat into the water and climbed aboard.

'That shall we see,' said Thor, and jumped in after him.

Hymir rowed mightily, far out into the ocean, and at last he laid the oars aside. 'Here are my fishing grounds,' he said.

'Let us go farther yet,' said Thor. And seizing the oars, he rowed on, until Hymir himself protested. Then Thor ceased, and Hymir baited his hook and soon he caught two huge whales. 'There is our supper, little one,' he said. 'Now let me see you catch a fish.'

Thor baited his hook with the head of the ox and flung it far into the sea, and after a while he felt a great tugging on the line. With mighty pulls Thor dragged his catch to the surface, while Hymir laughed, 'What have you caught, my friend, a flounder? Or perhaps a sprat?'

But he did not laugh any longer, when, above the sea, close beside the boat, appeared the head of Iormungand, the Midgard-Serpent, caught fast on Thor's hook, thrashing his enormous coils about until the sea was churned into froth and the giant's boat rocked as though at any second it would surely be capsized.

'Quickly, Hymir,' gasped Thor. 'Hold you the line for me, while I strike at the monster with Miollnir, and so shall I be avenged for the grey cat which I could not lift in the lord of Utgard's hall.'

But Hymir was afraid for himself and for his boat, and

taking the knife from his belt, he cut the line, and Iormungand, with a mighty roar, sank back into the sea.

'That was a foolish thing to do,' shouted Thor, furiously. 'I have ever thought the giant-people to be stupid, but never did I think that even one of them could do a thing such as you have done this moment.' And he snatched up Miollnir and swung a blow at Hymir, and missed him as the giant leant aside, while the boat rocked and all but overturned; so that Thor was forced to desist, and flung down his hammer. Then angrily and in silence they rowed back to the shore.

When they reached land, Hymir leapt out on to the beach, and slinging the two whales over his shoulder, he started off for his house; upon which Thor picked up boat and tackle and oars and carried those up to the gate.

That evening as they sat at their meal, Hymir said grudgingly, 'Well did you row today, little Thor, and well did you fish, but I will call no man truly strong who cannot break my cup.' And he held out to Thor the glass goblet from which he drank his ale.

'That will be easy,' laughed Tyr, as Thor took the cup and smashed it down upon the table top. But the cup dented the wood and was not even cracked.

And Hymir laughed, 'Try again, little Thor, try again.'

Angered, Thor rose and flung the cup with all his might against one of the pillars of the hall, but the wooden post fell in splinters, while the glass cup was whole.

And Hymir laughed, 'Perhaps you are not strong enough, my friend.'

Thor dashed the cup down upon the floor, but still it remained unbroken, and he became more angry every moment; while Hymir laughed on, throwing back his ugly head and holding his shaking sides.

Then, unseen by anyone else, Hymir's wife came close

to Tyr, and under pretence of pouring his wine, she whispered, 'Hymir's head is harder even than his goblet.'

'Smite Hymir's skull,' said Tyr to Thor; and with a shout, Thor struck the giant on the head with the goblet, so that it was shattered and fell into a thousand pieces on the floor.

Hymir at once ceased his laughing and stared ruefully at the broken cup, and it was Thor's turn to laugh. Then Hymir said, 'Sorry indeed am I to lose my glass goblet, for it was a rare treasure, but you have proved to me your strength, and I would be willing to give a fine gift to one as strong as you. Ask what you will of me, and maybe I shall give it to you, if I see fit.'

Promptly Thor replied, 'I would have the cauldron in which you brew your mead.'

'Sad was I to lose my glass goblet, and yet sadder would I be to lose my cauldron, but even that will I give to you, if you can carry it away.' And Hymir smiled, for he thought that never would Thor be able to take his huge cauldron from the house.

Tyr rose at once, and going to where the cauldron stood, he tried to lift it, but not an inch could he raise it off the floor, though he tried with all the strength of his left hand. 'Try what you can do, Thor,' he said. And Thor seized hold of the rim of the cauldron, and with a mighty heave, he raised it up and placed it on his head, and with a loud whisper to Tyr, 'Come, my friend, it is time for us to be going home,' he walked the length of the giant's hall and out through the door, across the courtyard and through the gate and away over the rocky plain, followed by Tyr.

And Aegir brewed such quantities of mead in Hymir's cauldron that all the gods were loud in praise of the good cheer in his palace; so that, ever after, at harvest time, they went to his sea-halls for the autumn feasting.

XV

Thor's Battle with the Giant Hrungnir

ODIN once rode into Iotunheim on Sleipnir, his eight-legged horse, who was the best of all steeds. From the gateway of his house, Hrungnir, the strongest of the giants, whose head was of stone and whose heart was flint, saw Odin ride by, and marvelling at Sleipnir's speed, wondered who the stranger might be. 'Who are you, in the golden helmet, who ride so fast?' Hrungnir called out.

'I am Odin from Asgard,' answered the Allfather, pausing in his gallop.

'I had heard much of Odin's horse, how great his speed, and now that I have seen Sleipnir for myself, I know that

113

what I heard was true. But swift as he is, your horse is yet not so swift as my Gullfaxi.'

Odin laughed. 'That is not possible,' he said. 'I would wager my head on it, there could be no horse in all Iotunheim so swift as Sleipnir.'

Hrungnir grew angry and shouted for Gullfaxi to be brought, and leaping into the saddle, he raced with Odin across Iotunheim. Over plains and mountains, over rocks and rivers they went, and as Odin had boasted, Sleipnir proved himself the better steed and gained steadily on Gullfaxi. On and on Odin galloped, followed by Hrungnir, across the borders of Iotunheim and right on into Asgard, and there he drew rein.

Hrungnir caught him up. 'You spoke truly,' he said, 'your horse is the very best there is.' And then he looked around him and saw how he had galloped even into Asgard, the home of his enemies, who now came from all directions to greet the Allfather on his return. 'Is this a trap into which you have led me?' he asked Odin. 'Have I ridden over the sea and across the land and through the sky, only to perish within the walls of Asgard?'

'That may no one ever say of the Aesir, that they have tricked one of the giant race into their home and slain him there,' said Odin. 'You are welcome, Hrungnir, to feast with us today in friendship, and I think you will not find our entertainment wanting.'

So Hrungnir stayed that day to feast in Asgard, and there was no one to condemn his company, for Thor, who alone would not have suffered a giant to enter Asgard, was away, as so often, adventuring.

The gods gave Hrungnir of their best, as though he were no enemy; and for his part, he much enjoyed the feasting. But the good mead given by the goat Heidrun was stronger than any he was wont to drink, and before long he had grown drunk and loudly boastful; and of all the goddesses, only Freyia dared pour for him.

'Give me more, more of this delicious mead, fair Freyia,' he shouted, 'for I vow that I will drink all the mead in Asgard, if I am but given time.' And the more she filled his drinking horn for him, the more boastful he became, until at last his words were more than mere discourtesy to his hosts. 'How small a place seems this Asgard,' he said. 'And the hall you call Valhall, why I could lift it up with one hand and carry it to Iotunheim. And so shall I do one day, for none of you puny gods can stand against the might of Hrungnir, once he is armed for battle. Yes, there will come a time, and not so far away—Give me more mead, Freyia—when I shall slay you all, yes, each one of you, and send Asgard crumbling into dust.' He once more drained the horn, and signed for Freyia to refill it. 'Yes,' he went on, 'each one of you shall I destroy, gods and goddesses alike, save only Sif and Freyia; Freyia because she poured my mead, and Sif for her golden hair. Those two shall I take with me into Iotunheim, to be my wives.'

Seeing him to be drunk, the gods had kept silence at Hrungnir's loud affronts, but just at the moment when he was speaking of Sif, how he would take her into Iotunheim to be his wife, Thor entered the hall, and angry as he would have been at the sight of a giant drinking in Asgard, he was yet angrier at hearing Sif's name on Hrungnir's lips. He strode forward, Miollnir held tightly in his hand. 'What means this?' he thundered. 'Who gave Hrungnir leave to enter Asgard? How should a giant drink with us? And why should Freyia pour mead for him, as though he were an honoured guest?'

With insolence Hrungnir turned to Thor and answered

him, 'It was your Odin himself who brought me here, and it is on his bidding that I drink in this hall. It is unfitting that you should question the Allfather's wishes, Thor who shouts too loudly.'

'You will soon regret that bidding which you so lightly took,' cried Thor, and he swung Miollnir above Hrungnir's head.

But Hrungnir cried back at him, 'Have a care, Thor, for it will be small glory to you to slay me here, an unarmed guest.'

And all the other gods called out to Thor to desist. 'For his words are true,' they said, 'and it would be an everlasting shame to us if he were slain weaponless in our midst.'

So, wrathful though he was, Thor heeded their warning, and laid Miollnir by, glowering all the while at Hrungnir.

The giant laughed and said, 'A greater test of your courage would it be, Thor, if you were to meet me at a place which we both should choose, at a time which we both should name, there in single combat to decide which of us is the better.'

Eagerly Thor agreed to this, and they settled on a place where they should meet to fight, and when. 'Foolish was I,' said Hrungnir, 'to ride to Asgard weaponless, for had I my shield and my battle-hone with me now, there need be no delay to our fighting.'

Then Hrungnir went out from the hall, mounted Gullfaxi, and rode away out of Asgard back into Iotunheim. And when the other giants heard that he and Thor were to meet to fight, they thought that they had much to lose, if Hrungnir perished at Thor's hands; for Hrungnir was accounted the strongest of them all, and it would go ill in the future with those weaker than he, if Thor were the victor.

'Since Thor will bring his squire with him,' they said, 'you too must have a squire, and he must be so mighty in stature that the very sight of him will put fear into the heart of the god of thunder.' But since there was, to their minds, none huge enough in all Iotunheim to be their champion's squire, they fashioned a man out of clay, nine miles high and three miles broad, and gave him the heart of a mare set in the midst of the clay.

Then Hrungnir and the man of clay awaited the coming of Thor and Thialfi, the farmer's son, who was his squire. And when Thor's mighty tread was felt, shaking the earth as he came, Hrungnir took up his shield which was made all of heavy stone and in his right hand he brandished his battle-hone, a huge whetstone of flint, and he glared most horribly, a terrible sight to behold. But the mare's heart in the breast of the clay giant fluttered and quaked, for the man of clay was afraid.

'I have an idea to help you, master,' said Thialfi, and he ran on ahead to where Hrungnir waited. 'Great Thor is coming,' he called out. 'My master, great Thor of the Aesir, comes.'

'I am prepared for him,' said Hrungnir. 'Let him come when he will.'

Thialfi laughed. 'Do you call yourself prepared, giant?' he asked. 'You who wait so ill-protected?'

'Indeed, I am not ill-protected,' said Hrungnir with indignation, 'for have I not my shield which no weapon can pierce and my hone which kills when it strikes?'

'You have them truly, Hrungnir,' replied Thialfi, 'but you hold your shield before you, and what use is that to you, since Thor is coming up from the ground against you? When the earth opens beneath your feet, what use will a shield be over your heart? Can you not hear the rumbling of the earth as it splits apart to let Thor forth?'

And the foolish Hrungnir believed Thialfi's words, and

immediately he stood upon his shield. 'Now am I well protected against all assault from the earth,' he said.

At that moment Thor appeared before him, the sparks of anger flying from his tawny beard, and he hurled Miollnir with all his might; and it was too late for Hrungnir to raise up his shield once more. Instead, with both his hands, he flung his hone at Thor. The hone met Miollnir in the air and they came together with a mighty clangour, and the hone broke in half. One half was shattered into a million pieces, so that all the earth around was evermore covered with flints, and the other half went deep into Thor's brow, so that he fell to the ground. But Miollnir struck the giant full upon his stone head and cracked it wide apart, and staggering forward, he fell dead.

Thialfi, flourishing his sword, rushed full at the clay giant, and since he was made of clay, for all the terror in his mare's heart, he could not run away, and Thialfi cut him down with one sweep of his sword. Then he turned to see how Thor had fared, and saw that he was lying with one of the dead Hrungnir's mighty legs across his neck. Thialfi ran to him and tried with all his strength to lift the limb that Thor might be freed, but he could not move it. He called upon all the gods to come and aid him, and in an instant they were there.

Yet they also could not move the mighty giant's leg, and it looked as though Thor would remain in that place, prisoned for evermore.

But suddenly his little son, Magni, came up and begged, 'Let me try what I can do.' And he took hold of the foot of the dead giant, and little though he was, and young, he lifted it easily off his father's neck; while all the gods marvelled at his might and said, 'When he is come to his full strength, he will be greater by far than us.'

Then Thor rose up and embraced his son, and gave to him

for his own, Gullfaxi, Hrungnir's horse. 'For,' he said, 'you have well deserved so fine a prize.' And all the gods rejoiced at the victory.

But the flint from Hrungnir's hone remained for always in Thor's head, and therefore among the Norsemen it was ever considered an ill thing to cast a hone to the ground, lest thereby the flint that was in the head of the thunder-god was disturbed and caused him pain.

XVI

How Loki Outwitted a Giant

A CERTAIN peasant and his wife lived with their young son
in a little house nearby the sea. The man was greatly fond of
playing chess, and frequent practice with his neighbours on
the long winter evenings had brought him much skill at the
game. One day a giant came to the cottage and demanded
that the peasant should play chess with him. Glad to match
himself with an opponent whom he had not tried before, the
man consented. 'But for what stakes do we play?' he asked,
for he much enjoyed winning a coin or two or a measure of
wheat from his neighbours.

'Whichever of us wins may ask the other for what he will
of his possessions,' replied the giant promptly.

And the man thought to himself, 'I am poor, there is but little among my possessions that a giant could covet, yet will he own much that would be of use to me, should the victory be mine.' And he agreed to the stakes, and they sat down to play together.

The game was a long one, and went on well into the evening, but at last the giant won. 'Now must you give to me out of all that you own that which I shall choose for myself,' he said.

'Choose and welcome,' said the peasant. 'It was a good game and I would not have missed it.'

'Give me your son,' said the giant. 'He is all I want of your possessions.'

The unfortunate man heard the words with horror; but in vain he and his wife implored the giant to take all else they owned and leave them their only child, for the giant did no more than laugh at their pleading. Yet at last, to their entreaties, he replied, 'I will leave you the boy for one night longer and tomorrow I shall come for him. And more, if tomorrow you have hidden him so well that I cannot find him, I will renounce my claim, and you may keep your son.' And with that he went away.

Weeping, the peasant and his wife wondered where they might hide the child, but they could think of no place where the giant would not look for him. Far on into the night they thought despairingly, and at last the woman said, 'Let us pray to Odin, he may hear us and come to our aid.'

So they prayed to Odin, and after a time there came a great knocking in the darkness on the cottage door. 'It is the giant returned,' said the woman fearfully. But her husband replied, 'It is not yet dawn, he will not come in the night.' And he went bravely to the door and opened it.

Outside stood a stranger in a grey cloak with a wide-brimmed hat, none other than Odin himself. 'I have heard your prayers,' he said. 'Give me your son and I will hide him for you, and maybe the giant will not find him when he comes in the morning.'

Gratefully the peasant and his wife gave the child to Odin; and Odin changed him into a grain of wheat and hid the grain in an ear growing in a wheatfield close by.

In the morning the giant came and looked once around the cottage. 'You have not hidden him here,' he said, and went outside. He looked all about him, and then, having some strange knowledge, he went straight to the wheatfield, while the peasant and his wife watched with troubled eyes. 'Give me a sickle,' demanded the giant, and the man dared not refuse him.

Rapidly the giant cut the wheat, casting aside each armful save one, and then he flung down the sickle and picked out a single ear of wheat from among the rest he held. Then he plucked off, one by one, each grain, until he held the very one which was the boy. The peasant and his wife wrung their hands in despair; but Odin, taking pity on them once again, blew like a puff of wind and tossed the grain of wheat out of the giant's grasp and back to the man and his wife, where it became once more the boy. 'I have done what I can for you,' said Odin. 'Now must you help yourselves.'

The giant strode over to the cottage. 'That was good,' he said, 'but it was not good enough. You will have to outwit me more cleverly than that, if you wish to keep your son. Tomorrow I shall come again to find where you have hidden him.'

All that night the peasant and his wife wondered what they should do, now that Odin could help them no longer; and at last they prayed to Hönir, the bright god, Odin's brother. And just before dawn, when the woman opened the door of the cottage to see if it was yet day, there outside stood Hönir, like a ray of light. 'Give me your son,' he said, 'and I will hide him for you, and maybe the giant will not find him when he comes.'

Gratefully they gave him the boy; and Hönir turned him into a tiny feather and hid him on the breast of a swan which swam on a stream close by.

In the morning the giant came and looked once around the cottage. 'You have not hidden him here,' he said, and went outside. He looked all about him, and then, having some strange knowledge, he went straightway to the stream and snatched up the swan and tore off its head. Then he plucked off its feathers one by one, while the peasant and his wife watched him with dismay. At last the giant held in his hands one fluff of white down which was the boy, and the father and the mother wrung their hands in despair.

But Hönir took pity on them and blew like a puff of wind and blew the feather into the cottage where it became the boy again. 'I have done what I can for you,' said Hönir. 'Now must you help yourselves.'

The giant came to the peasant and said, 'That too was good, but it was not good enough. Tomorrow I shall come again to find where you have hidden him.'

Once more the man and his wife wondered all night what they might do to save their son, now that Odin and Hönir could not help them; and towards dawn they were still sitting over the ashes of their fire, their faces white and drawn.

The man shivered. 'The fire is dying,' he said. And glad to do something other than think, the woman raked the ashes and laid wood on them. Suddenly she said, 'There is yet Loki.'

'Why should Loki help us?' asked her husband.

'We can but pray to him,' she said.

So they prayed to Loki that he would save their son, and waited in the grey darkness for an answer. And suddenly the wood caught fire and blazed up, and in the light of the flames, there stood Loki in the room. 'Give me your son,' he said, 'and I will hide him for you, and maybe the giant will not find him when he comes.'

They gave the child to Loki, who changed him into the tiny egg of a fish, and went from the cottage down to the sea and hid the egg in the roe of a flounder that swam far from the shore.

When the giant came he looked once around the cottage and said, 'He is not here, he is outside.' And he went out and looked about him. Then, having some strange knowledge, he hurried off to fetch his boat and dragged it down to the shore, while the peasant and his wife watched him with terror. But as the giant climbed aboard, Loki came up to him. 'Take me fishing with you,' he demanded.

'Willingly,' said the giant, and they put out to sea together.

In the middle of the ocean the giant baited his hook and fished; but each fish that he caught he flung overboard again, until he caught a certain flounder, and placing it carefully in the bottom of the boat, he rowed once more for the shore.

On the beach he took out his knife and cut the fish open to take out the roe. Splitting the roe, he looked each egg over until he held the one which was the boy between his finger and his thumb. 'This time have I caught you,' he laughed.

'What have you there?' asked Loki.

'No more than a flounder's egg,' said the giant.

'No one would take such care of a flounder's egg,' scoffed Loki. 'Show it to me.'

The giant moved aside his thumb so that Loki could see he spoke the truth, and in that instant Loki snatched the egg and it became once more the child. 'Go, hide yourself in your father's boathouse,' said Loki. And the terrified boy ran across the beach to the little boathouse, and going in, shut the door behind him.

The giant instantly started off in pursuit, flung open the boathouse door and thrust his head inside, shouting to the boy to come out. But as Loki had thought he would, the giant forgot how small the boathouse was, and he struck his head on a beam and fell down senseless. Loki immediately ran up and killed the giant with his own fishing knife, and the boy was saved.

And ever after, the grateful peasant and his wife considered Loki the greatest of all the gods, for he alone had not said to them, 'I have done what I can. Now must you help yourselves,' but had stayed to see his trick through to the end.

XVII

Odin and Rind

THERE came a time when Odin, with his power of seeing those things which were yet to come, grew greatly troubled; for, looking forward into the future, he saw how one of his sons was doomed to die by the hand of another, bringing much grief to Asgard and all the gods. But because nothing was hidden from him, the Allfather saw also how another son of his would be born who would avenge his brother's death. The name of this son would be Vali, and his mother would be Rind, a princess in an eastern kingdom of Midgard. So, heavy at heart for all the unhappiness that was yet to come, Odin went down to earth and set himself to woo and win the princess who was to be Vali's mother.

Rind was very beautiful, and exceedingly proud; and one after another she had rejected all her suitors, saying that they were neither great nor noble enough to wed her, until her father despaired of ever finding her a husband.

But he soon had other troubles beside his daughter's wilfulness, for an enemy gathered together a great army and marched against his kingdom; and being old, the king knew himself to be but a poor warrior, though he had been accounted of much prowess in his youth. He sat upon his throne and thought over all his captains, wondering to which of them he might give the command of his army, and in his mind he doubted the abilities of each one.

While he sat, thinking unhappily, a stranger of middle age, wearing a grey cloak and a wide-brimmed hat and having but one eye, came into the hall and spoke to him. 'Give me the command of your army,' he said, 'and I will win the battle for you.'

The stranger's words were boastful, but there was something in his bearing that made the king believe them, and it was without misgivings that the old king sent forth his men against the enemy with the stranger at their head.

And Odin, for it was he, made good his words, and the enemy was utterly destroyed. Overjoyed, the king welcomed back the stranger, saying, 'Any reward that you claim is yours. Ask what you will of me.'

'All I ask,' said Odin, 'is leave to woo your daughter.'

'It is yours,' said the king, 'and may you be successful.' And he thought how from gratitude at least, Rind might look kindly on the stranger who had saved her father's kingdom.

But when Odin went to Rind and declared himself her suitor, never a smile or a word of thanks did the lovely maiden offer him. She did no more than look him up and

down and frown a little. 'The man I marry must be young,' she said, 'and you are of middle years.' And she turned away and spoke no more to him.

Odin went from the king's house, and the old king was sad to see him go and angry that Rind should have slighted him. But before many days had passed, Odin returned in the guise of a worker in metals and precious stones, young and handsome.

The king welcomed him for his craftsmanship, and he made for the king rings and brooches and silver cups, while for Rind he made necklaces and other jewellery which gave much pleasure to her. Well pleased by his skill, the king wished to reward the young smith for his work. 'What would you ask of me?' he said. 'For I would give you a gift.'

Odin smiled. 'There is nothing I would ask of you, save permission to woo your daughter.'

'It is yours,' said the king, 'and may you be successful.'

But pleased as she had been by his skill and by the jewels he had wrought for her, Rind had no smile or word of greeting when Odin came to her; she only looked him up and down and said with scorn, 'You are young and handsome, yet you are no more than a smith. The man I marry must have proved himself a brave and noble warrior.' And she sent him away from her without another word.

The king was sad to see him go, for he feared that there would be no pleasing his daughter, and that in the end she would die unwed through her great pride. But before many days had passed, Odin came again to the king's house, this time as a warrior, young and bold, rich, noble, and handsome. He greeted the king with respect and begged that he might be allowed to woo his daughter.

The king's heart lightened at the sight of Rind's latest suitor. 'Surely,' he thought, 'no maiden could refuse so fine a man.' And eagerly he welcomed Odin. 'Go to my daughter, stranger,' he said, 'and may your wooing be successful.'

'I have long admired your beauty, fair Rind,' said Odin, 'and I have come from far away to ask you to be my wife.'

Rind looked him up and down and she hesitated, so that her waiting-women glanced at one another and smiled, thinking, 'This time her hand is won.'

But at last Rind spoke. 'Stranger,' she said, 'you are handsome, and your garments show you to be rich; you seem to me to be a mighty warrior, and your bearing proves you noble. Such a one as you would be a worthy husband for any maiden save myself. But my beauty is not for any mortal man.' And she turned her head away from him.

Then Odin grew angry. 'This time, fair Rind, you have scorned me once too often.' In a voice so quiet that only she could hear him, he spoke magic runes over her, and with a cry she fell senseless into the arms of her attendants. And flinging his cloak around him, Odin strode from the room.

The king's distress was great, for he thought that Rind was dying, but after a time she recovered her senses. Yet it seemed as though she had lost her reason, for she no longer smiled or laughed, she would speak to no one, and, day after day, would do no more than sit staring before her at nothing at all.

In vain the king called to his house all the women of his country who were known for their skill in medicine, for no one of them could tell him what ailed her. 'She has angered the gods,' was all they could say, 'and the gods alone can help her.'

And then one day Odin came again to the king, and this time he was in the shape of an old woman, poor and ragged. 'I can cure your daughter,' he said to the king. 'Let me but speak with her alone.'

So the king led the old woman to the hall where Rind sat

and he dismissed all her attendants. 'There is my daughter, alone and in your power, old woman,' he said. 'If you can cure her, there is nothing you may not ask of me.' And he went from the room.

'Rind,' said Odin quietly, 'would you be satisfied with a husband from among the gods?'

Rind looked at him suspiciously. 'What can you know of my wishes, old woman?'

'Fair Rind, you scorned me as the captain of your father's army, you despised me as a smith, you rejected me as a warrior, what will you say to me as a god?' And Odin took his own true shape, bright and shining and glorious to look upon, and in terror Rind fell upon her knees and besought him to forgive her.

Odin smiled. 'You have given me no answer yet. Will you be the wife of a god?'

'Willingly,' she whispered.

'It will be only a short time that we can be together,' Odin warned her gravely, 'since before many days are passed I must return to Asgard, and you may never see me again. Yet you will be held in respect above all women and a son shall be born to us who will do great deeds. Think you the honour worth the price?'

Rind rose and looked into Odin's eyes. 'I have ever known,' she said, 'that I was destined to great glory.'

So Rind was married to Odin, yet he dwelt with her in her father's house for no more than a little space, as he had foretold. And one day he said to her, 'I must leave you now, fair Rind. When our son is born, name him Vali, and send him forth to find his father, for there will be a task for him to perform. Farewell.' And before she could reply to him or seek to keep him with her, he was gone, as though he had never been there.

XVIII

The Death of Balder

BALDER, the beautiful young sun-god, was the happiest of
all the gods, for ever gay and joyous, unlike his melancholy
blind twin brother, Höd, the god of darkness; and he was the
best loved of all who dwelt in Asgard. But there came a time
when Balder grew pale and sad, as though something troubled
him, so that Nanna, his beloved wife, seeing him so downcast,
asked him what was amiss.

'It is,' he replied, 'that I am distressed by a dream which I
have had, night after night, of how my life is to be taken, by
whom I know not, and no one of all the gods may save me
from the house of the dead, where grim Hel rules.'

Grieved at his words, Nanna went to Odin and Frigg and
told them of their son's dreams, and they heard her gravely.
'We must call the gods and goddesses to a council, to decide

what should be done for Balder's safety,' said Odin, 'for such dreams can bode no good to him.'

But before he went himself to the council, Odin climbed to his throne on his watch-tower, Hlidskialf, and looked out over Midgard and Iotunheim and down into misty Niflheim even to the house of Hel, Loki's terrible daughter. And he saw that her halls were swept and garnished, her high chairs hung with coverings, and the cups set out on her tables as for a feast; and he knew that her house awaited the coming of a greatly honoured guest. 'This,' thought Odin, 'is the beginning of that end which is to be.' And with a heavy heart he joined the other gods at their council.

After they had debated long, it was decided that Balder's safety could only be assured if oaths were taken of all things that they would not harm him. And forthwith Frigg herself sent out her messengers to ask of each thing there was that it might promise no hurt to her son. Fire and water, the trees, the plants and the flowers, stones and rocks, the earth and the metals beneath the earth, sickness and plagues, birds and all animals, each one swore to Balder's safety. And when that had been done, all the gods save only Odin smiled and said, 'Now can Balder be harmed by naught.' But Odin still feared, though he spoke not of his fears.

And it became a great sport with the gods to cast at Balder all manner of weapons, and sticks and stones, to see him quite unharmed by them; and they would laugh greatly and rejoice, for they held Balder very dear.

But Loki alone of all the gods did not rejoice, since fire must ever be jealous of the sun, which is more bright and better loved, and Loki longed that Balder's beauty and light might be put out for ever, and he sought a way to harm him. In the likeness of an old woman he went to Fensalir, where Frigg sat spinning the clouds, and he greeted her.

'Have you passed by the courtyard where the gods are gathered?' asked Frigg. 'What do they there?'

'They cast stones and weapons at Balder, your son,' said Loki, 'and he stands unharmed.'

Frigg smiled happily. 'Each thing there is has sworn to me that Balder will be safe from it,' she said.

'Are you certain that each thing has sworn?' asked Loki. 'Is there no thing at all that you have forgotten?'

'No thing at all has been forgotten,' said Frigg. 'One thing alone has not sworn, though I did not forget it. It is the mistletoe that grows on the oak-tree that stands at the gate of Valhall. It is such a little thing that it could harm no one, so I did not think to take an oath from it. It will do no hurt to Balder.'

'Indeed, why should it harm Balder?' said Loki. 'Do not all things love him?' And bidding Frigg farewell, he went from Fensalir. Immediately, taking his own shape, he hastened to the oak-tree that grew at the gate of Valhall and cut the little branch of mistletoe and fashioned it into a dart. Then he went to the courtyard where the gods were gathered, with Balder in their midst, following their favourite game of throwing weapons at him, while he stood there laughing and unharmed.

Only blind Höd waited alone, apart from the others, because he could not see to aim a weapon or a stone. To him Loki went and asked, 'Why do you not play with the others, Höd? They have great sport.'

Bitterly Höd answered him, 'It is always dark where I am, so how can I see the sun?'

'Here is a shaft,' said Loki, putting the mistletoe dart into his hand. 'Turn around, and I will guide your aim.'

Höd smiled. 'You are kind,' he said. 'I am always lonely because I cannot join the others in their games, but now you have lent me your own eyes.' And he took aim as Loki guided him and cast the little dart. And it pierced Balder through the heart so that he fell down dead; and with a smile, Loki stole away.

The gods' gay laughter died, and a deep silence fell; and in the silence Höd asked, 'What is amiss that no one speaks?' And someone answered him, 'Balder is dead and you have slain him.' And all the gods fell to weeping. With a cry, Höd ran from the place, stumbling and afraid; and going for ever from Asgard, sought the shelter of a dark forest, where he groped his way among the trees, always listening lest the others might come after him to destroy him for his unwitting crime.

Frigg came from Fensalir to see how her son was slain, and bitter were the tears she wept for him. After a time she spoke and said, 'If there is any one among the gods who would have my love for evermore, let him go down to the house of Hel and offer her a ransom, that Balder, my dear son, may be returned to us. For without Balder our days are dark indeed.'

And bold Hermod, the messenger, stepped forth and said, 'I will go down into the house of Hel and speak with her.'

Odin gave to him his own horse, Sleipnir, to carry him along his dreadful road, and sped by the hope of all the gods, Hermod rode away to misty Niflheim.

The gods carried Balder's body to the sea and laid it on his own ship, Hringhorni, and placed his armour and his sword by him, and heaped all around him resin-scented pine logs. But when the bale-fire was built, they found that they could not launch the ship, for she was too heavy. So the gods sent into Iotunheim for the help of the giant-woman Hyrrokkin, and she came riding on a huge wolf bridled with snakes. She went to the ship, and with one mighty thrust, she sent her down the beach into the sea.

Then, before all the assembled gods, and before many of the giants who had come from Iotunheim to bid a last fare-well to Balder, whom all, gods and men and giants alike, had loved, save only Loki, Odin took up a flaming torch and went to fire the pile. But as she watched, Nanna's sad heart broke when she thought how she would never see her hus-band more, and she died. So the gods laid her gently on the pyre beside Balder, and Odin placed by them his arm-ring Draupnir, that Sindri the dwarf had made for him, and he thrust his torch among the wood, and the flames blazed up, as the ship moved slowly out to sea. And from the shore the gods watched her, weeping, until she was quite consumed by fire.

For nine nights Hermod rode through the darkness until he reached the bridge that spanned Gioll, the river that flowed through Niflheim, and Modgud, the maiden who kept the bridge, called out to him, 'Stay, and tell me your name and your errand, you who ride by so fast. Yesterday did five companies of dead men pass this way, yet they made no sound as they crossed my bridge. But your horse's hoofs have a noise like thunder, and your face has not the colour of death. Say who you are and what is your will.'

'I am Hermod from Asgard, and I seek out Hel, that I may ransom Balder. Has Balder passed this way?'

'He has passed this way, he and his wife, and they are even now in the house of Hel,' said Modgud.

So Hermod rode on until he saw the walls of Hel's house before him, and her gate, with Garm, her huge hound, guarding it. But there was no one there to open to him, so he rode Sleipnir at the gate, and Sleipnir leapt right over, into the home of Hel.

Hermod rode across the dark and silent courtyard, and dismounting, went into Hel's great hall where she sat upon her throne. Close beside her, in that dread place, sitting in silence at the high table, hand in hand, were Balder and Nanna, pale and dim, with the light all gone from Balder's face. And they both arose and embraced Hermod with joy, and greeted him.

Then Hermod knelt before Hel and asked her to name a ransom for Balder. 'For,' he said, 'the gods will never have done weeping for him, and all things sorrow at his death. Release him, mighty Hel, that he may return to us.'

And Hel looked at him with her deep, dark, sad eyes, that no one might see without shuddering, and in her harsh voice she replied, 'If Balder is so truly beloved as you tell me, then may he return to life. But if there is found one thing that will not weep for him, then he remains here with me.'

With hope Hermod bade farewell to Balder and Nanna, saying, 'May it be soon when we meet again, and in joy.' And Balder took from his arm the ring Draupnir and gave it to Hermod. 'Take this to my father from me,' he said, 'as a remembrance.'

And to Frigg Nanna sent the robe she was wearing, and a golden ring from her finger to Fulla, Frigg's handmaiden. And at the gateway of Hel's house Balder and Nanna stood and watched Hermod ride off on Sleipnir, back to life and Asgard.

Hermod told the gods of all that he had seen and heard in the house of Hel, and immediately messengers were sent out to bid all things weep, that Balder might come back to them. And all the things there were wept; the gods, the giants, the dwarfs and the elves, all men and women, the flowers and the trees, even the rocks and the stones, all things in every place; so that everywhere the sound of lamentation filled the air. But as the messengers were hastening back to Asgard, believing their task completed, they passed by a cave where a giant-woman sat whom they had not seen before. 'Who are you?' they asked her.

'I am called Thökk,' she replied.

And they bade her weep Balder out of the house of Hel, and she answered them, 'Why should I weep for Balder? I loved him not. Let Hel keep what she holds.' And she laughed and was gone.

Sadly the messengers returned to Asgard and told how of all things one giant-woman only had not wept for the god of the sun. And they told how to their ears, her laugh had seemed like the mocking laugh of Loki, who was so skilled at changing his shape. And there was great grief in Asgard, that Balder had to remain in the house of Hel, with his death yet unavenged.

But on a certain day there came a youth to Asgard and demanded admittance to Odin's hall, and the doorkeeper would not let him pass. 'I am awaited,' said the boy quietly, and he thrust the doorkeeper aside and went through the hall to where Odin sat. Standing before Odin, young and proud, with his bow in his hand and a quiver of arrows slung at his shoulder, he said, 'I am Vali, and my mother Rind has sent me to you, for you have a task for me to perform.'

Odin smiled sadly. 'You know your task,' he said. 'Go now and do it.'

And Vali turned and left the hall, while the gods marvelled at him. He went to the wood where Höd wandered fearfully, and going swiftly among the trees like a ray of light, he fitted an arrow to his bow. And Höd heard his footsteps and knew that the end was near for him, and he was not grieved, for his life had grown weary. Vali's arrow sped true and found its mark, and Höd went down to the house of Hel, where his brother Balder greeted him in love and kindness. And thus did all things come to pass as Odin had known they would.

XIX

How Loki was Cast Out by the Gods

THOUGH the gods still mourned for the loss of Balder, when the time came round again when they were wont to go to feast with Aegir in his palace under the sea and drink the mead which he brewed in the cauldron of Hymir, they went as was their custom, all save Thor, who was journeying in the north, in Iotunheim, for they wished to do courtesy to Aegir. In Aegir's halls, lighted by the glittering gold that shone upon the walls in place of torches, the gods set themselves to forget their sorrow and enjoy the entertainment offered them, eating the good meat put before them and drinking the abundant mead; and there was great peace among them.

But while they feasted and told tales of their feats of arms, Loki, who had been apart from them since Balder's death, came to the door of the hall and made to enter. Eldir, Aegir's serving-man, would not let him pass, saying, 'These are no friends of yours gathered here today, Loki. Go you back whence you came.'

'I have come to feast with the other gods as is my right,' said Loki, 'whether they wish my company or not.' And he went on into the hall.

And when the gods saw that he had come among them, they all fell silent, and there was not one of them who was glad to see him there; not even Sigyn, his wife, for she was afraid for him.

Loki looked around the hall and laughed. 'I am thirsty,' he said, 'and I have journeyed far to drink of Aegir's mead. Why are you all so proud and silent? Why do you not bid me sit and drink with you?'

And Bragi, the god of poetry, answered him, 'Your place is no longer with us, Loki, for you have forfeited the right to our friendship by your evil deeds.' And the other gods murmured their agreement with his words.

Loki turned to Odin. 'Do you remember, Odin, how once we took an oath to be as brothers in all things? There was a time when you would not have drunk the ale that was poured for you, unless it were poured for me also.'

And because he spoke the truth, Odin could not gainsay him, and he turned to the others and bade them make room at the table for Loki. 'The father of Fenris-Wolf would sit and drink with us,' he said. 'Bring a cup and mead for him.'

Odin's son, Vidar, the silent god, rose and gave his place to Loki and poured out mead for him. Loki took the crystal cup and raised it. 'Greetings to you all, brave gods and fair goddesses. I wish you well, all save Bragi yonder, who would have sent me away.' And he laughed and drank.

Quietly Bragi answered him, 'I would give much, Loki, if I might prevent strife and quarrelling here this day.'

Loki laughed again. 'I do not doubt it, Bragi, for of all the Aesir and the Vanir who are gathered here, you are the least valorous in battle, and ever ready to avoid a quarrel.'

Angrily Bragi answered him, 'If we were not guests in Aegir's hall, your head would pay for your lies.'

But Idunn, his wife, laid her hand upon his arm and pleaded, 'He is Odin's sworn brother, Bragi, speak to him gently. Harsh words avail nothing.'

'Hear how Idunn from Svartalfheim seeks to keep the peace that her Bragi may not be called upon to fight,' mocked Loki.

'Come, Loki,' said Odin, 'this is no place for wrangling. Drink and be at peace with us while you may.'

'Are you afraid, Odin, that I shall tell aloud of how you have not always been wise or just when you wandered amongst men? Or of how you worked as a thrall for a giant, when you reaped Baugi's fields for him?'

'What do old tales matter to us here today?' said Frigg gently. 'Forget what you and Odin may have done in the past. And if it is folly that is forgotten, it is so much the better for that.'

Quickly, Loki turned to Frigg. 'I do not doubt, Frigg, that you would prefer that I should forget also how you cheated Odin once when you sent a lying message to Geirröd the king, that you might not lose a wager you had made.'

'If my dear Balder were still with me, no one would dare to speak to me thus,' said Frigg bitterly.

'You have me to thank that he is not, good Frigg.' Loki smiled and raised his cup to his lips.

'You are out of your mind, Loki,' exclaimed Freyia, 'that you boast of your shameful deeds here, before us all.'

Loki put down his cup and turned to Freyia. 'I did but speak a few true words, Freyia, where is the shame in that? You, I see, are wearing Brisinga-men, here, before us all. Do you remember how, in Svartalfheim, you paid with kisses for your necklace? You, the lady of the Vanir?'

Freyia blushed and looked away confused, having no answer that she could give him; but Niord, her father, spoke for her, 'However many slanders you may speak against fair Freyia, Loki, at least you can never say of her so strange a thing as that she was the mother of an eight-legged foal.' And all the gods and goddesses laughed at his words, and even Loki himself smiled, for he never could resist a jest. 'And of Frey, my other child,' went on Niord, 'surely not even Loki's malice can find evil to speak.'

Tyr, the god of war, who had until then been silent, now spoke up in praise of Frey. 'Indeed, Niord, he is the best of all gods, brave and gentle and kindly. A good friend is Frey.'

At once Loki sneered at Tyr. 'A good friend! Maybe the words fit Frey, but a good friend is a name which even your friends could never give you, you whose chiefest delight it is to stir up strife and bloodshed, you who are ever near where there is battle and slaughter. Surely there could be found some more peaceable occupation for a god who lacks a right hand to hold a sword?'

'I may lack a hand,' answered Tyr angrily, 'but you lack your son, Fenris-Wolf, who stays in chains until the end of all things comes. And there is no one here save you, Loki, who would think to mock me that I must wield my weapons with my left hand because I once did a service for Asgard.'

Just as Tyr had spoken for him, so now Frey spoke for Tyr. 'Tyr is the bravest of us all, Loki, and you do rashly to speak so to him. Beware lest you yourself join your monster-child in chains.'

Loki smiled. 'How foolish you are, Frey, to provoke my words, it would have been wiser to have remained silent. Do you wish that I should remind you of how you once sat on the Allfather's throne and saw a certain giant-maid and grew sick with love for her? Unfortunate Frey, she would not receive your gifts, and at last you paid for her love with a sword which you gave to Skirnir. When the end of all things comes, and you have no sword to defend yourself, you will regret that you gave your sword to win yourself a wife.'

At this Skirnir called out in defence of his master, 'Were I great Frey, I would not wait to hear further evil from the lips of Loki, that speaker of ill. I would break and crush him until he was no more.'

Loki drained another cup of mead. 'It seemed to me then as though I heard a voice which spoke my name. What little creeping creature spoke of Loki?'

'I am Skirnir and proud to serve great Frey. And proud too am I that because of my master the gods permit me to drink with them today.'

'Ah yes,' smiled Loki, 'Skirnir is your name. I have noticed you, following after Frey like an obedient dog, and running errands for him.' And from shame and anger Skirnir did not answer him.

'Loki, you have drunk too deeply of Aegir's good mead, and you do not know what words you speak,' said Heimdall, who sought to prevent more quarrelling.

'Why, Heimdall, are you, too, here today? Have you then grown weary of watching from your post upon Bifrost? A good watchman never leaves his post to go feasting with his friends.' Loki laughed. 'Do you remember, Heimdall, how we once fought for Freyia's necklace?'

Skadi, who had been silent ever since Loki had entered the hall, now could no longer refrain from speaking; frowning and angry, her voice bitter with hatred for Loki whom she blamed for the death of her father, Thiazi, she called across the hall from where she sat. 'Beware, Loki, for one day an evil fate will come to you, and when that day arrives, I shall smile and be glad.'

'Fair Skadi,' he answered her, 'no one will prevent you if you wish to smile and be glad at my ill fortune, yet all your smiles and gladness will not bring back to you Thiazi, the old eagle. There is naught left of him now save two stars set in the sky.'

'And I shall ever hate you for that, Loki,' she said in a low voice. But he only laughed, and looked into his cup which was empty again.

Then Sif, Thor's wife, thinking how his mocking tongue had spared her until then, and seeking to win his favour with soft words, rose and came to Loki with a jar of mead, and smiled at him, and filled his crystal cup and said, 'Drink, good Loki, and be friends with us. Of almost all who are gathered here today, have you spoken ill words, yet in me you have found no fault; for I am blameless, am I not, good Loki?' And she smiled again at him.

Loki took the mead she gave him and drank, then he set down the cup and looked at her and laughed a little. 'If I have spared you, Sif, it was because I had forgotten you, or did not notice you among so many fairer goddesses. For all your sly smiles, Sif, and the mead you pour for me, you are no better than the others here. Shall I tell them some tales of you, that you may hear them laugh?'

But before Sif could reply, there was a heavy tread without and a shadow at the doorway, and Thor entered the hall, followed by Thialfi, and with a cry Sif ran to him for his protection. 'What means this,' demanded Thor, 'why drinks that traitor with us? He would not have dared to speak Sif's name had I been here when he began his slanders. Have a care, Loki, lest Miollnir break your skull for you.'

'Your threats were ever loud, Thor, but I do not think that you will find much time to talk when the end of all things comes, as come it shall. Then you will have to act, not threaten.'

Thor thrust Sif aside and strode forward. 'Be silent, Loki, or I will pick you up in one hand and fling you northwards, even into Iotunheim, where you belong.'

Loki laughed. 'If I were Thor, I would not speak of Iotunheim. Do you remember, Thor, that time we travelled northwards and slept in a glove? You sat all night, afraid, with Miollnir nursed in your arms, like a woman with her child, waiting to be attacked by unknown enemies. And it was no more than a giant's snoring that you feared, brave Thor.'

'If you do not cease your mockery, Loki, I shall truly slay you.' Thor was now so angry that there is no doubt that he would have done as he threatened, had not Odin intervened. 'Peace, Thor,' he said, 'do not desecrate the halls of Aegir, who is our host.' And Loki rose and moved so that he stood between Thor and the door of the hall, while Thor lowered Miollnir and scowled furiously.

'Come, sit and drink with us, good Thor,' said Aegir, in his voice that was like the rumbling of the mighty waves. 'You have come late to the feast, but you are no less welcome for that. Tell us what adventures you have had. Did you slay many giants on your journey?'

'It is not a giant that I would slay at this very moment, if I had my way,' said Thor.

Loki stepped a little nearer to the door, for he knew of old Thor's thunderous rages, and feared lest there might soon be found no one, neither Odin nor another of the gods, to speak for him and so save him from Thor's wrath. He laughed again. 'I have said what I wanted to say to you all, and much mirth has it given me. But when Thor loses his temper, it is best to be far away.'

And all the gods cried out how they would be glad to see him go. 'And come not near us again, Loki, lest you regret it,' they called to him.

Loki shrugged his shoulders. 'I thank you for your good mead, Aegir,' he said, 'I shall not drink with you again. Farewell, Aegir, and farewell to you all, Aesir and Vanir. You have cast me out; seek not to find me fighting at your side when the end of all things comes.' And he was gone from the hall and away.

And there was no one there who was not glad to see him go, not even Sigyn, his wife. Yet Sigyn wept, while Frigg sought to comfort her; but she would not be comforted.

Loki, knowing that once he had declared himself their enemy, the hands of all the gods would be against him, hid himself on the top of a high mountain, in a house which had four doors, one in each of its four walls, so that he could see in all directions at one time and might not be taken by surprise. Close by the house there was a mountain stream and a waterfall, and here would Loki often swim in the shape of a salmon.

One day, as he sat in his house by the fire, to pass away the time he took twine and knotted it into a net, such as Ran, Aegir's wife, was wont to catch the sailors in. But suddenly he looked down into the valley and saw how Odin and Thor and others of the gods were climbing up the mountain side. 'Odin will have spied me from Hlidskialf,' he thought. 'But they will not find me here when they come.' And throwing his net into the fire, he went out from the house and leapt into the stream, changing himself into a salmon.

147

When the gods reached the house, they found it empty. 'He has gone,' said Thor angrily.

But Odin picked out from the ashes of the fire a half-burned net. 'He has been here but a short while ago,' he said. 'See, he has made himself a net for fishing.' And the gods looked out to where the stream flowed, and wondered if Loki had hidden himself in the water.

So they too made a net, and going to the stream, cast it into the water, and with Thor holding one side, and all the remaining gods the other, they dragged it up the stream. But Loki lay still between two stones on the bed of the stream, and the net went over him. A second time they cast the net into the water, having weighted it so that nothing might remain beneath it, and this time Loki leapt high out of the stream and the net passed under him.

The gods all called out to one another that they had seen him. 'He will try to swim down to the sea where he will be safe,' they said. And they went back again and divided into two groups, one on either side of the river, and so dragged the net along, down towards the sea, while Thor waded out into the middle of the stream, between Loki and the river mouth, and watched and waited.

And Loki saw that there were but two things left for him to do, to attempt to swim past Thor, down to the sea, or to jump once more over the net and swim back up the stream. And having little hope of evading Thor, he jumped again; but he was weary and he jumped not far enough, and Thor caught him by the tail; which is why, to this day, the salmon has a tail that is thinner than that of any other fish.

Loki struggled, but when he saw how all escape was hopeless, he took his own shape once again, that he might face whatever judgement the other gods put on him.

They took him to a cavern beneath the earth, and there

they bound him to a rock, so that he should remain there until the end of all things came. And Skadi, in her spite, now that Loki was powerless against her, brought a venomous serpent and fastened it above him, that the poison which trickled through its fangs might drip upon his face. 'So shall my father be avenged at last,' she said, and laughed.

But when all the gods were gone and had left him to his torments, Loki saw Sigyn come forward from the shadows. 'Why do you not go with the others?' he asked her.

She smiled through her tears and stroked his red hair. 'I would rather be with you,' she said. And she remained with him in the cavern, holding a cup above him to catch the drops of venom, so that it was only when she turned away to empty the cup that any of the poison touched him, and then he struggled so greatly that the whole earth trembled, and men called it an earthquake.

XX

The End of All Things

BUT the Norsemen believed that, as Odin had foreseen, the gods were doomed one day to perish, and this is how they told that it would come to pass.

First would there be three winters more terrible than any that had ever gone before, with snow and ice and biting winds and no power in the sun; and no summers to divide this cruel season and make it bearable, but only one long winter-time with never a respite. And at the end of that winter, Skoll, the wolf who had ever pursued the sun, would leap upon it and devour it, and likewise would Hati with the moon. And the stars which had been sparks from Muspellheim would flicker and go out, so that there would be darkness in the world.

The mountains would shake and tremble, and the rocks would be torn from the earth; and the sea would wash over the fields and the forests as Iormungand, the Midgard-Serpent, raised himself out of the water to advance on the land. And at that moment all chains would be sundered and all prisoners released; Fenris-Wolf would break free from Gleipnir, and Loki rise up from his prison under the ground. Out of fiery Muspellheim would come Surt the giant with his flaming sword; and out of her house would come Hel, with Garm the hound at her side, to join with her father, Loki. And all the frost- and storm-giants would gather together to follow them.

From Bifrost, Heimdall, with his sharp eyes, would see them come, and know that the moment which the gods had feared was at hand, and he would blow his horn to summon them to defend the universe. Then the Aesir and the Vanir would put on their armour, and the spirits of the dead warriors that were feasting in Valhall take up their swords, and with Odin at their head in his golden helmet, ride forth to give battle to the enemies of good.

And in the mighty conflict which would follow, all the earth, all Asgard, even Niflheim itself, would shake with the clang and cry of war. Odin would fight against huge Fenris-Wolf, and hard would be the struggle they would have. Thor, with Miollnir, would kill the Midgard-Serpent, as had ever been his wish to do; but he would not long survive his victory, for he would fall dead from the dying monster's poisonous breath.

Tyr and Hel's hound, Garm, would rush at each other and close to fight, and with his good left hand, brave Tyr would hew down the mighty beast; but in its last struggles it would tear the god to pieces, and so would they perish both.

Surt with his flaming sword would bear down on Frey,

but Frey had given his own sword to Skirnir, and as Loki had foretold, bitterly would he regret it, for he would have no more than the antler of a deer with which to defend himself. Yet would he not perish without a struggle.

As they had met and fought once before, over Freyia's necklace, so Loki and Heimdall would come together in battle once again, and Loki would laugh as he strove with his one-time friend. And in the same moment, each would strike the other a deadly blow, and both alike fall dead.

Though Odin would fight long and bravely with Fenris-Wolf, in the end that mighty monster would be too strong for him, and the wolf with his gaping jaws would devour the father of the gods, and then perish at the hands of Vidar the silent.

Then fire from Muspellheim would sweep over all, and thus would everything be destroyed; and it would indeed be the end of all things.

But the Norsemen believed that one day, out of the sea that had engulfed it, and out of the ruins, the world would grow again, fresh and green and beautiful; with fair people dwelling on it, born from Lifthrasir and Lif, the only man and woman to escape the fire. And they believed that out of the ashes of old Asgard would arise another home for the gods, where would live in joy and peace the younger gods, who had not perished; the two sons of Odin, Vidar the silent god, and Vali the son of Rind. And with them would be Magni, the strong son of Thor, mightier even than his father; while out from the house of Hel, at last, would come Balder, and Höd, his brother. And everywhere would be happiness.

Part Two

TALES OF THE NORSE HEROES

I

Svipdag and Menglod

THERE was once a king named Solbiart, whose much-loved queen, Groa, fell sick, and her sickness was such that all knew that she must die. Though her last faint smiles were for her lord, her dying words were for Svipdag, their little son. 'If ever you need my help, Svipdag, in the days to come, go to the grave where I shall have been laid and call to me, and I will come to you, even from the halls of Hel.'

For some years King Solbiart mourned the loss of Groa, and then, while Svipdag was yet a boy, he took another wife. The new queen hated her stepson, but because of his father's great love for him, she dared do him no harm.

When, however, he had grown into a tall and comely

youth, one who showed great promise of being always at his father's side both in counsel and in battle, she made up her mind to be rid of him. Smiling, she said to him one day, 'It is not fitting, dear stepson, that you should ever be at home in your father's house, when there are great deeds to be done in the world beyond. Go forth, prove in some high adventure your father's house, when there are great deeds to be done to take your place beside your father, ruling his lands with him.'

The king was well pleased by her words. 'Indeed, you have spoken well,' he said. 'Go forth, Svipdag, and may the gods prosper you.'

Svipdag smiled, glad that his father was trusting him to venture far into the world alone. 'I will do as you say,' he said, 'and when I have some noble deed to tell you of, I will return to you.'

'What more noble deed could there be,' asked his stepmother craftily, 'than for a brave youth to venture up the hill that is called Lyfiaberg to the house which Loki built, where waits, under an enchantment, the lovely maiden Menglod for him who is bold enough to win her for his bride?'

His eyes shining, Svipdag said, 'I will come home with Menglod, or I will never come home again.'

He began at once to make preparations for his journey, polishing his sword and seeing to the harness of his horse, longing eagerly to be away on his quest; and to all who asked him whither he would go, he answered, 'To the hill that is called Lyfiaberg, to seek the maiden Menglod in the house that Loki built.'

But each one that heard this answer shook his head and said, 'Many have gone on that quest, but no one of them has returned. There is no hope at all for you, Svipdag.'

His spirits became more downcast with the words of each

that spoke, and at last it was plain, even to his trusting heart, that his stepmother was sending him on a quest on which she hoped he would perish. But since only a coward would draw back from an adventure when he found it to be over-dangerous, he could in no way alter his decision. And one day, after bidding farewell to all there, he rode forth from his father's house with a heavy heart, for he feared that he would never see it again.

But before he left King Solbiart's lands, he went to the grave-mound of his mother, and standing before the green barrow, he called to her. 'Many years ago, mother, you bade me call to you, if ever I needed your help. Dear mother, come to me, for I need it now.'

And from the grave-mound the voice of Queen Groa answered him, 'What ails you, my son, that you call on your mother for help?'

'My father's wife has sent me forth to win the maiden Menglod for my bride, but none may enter the house where she waits, and many have died on that quest.'

The voice came again from below the grass. 'It is indeed an evil fate that wicked woman hopes for you, my son. But have courage, for you may yet succeed where all others have failed.'

'Give me a charm, dear mother, to aid me and keep me safe, for I am young to die.'

And after a time he heard her voice once more. 'Nine charms will I give you, Svipdag, my son, to help you on your way. The first shall give you strength in yourself, that you may trust your own counsel above that of all others. The second shall keep your feet safe on any path they may tread. The third shall protect you from all rushing rivers whose waters you may have to cross. The fourth shall give you the victory in arms over any mortal enemy. The fifth shall loosen all bonds by which you may be bound. The sixth shall protect you at sea, so that never may you be drowned in the nets of cruel Ran. The seventh shall wrap you around like a cloak and keep from you the chilling cold of the frost. The eighth shall guard you from the curses of a witch. And the ninth shall give you wit and wisdom and words with which to answer the words of others.'

'I thank you, mother, for all your care of me,' said Svipdag.

'Now go forth, my son, and may you prevail, and may the lovely Menglod be your bride.' The voice from the burial-mound grew fainter until it faded away altogether; and though Svipdag waited many minutes, it spoke no more to him, so he mounted his horse and set off on his quest.

Protected by his mother's charms, he travelled far; and after many perils safely passed, he came at last to the foot of the hill at the top of which stood the house where Menglod dwelt. Full of hope, since he had reached so far unharmed, he rode up the hill towards the house which Loki had built, and saw, when he came nearer, that it stood tall and grey and grim, with a great doorway that was closed and unwelcoming. Beside the house grew a tree whose branches overshadowed the roof, and on the topmost bough of the tree there perched a cock with red and golden plumage. 'The house has no welcome to offer me,' said Svipdag to himself, 'yet I can but knock on its door and see what befalls.'

But as he came close, a ring of flame sprang out from the ground and encircled the walls, and the door opened and a huge giant came forth, brandishing a club; and before the door shut again, the giant was followed by two great hounds. And Svipdag understood why no one had ever won the lovely Menglod or returned alive from seeking her. But he was of good courage and he called out to the giant, 'Who are you, tall one, that greet a wayfarer so fiercely?'

'My name is Fiolsvid and I have no welcome for any travellers,' roared the giant. 'Begone while there is yet time to go.'

'I have come a long way to reach this house,' said Svipdag boldly, though he was not a little afraid, 'and I shall not turn back until I have stepped through the doorway and seen what I have come to see.'

'You speak big words, little one,' scoffed the giant, 'but you will not speak for long. Who are you, that dare to scorn the might of Fiolsvid?'

'If I tell him that I am no more than a mortal man, Svipdag, the son of Solbiart the king,' thought the youth, 'then he will despise me and kill me at once. But if I deceive him and tell him that I am of the frost-giants, he may respect me and let me live a little longer.' So he answered the giant, 'My name is Wind-Cold, and my father is Winter-Cold and his father is Great-Cold, and I am kin to the frost-giants. And now do you answer a question in your turn, brother giant, and tell me who rules in this house.'

'It is Menglod of the golden necklaces who rules in this house, and none may approach her, for I am here to guard her home.' And the giant tossed his great club from one hand to the other.

'But should one succeed in worsting you, might he not enter the house, and see its lovely mistress?'

The giant laughed. 'Small chance has any man of that. But if he should go by me, he would have the hounds to face, that wait for him. And if he should evade the hounds, why then the house door is so built that if he but lays his hand on the latch, he is trapped and held fast till he dies. Oh no, little stranger, there is no way into Menglod's house by force for such as you.' The giant laughed again, and strode a pace to-wards Svipdag, flourishing his club, while the two hounds growled. The giant glanced at them. 'See them,' he said, 'do you think that they would ever let you pass?'

'Sometime,' said Svipdag, 'they must surely sleep. Then might a man evade them and have only you to reckon with.'

'They sleep, one by day and the other by night,' replied the giant, 'and the barking of one would arouse the other and bring him forth to the fight.'

'While the door was open,' said Svipdag boldly, 'might not a man slip through, if he flung the hounds some meat, so that by the time they had eaten their fill, he would be within the walls?'

'He might indeed,' said the giant, 'but only if he fed them with the wings of the red and golden cock that perches on the topmost bough of the tree that overhangs the house. That meat alone would lure them from their task of watching Menglod's house.'

Svipdag reflected that this was the first answer to his questions that had given him any hope, and eagerly he asked, 'With what weapon may that cock be slain, for I guess it to be a magic bird, not to be killed by an ordinary arrow?'

The giant leant upon his club and looked down upon Svipdag. 'You are right,' he said, 'that cock is a magic bird, and may only be slain by the arrow that is hidden in the coffer which is kept by Sinmora the giant-woman.'

'And might a man take this arrow from Sinmora's coffer?' asked Svipdag quickly.

The giant laughed. 'Truly, little one, you seek to know much,' he said. 'But I will tell you what you want to know. Sinmora will give the arrow from her coffer to the man who brings her that which she most desires.'

'And what is it that Sinmora most desires?'

'The tail feathers, bright as gold, of the cock that perches on the topmost bough of this tree.'

Svipdag looked up at the cock. 'But how can I take its tail feathers to Sinmora and give them to her in exchange for her arrow, if it is only with her arrow that I can kill the cock?'

'How indeed?' mocked the giant, and he held his sides with mighty laughter. 'How indeed, little stranger who thought to enter Menglod's house?'

Svipdag sighed. 'So shall I never win even to a sight of the lovely Menglod,' he thought, 'and I must either return home to be taunted by my stepmother and all others who hear how I have failed, or I must fight with this giant and be killed. Indeed, it were better to die here bravely than to face the scorn of others.' And to the giant he said, 'Thus it seems that Menglod will never be won by any man. Yet though I may not win her, I shall strike one blow at least against the strength that keeps her hidden from my eyes. But before we fight, giant, and before you send me to my death, tell me, is it fated that never shall any man win Menglod for his bride? Must she for ever remain in her house unwed?'

'It is decreed, and has been from all time, that to one alone shall the doors be opened, and him shall Menglod marry.'

'One question more, giant, the last that I shall ask of you, or indeed of anyone at all in this world. What is the name of the man who is fated to make her his wife?'

The giant raised his club above his head and swung it round. 'Your question shall I answer,' he said, 'and then no more questions shall you ask, whether you will or no, for I shall have stopped your questioning for ever. Know, little one who is kin to the frost-giants, that the man who will win Menglod of the golden necklaces is Svipdag, the son of Sol-biart. So has it been decreed from all time.'

For a moment Svipdag could not believe what he had heard, and in that moment the giant's club almost fell and crushed him. But barely in time he cried out, 'Hold back your club and open wide the door, for I am Svipdag, the son of Solbiart.'

And even as he spoke, the flames that ringed the house died down and the door flew open of itself and the hounds ran forward and fawned at his feet. With a shout of joy the giant ran into the house, calling to Menglod to come; and followed by her nine handmaidens, she came out to where Svipdag stood, and he gazed at her beauty entranced, for the gold of her hair shone no less brightly than the gold of her many necklaces.

'Are you indeed Svipdag, the son of Solbiart, he who shall be my lord?' she asked.

'I am, and I have travelled far to find you.'

Menglod smiled. 'And I have waited long for you, alone in the house which Loki built. But now I shall be alone no longer. Come, you are the more welcome for the long delay.' And she held out her hand to him, and he took it, and together they went into the house, followed by the nine handmaidens, singing joyfully. And the hounds wagged their tails in pleasure, and the cock crew on the tree that overhung the roof, and the giant laughed and tossed his club away, for he needed to guard the house no longer.

II

Völund the Smith

THREE brothers once lived on the shores of a lake, and their names were Slagfid, Egill, and Völund. In their veins flowed a certain measure of elf blood, which made them skilled and wise above other mortal men. Slagfid and Egill were crafty hunters, but Völund was not only mighty in the chase, he was also a most cunning smith, and the work he wrought in gold and silver and bronze was the finest ever seen.

One summer morning the three brothers came out from their house and saw, sitting among the flowers at the edge of the lake, three fair young maidens. One of them was twining herself a garland of blossoms; another was combing her hair, leaning over to look at her reflection in the water; while the

163

third sang softly to herself. And beside each one of them lay a garment of white swan feathers.

The three young men went to them and greeted them and asked who they might be, and the maidens looked up and smiled. And the first, setting the garland on her head, answered, 'We are three Valkyrs, three of Father Odin's warrior-maidens from Valhall where the dead heroes dwell. As we flew above the clouds on the white wings of our swan-robes, we saw this lake and thought how it would be pleasant to while away an hour or two, sitting by the water.'

'How are you named?' asked Slagfid, gazing at her with admiration for her beauty.

'I am Hladgud,' she answered, and smiled at him.

'And how are you named?' asked Egill of the maiden who was combing her hair, and who seemed to him the loveliest sight in the world.

'I am Olrun,' she answered, and smiled at him.

In all this time Völund had not ceased to watch the maiden who had been singing, and now he asked her, 'And how are you named?'

'I am Hervor,' she answered, and smiled at him. And her voice when she spoke was no less sweet than it had been when she sang.

The three brothers sat down on the grass beside the Valkyrs. 'I would that you were here for longer than an hour or two,' said Slagfid.

'We may well remain till sunset, since we have found a welcome,' said Hladgud.

'What is a single day out of a lifetime?' asked Egill.

'You are right,' said Olrun. 'It is but a short time. We might well remain for longer.'

But Völund took Hervor's hand in his and said, 'Could you not remain for ever?'

And Hervor turned to the other maidens and asked, 'What say you, my sisters, shall we call this place our home?'

They considered a moment, then Hladgud said, 'I am a little weary of battles and the din and stress of war, and I should be glad of the peace by this lake.'

'And I,' said Olrun, 'am a little weary of the feasting and the combats in Valhall, and I should be glad of the quiet that is found in a small house.'

'And I,' whispered Hervor, 'am a little weary of being a warrior-maid, and I should be glad to be some good man's wife.'

So the three Valkyrs stayed with the three brothers in the house by the lake, laying their swan-garments by in a wooden chest. And Slagfid took Hladgud for his wife, and Egill took Olrun, while Völund wedded with the maiden of his choice, fair Hervor.

For seven years they could not have been happier, but in the eighth year a longing came on Hladgud and Olrun and Hervor to fly again through the air, and to hear once more the sounds of battle and rejoice in the deeds of warriors. And though at first they said nothing of this to each other, one day Hladgud spoke. As the three of them sat by the fire, their husbands being out in the forest hunting, she said, 'Is it not over-quiet here, my sisters, beside this silent lake?'

'In Valhall,' said Olrun, 'at this moment, the warriors test their strength in the courtyard with golden swords, and soon they will enter the hall to feast on boar's flesh and mead.' And she sighed.

'Sometimes,' said Hervor slowly, 'I long to wear once again my flashing helmet and ride through the sky at the Allfather's bidding. Do you not remember what it was like, my sisters?' And she brushed away a tear.

'A Valkyr should not weep,' said Olrun.

'A Valkyr need not weep,' said Hladgud, and she rose and went to the wooden chest and took out the swan-garments that they had not looked upon for seven years. And the others came to her, and as each took in her hands her own robe of swan feathers, the longing grew too strong for her; and they all three cast off the keys from their girdles and the bands that bound their hair, and they slipped on their swan-garments and stole from the house. And with a heavy beating of wings, three white swans rose up into the air and flew across the lake and away beyond the clouds.

When the three brothers returned from hunting, they called out gaily to their wives to show them the game that they had caught; but never a sound answered their glad greeting.

'What can ail them?' asked Slagfid.

'Perhaps they jest with us and hide themselves,' said Egill.

But Völund said nothing, for there was a strange wild terror in his heart as he remembered the three white swan-garments of the Valkyrs, and in silence he went to the chest where they had been hidden, and found it open and empty; and he stood there, still and staring. As though they came to him in a dream or from a long way off, he heard his brothers' voices calling, 'Hladgud, Olrun, Hervor, where are you? Come and see the deer that we have killed.' And after a time he said, 'They cannot hear you. They are gone.'

'Where are they gone?' asked Egill. 'Had they gone to fetch water or kindling, we should have seen them as we returned.'

'They are hidden somewhere,' laughed Slagfid. 'The house is not so large, we shall find them soon enough.'

'They are gone,' repeated Völund, pointing at the empty chest. 'Look.' And his brothers looked and saw, and they too stood still and staring, unable to believe.

But at last Slagfid said, 'I am going out to seek my Hladgud. If I travel fast enough, one day I shall overtake her.' And he strapped on his snow-shoes and took his sword and his bow and set off to the south.

And Egill said, 'I am going out to seek my Olrun. If I wander far enough, one day I shall find her.' And he strapped on his snow-shoes and took his sword and his bow and set off to the east.

But Völund closed the chest softly and thought to himself, 'I will wait here for my Hervor, and maybe one day she will return to me.' So he made up the fire and put to rights the empty house and waited.

And the idea came to him to make each day a golden ring for Hervor, that he might give them to her if she returned; so every morning he wrought and hammered the shining metal and made a ring for her, and each ring he strung on to a long cord which he hung from the low rafters of the hall to await her coming. And so the months passed until there were 700 rings, 700 golden rings shining in the firelight, strung from beam to beam across the end of the hall. But Hervor never came home to wear them.

Now there lived a king across the hills by the sea, Nidud the cruel, and he heard how, alone in a house beside a lake, dwelt one in whose veins ran the blood of the elves, and who was said to be the finest smith the world had ever seen. And he sent for his men and bade them go to Völund's house and bring back to him some thing which this smith had wrought, that he might see for himself how great his skill might be.

When they reached the house, Völund was in the forest hunting, but their leader pushed open the door which was always ajar against Hervor's return, and the men entered and saw the rings strung on a cord stretched from wall to wall of the hall. 'One of these rings shall we take back to our king,' said the leader; and he slipped a single ring off the cord and they left the house.

When Völund returned home he counted the rings, as was his daily custom, and found that one was missing. 'Perhaps it was Hervor who came and took it for herself,' he thought, and his heart beat fast with hope, as he set to work to make her yet another golden ring.

King Nidud looked at the ring his men had brought him, turning it this way and that in his hands; and at last he said, 'I have no smith in all my lands who can do such work as this. I would that Völund wrought for me alone and for no other man.'

Bodvild, his only daughter, stood close beside his chair and clasped her hands together. 'He must indeed have marvellous skill,' she whispered.

Nidud looked up at her and his hard face softened a little as he held out the ring to her. 'It is yours, my child,' he said. 'Wear it and take good care of it.'

With joy she put it on her finger, and with joy she kissed him. 'Dear father, thank you for such a truly wondrous gift.'

Nidud smiled. 'This Völund shall make other jewels for you and for all my house,' he said. He turned to his men and his voice was harsh again. 'Go, bind me this smith and bring him here, for he shall be my thrall.' And his men hurried from the hall, for they knew King Nidud gave no order twice.

But fair Bodvild gazed at the ring upon her finger and thought, 'Whatever other jewels my father may give me of the elf-smith's or any other man's making, this shall ever be my favourite among them all.'

So Nidud's men returned to the house by the lake, and in the moonlight they rode up to the door; and entering, they fell upon Völund even while he slept and bound him with strong ropes, and rode with him back to their master's halls, taking with them, for the king, Völund's sword which was of skilled and curious workmanship.

King Nidud looked at the sword and tested its strength and was well pleased. 'Is this your work?' he asked Völund.

'Whose else should it be, since your men stole it from my house?' answered Völund.

'And did you make the ring which my daughter wears?' asked Nidud.

'I made no ring for your daughter, nor for any other woman in your house,' replied Völund.

'Go, fetch me Bodvild's ring,' ordered Nidud, and someone ran to do his bidding. But his wife, the queen, came herself from the women's quarters, bearing the ring, for she wished to see with her own eyes what the smith was like who could work so skilfully.

When Völund saw the ring that he had made for Hervor and knew that another had worn it, he was angry. 'Give me back what is mine, you thief,' he demanded of the king, and would have fallen upon him, disarmed though he was, but that the king's men held him fast.

The proud queen looked him up and down and her eyes were cold. 'He is savage and unfriendly, this smith from beside the lake,' she said.

'I like your work well,' said King Nidud. 'Will you make for me and my house the things which we desire?'

'I will make nothing for you,' said Völund. 'Let me go. I am not your thrall.'

The king laughed; and the queen said quietly, 'You will do as we wish, Völund the smith.'

'I will make nothing for you,' repeated Völund, 'and I will be gone from your hated house as soon as I may.'

'It would be a pity if we were to lose you,' said King Nidud, 'and it must be prevented.'

'It were best,' said the queen, 'that we cut the sinews of his knee-joints and set him on the island of Saevarstad, lest he try to wander away from our lands.'

'That is well thought of,' said King Nidud, and he ordered it done. His two young sons came to look on and mock at the helpless Völund whose pleas and protests were in vain; but his daughter, the Princess Bodvild, sat spinning among her mother's maidens, waiting for her golden ring to be returned to her, and wondering what he was like who had fashioned it, and if he were unkempt and wild, with strange elfin eyes.

And when the sinews of his knee-joints had been cut, Völund might never run again, and he could only walk with pain. He was rowed in a boat to Saevarstad, a small island a little way out from the shore, where there was a house with a forge; and here he was left with gold and precious stones and tools to work them with. And every third day the king went himself over to the island with food and drink for Völund, and to fetch the things that the smith had wrought. And if he had made nothing, then no food or drink was left for him, so that he was forced to make for King Nidud and his family all the things which they desired: daggers for the two young princes, gold cups for the king, brooches and necklaces for Bodvild and the queen, and many things beside; whatever they demanded of him.

And with every hour that he remained prisoned on the island, toiling for him, Völund's hatred for the cruel king grew deeper, and he swore to be revenged one day, not only on the king, but on all his family; and while he hammered out the glowing metal and shaped the rich ornaments, he thought only of how he might escape. And at last he considered how with his elfin skill and knowledge he might fashion for himself a pair of wings, that since he could walk no distance, he might fly away. So with feathers taken from the birds upon the island and with scraps of metal taken from the king's hoard, he set himself to his task with a will; but sparing for it only a little time each day, so that the work he wrought for Nidud might not appear to be less than formerly.

While Völund longed for vengeance and worked upon his wings, in the king's house, Bodvild, with each new jewel that her father brought her from the island, wondered more and more what Völund could be like, and thought of him for a longer time each day.

And the two boys, King Nidud's sons, thought much on Völund also, and wished that more of the things he made might be theirs, than only those things which their father gave to them. And they talked together of it and wondered if they might not persuade Völund by promises or by threats to make them each a sword as fine as that which the king had stolen from him and which he ever wore at his belt, boasting of it to friends and strangers alike. And at last they made up their minds to row over to the island themselves, unknown to their father, and bid Völund fashion them two swords.

Saying no word to anyone, they rowed the little way to Saevarstad early one morning on a day when Völund's work on the making of his wings was well advanced. 'Make us two swords such as the one you made before, which our father wears,' they demanded. 'But tell no one of it.'

Völund looked at their greedy eyes and the hard lines of their young mouths, and the thought of his longed-for vengeance came into his mind. 'Did anyone see you come to the forge?' he asked.

'There was no one about to see us, smith.'

'Did you tell anyone that you had it in your minds to come to Saevarstad?'

The boys laughed. 'Do you take us for fools?' asked the elder. 'Whom should we tell that we wish you to use our father's bronze to make us weapons with? Our father, so that he may prevent us?'

'And if you should see fit to tell him yourself,' said the younger prince slowly, 'we shall say that you lie, and we shall bid our father devise fresh torments for you, so beware.'

'I shall not speak to your father of this,' said Völund quietly. 'I give you my word on that.'

'Then set to work and fashion us our swords with speed, and when seven nights are passed we shall return for them. And remember, not a word to the king,' said the elder prince.

'While we are here, brother,' said the younger, 'why do we not take with us as much as we can carry of our father's gold? It may be worth our keeping.'

'Show us where you have our father's gold,' they demanded of Völund; and he smiled and led them to a great chest which stood by the wall. 'In there is the gold,' he said. 'Open it and see, and take what you will of it, for it is not my right to prevent you.'

The princes raised the heavy lid of the chest and saw the gold all shining within, and cried out in their pleasure at the sight. And Völund backed a little way from them, to where an axe stood leaning up against a wooden pillar.

'Come, let us take the largest pieces,' said the elder brother; and they both knelt down on the floor and reached into the chest, running their hands through the glittering hoard. And Völund took up the axe and moved softly behind them.

'This piece is mine,' said the younger boy. 'See, how large it is.'

'It is the largest of all,' said the elder, 'and it should be mine, since I have seen more years than you.'

'I found it first,' retorted his brother, 'and the best prize goes to him who has the sharpest eyes.'

'I saw it as soon as you, brother, but you cheated and snatched it from beneath my hands.'

'That is a lie,' said the younger boy; but his brother made to take the piece of gold from him.

Yet even while they struggled for possession of their father's wealth, Völund raised the axe and struck. Twice he struck and twice the axe fell and the two boys died, still clutching at the gold. And Völund laughed a little to himself. 'They were fit sons of such a father,' he thought. 'And now is my vengeance begun.'

He drew up the boat from the beach and burnt it, so that no one might know that the princes had been to Saevarstad, and then he buried their bodies, all save the heads, beneath the sooty floor of the forge. But the two skulls he took and set in silver and made of them two drinking cups for Nidud the king, and with elfin runes he changed their eyes into gems for their mother the queen, while their teeth he set in a golden brooch for Bodvild their sister. And when King Nidud came again to the island, Völund smiled on him and gave him the gifts, and King Nidud bore them away, little knowing what they were.

In the king's house it was thought that the two boys had gone hunting, and would be home after a few days had passed, so that at first no one grieved for them. And on the island Völund smiled grimly to himself, and worked long into the night, by firelight, fashioning his wings.

And when he had but a day's work left until they should be completed, Bodvild broke the golden ring that Völund had made for Hervor his wife, and she wept, for it was her favourite jewel. And though she longed that the break might be welded, she dared not tell her parents of it, for she feared that her mother might call her clumsy and her father might chide her for not keeping her jewel more carefully, and she thought, 'There is no one to whom I would dare to speak of this and ask his help, save only him who made the ring.' And because she longed to have her ring whole again that she might wear it as she was wont, and because she longed to see Völund for herself, she slipped early from her father's house, and rowed over to Saevarstad in a small, light boat. She knocked on the door of the smithy and Völund opened it and saw her standing there.

'You are welcome, princess,' he said, and stood aside to let her in.

Half afraid, she entered, her cloak clasped around her. 'You are alone?' he asked.

She nodded. 'Quite alone.' Then quickly she pleaded, 'You will not tell my father I was here, when he comes to you again?'

'She is alone, and no one knows her to be here,' thought Völund. 'Now will my vengeance be completed.' And he laughed in his heart. 'I shall not tell your father, princess,' he said, and closed the door. 'But why are you here, on Saevarstad?'

Shyly, she held out the ring to him. 'I have broken my ring. Will you mend it for me?'

When he saw again the ring that he had made for Hervor, he frowned and almost snatched it from her, so that she thought he was angry at her carelessness. 'I am sorry,' she said timidly. 'It was clumsy of me to break it, but I would not have had it broken for the world, for it is my favourite jewel.'

'You would have me mend it for you?' he asked.

'If you will.' She watched him as he looked closely at the break, and thought how he did not seem the wild elfin crea-

174

ture her mother had said him to be. She was glad that he was young, and though his looks had been spoilt by lines of suffering, he appeared to her eyes to be all that she had ever dreamt he might be. 'If only he would smile,' she thought, 'just smile once for me.'

Völund stared at the ring, but he did not see it, for he was thinking. 'The two boys are dead and here stands the maiden. A high price shall you pay, King Nidud, you and your queen, for your cruelty.' And he looked up, and from the triumph in his mind, he smiled at Bodvild; and because her eyes saw him with love as through a veil, she thought his smile was kindly and her heart rejoiced.

'Sit here and rest, while I mend the ring,' he said, and led her to a chair. He filled a cup with ale and brought it to her. 'Drink, princess,' he said. And she thanked him and took the cup.

He looked across to the pillar against which stood the axe with which he had killed her brothers. 'First,' he thought, 'must I weld the break in Hervor's ring, it must not be left broken longer.' And he went to heat gold to mend it.

The ale was a strong man's drink, and the cup was large; but Bodvild thought that it would be discourteous in a guest to leave the cup unemptied, so she drank the ale, down to the last drop. After, she put the cup carefully on the floor, and sat thinking for a little while; then, her heart made brave by the drink, she rose and walked a little unsteadily to where Völund worked on the ring beside the smithy fire. She stood there watching him until he was almost done, and then she spoke to him. 'Völund.'

He looked round, surprised to see her there. The flames shone on her golden hair and on her gentle eyes, and on her cheeks, flushed by the ale and by her own boldness. 'What do you want?' he asked.

'Only to tell you that I love you, Völund,' she said. 'And that it is a painful thought to me, the cruelty my father has shown to you.'

Völund smiled bitterly. 'You have drunk too much ale, and you do not know what you are saying.'

'I have drunk too much ale,' she said, 'but for all that I know what I am saying, and it is the truth. Yet if I had not drunk your ale, I would not have dared to say the truth to you.'

'Do you expect me to rejoice in such words from King Nidud's daughter?'

The tears shone in her eyes. 'I am not to blame for his cruelty,' she whispered.

Völund hardened his heart against her. 'That is nothing to me, princess.'

The tears trickled down her cheeks. 'Now that I have seen you, I shall always hate my father and my mother for what they have done to you,' she said. 'All my life I shall hate them. How could I do otherwise, loving you so well?'

And watching her, Völund realized that his vengeance was complete, for King Nidud and his queen had lost their daughter, more surely and more cruelly than though she lay dead beside her brothers beneath the floor of the forge; and for the first time he saw her as Bodvild, and not as Nidud's child.

She twisted her hands together. 'I shall never love another man in all my days, yet if I may not have you for my husband, at least I may help you to escape from here.'

'I can leave this island without your help,' he said, but his voice was less harsh than it had been.

'Will you not take me with you?' she whispered. 'Even though I am my father's daughter, I would ever strive to make you a good wife.'

Völund took her hands in his and said gently, 'I had a wife named Hervor once, and she is the only woman I could ever love. I lost her, but I still hope that one day she may come back. Can you understand how it is with me?'

And after a time she took her hands from his and said, 'I understand well,' and tried to smile.

He took Hervor's ring from the anvil and held it out to her. 'Here is your ring,' he said. 'See, I have mended it for you.' And he slipped it on her finger.

When she went, he took her down to the shore, limping slowly to the water's edge, and helped her push the little boat out from the beach; and there they parted without a word.

A few hours' more work on his wings, and they were finished; and before the house on the island, Völund tested them and found that they would carry him. With great triumph in his heart, he flew across the little stretch of sea to the mainland, and through the air to Nidud's house. There he alighted on the highest point of the roof and called to King Nidud to come forth from his hall.

And Nidud came out and stood before his house and looked up at Völund, and his face was drawn with anxiety, for his sons had not yet come home, and never before had they been gone so long. 'How came you here, Völund?' he asked.

'On the wings that I made for myself. Think you not that I am a mighty smith?' And Völund laughed. 'Where is your daughter, King Nidud?'

'She sits by the fire and weeps, and will speak to no one, and she looks on me and on the queen as though she hated us.'

'And where are your sons, King Nidud?' mocked Völund.

'They are hunting in the forest,' answered the king, 'and if they do not come home soon, I must go forth to seek them.'

Nidud's queen came out from the house, and her face was pale and wan as she looked up at the roof.

'If you would seek your sons, King Nidud,' said Völund, 'there is no need to go to the forest. Look under the floor of the forge that you built for me, and there you will find your sons. Their skulls I set in silver to grace your feasts, their eyes are gems for your queen, and your daughter wears their teeth in a brooch on her gown.'

Nidud gave a mighty cry, and the queen fell senseless to the ground. Völund laughed again. 'Now are you both paid for your cruelty,' he said, and spreading wide his wings, he rose into the air. The king called for his men to come with their bows; but when they came, Völund was too far away for their arrows to reach.

And never again in King Nidud's house was there peace or joy or love, but only hatred and despair. And always Völund flew onwards and onwards through the clouds, right across the world, ever seeking Hervor the Valkyr, his wife.

III

The Story of the Volsungs

I

THIS is the story of the Volsungs, a family which Odin loved; and of the Giukungs, who dwelt by the Rhine; and of Brynhild, who had been a Valkyr.

There was once a king in Gautland, in Sweden, named Rerir. He was rich and powerful and much respected by his people, and he had a queen whom he loved greatly. Indeed, his only sorrow was that no children had been born to him and his wife, and he often prayed that the gods might send him a son; though it seemed for a long time as though his prayers had not been heard. But Frigg, the queen of the goddesses, had not forgotten him, and in her own good time she answered his prayers and sent him a sign.

One day, when Rerir was sitting alone, deep in thought, on a green bank near by his house, Frigg, in Fensalir her palace, called Gna her messenger to her and handed her an apple. 'Go,' she said, 'take this to King Rerir where he sits alone, that he may know it for a sign from the gods.'

Gna took the apple and mounted her horse, Hofvarpnir, that could gallop through the air as swiftly as the wind, and in a moment she was gone from Asgard. King Rerir looked up and saw the clouds parting before a maiden on a great horse, and while he could do no more than wonder at the sight, Gna had dropped the apple into his hands and vanished.

Rerir looked a long time at the apple and thought, 'This will be a sign from the gods at last, that they have heard our prayers.' And he went home to his queen and told her what had befallen. Then they divided the apple that was Frigg's gift, and each ate half of it.

A very few months later it happened that a neighbouring king harried the borders of King Rerir's lands, and he was forced to call together his warriors to drive away the enemy. But even as he was journeying to give battle, he fell sick upon the way, and died, to the great sorrow of his men.

When the queen heard of his death her unhappiness was more than she could bear; she became pale and ill from grief, and could not rejoice even when a son was born to her, but only closed her eyes and died.

The little boy who had been born a king was named Volsung. He grew tall and strong and brave, and the fame of his courage and his battle-craft spread far and wide and won him much renown, both for himself and for his family; so that all those of his line who came after him were known by his name as the Volsungs, and reckoned it a great pride to be of his blood.

King Volsung married a good and gracious wife, and they

had ten sons and a daughter, whom their father greatly loved. All the sons of King Volsung were brave and handsome above other men, but each one of them was surpassed in courage and in beauty by the youngest, Sigmund, who was twin to Signy, the king's only daughter. Moreover, to Sigmund at his birth, the gods had given the gift of being unharmed by any poison that he might eat or drink.

For his family, Volsung built a great house, far larger and finer than that which had sufficed his father Rerir, and the hall of this house he raised around a huge oak-tree, so that the tree was growing in the midst of the hall, with its branches away up above the roof of the house, overshadowing it on every side. And this oak-tree they called the Branstokk, and very proud was Volsung of it.

King Volsung and his eleven children, their mother being dead, lived together in peace and happiness until the time that Signy reached an age at which she might be married; and then a king who lived across the sea, King Siggeir of the Goths, sent to Volsung and asked that he might be considered as a suitor for his daughter. Volsung was glad, for Siggeir was rich and ruled over many men, and he was for answering Siggeir's request with favour, as were his sons; and of them all, only Signy was unwilling.

'King Siggeir is a good match, my child,' said Volsung. 'Were you to wait a lifetime, you would not find a better. How say you to his wooing?'

Signy looked at his kindly smile, and then she looked from one to another of her brothers, and saw in the smiles of each of them, save only Sigmund, the eager hope that she would agree without persuasion to what they wished. But Sigmund, her twin, was not smiling; in his eyes she saw pity and understanding, and a great sorrow that he must lose her company if she married with King Siggeir.

Yet Signy bent her head so that her hair might hide her face and her father not see her tears. 'In this as in all things else, dear father, will I be guided by you. If it seems good to you to give me to King Siggeir, then I will speak no word against it.'

Mightily pleased, King Volsung kissed her, and sent to Siggeir to come to fetch his bride.

Great preparations for the marriage feast were made in Volsung's house; ale was brewed against the coming of King Siggeir and his men, venison and ox-flesh were roasted on spits over open fires, great baskets were piled high with loaves of barley bread, and earthenware bowls were filled with buttermilk. The floor of the great hall was swept and strewn with fresh rushes, and all down that side of the hall where stood the king's high seat, with his shield and his weapons hanging above it on the wall, the floor was spread with woven cloth, a carpet for King Volsung and his guests.

When the day was come, in the women's bower there was much talking and laughter as the women and young maidens arrayed themselves in their festive clothes. Only Signy was silent and unsmiling as they decked her in a new kirtle of dyed linen and a bridal veil sewn with golden thread. There were wide rings of gold about her arms and a broad collar of gold around her neck, and no bride in King Volsung's house had ever looked more fair. But her heart was heavy, and she had a strange foreboding that no good would come of the marriage.

King Siggeir was tall, with crafty, narrow eyes, and, like all his followers, richly clad. He smiled often, even where many another man would have frowned, but in his smiles was neither mirth nor affection. He greeted Signy with courteous words, raised a little the veil which hid her pale face, and smiled. 'You are even fairer than I had dared to hope,' he said. But Signy could give him no smile in return.

'You are as yet a stranger to her, and she is shy,' said Volsung, and he led Siggeir away to the place of the most honoured guest, beside his own high seat. But Signy whispered to her brother, 'Oh, Sigmund, I like him not. Why must I marry him?' And Sigmund could find no words of comfort to offer her, and only held her hand in his.

While the feasting was at its most joyous, and the drinking horns had been refilled not once, but often, and the long fire that flared in a trench down the length of the great hall had burnt many logs to ashes, a stranger came to the porchway of the house. He was an old man, wearing a cloak with a hood, and there was a wide-brimmed hat on his head; his feet were bare and he had but one eye, and he was holding something beneath his cloak.

Because King Volsung would never have turned away a traveller, the servants bade the stranger welcome, and he stepped into the hall, standing for a moment in the doorway, looking down the great room with its two lines of carved wooden pillars to support the roof and the two rows of benches and trestles, one along either wall; where sat, on the one side, the king and his chieftains and King Siggeir and his noblemen, and on the other, their warriors and followers and, in the lowest place, the thralls; all drinking, talking, and laughing. He looked at the crackling fire which lighted the whole room; and in the very midst of all, the trunk of the Branstokk reaching up into the dimness of the rafters, with its branches outside, spreading over all, unseen.

Then the stranger walked slowly down the hall beside the fire trench, and, as he passed them, on either side of him the feasters fell silent and their jests died down. Looking neither to the right nor to the left, the stranger went on until he stood before the Branstokk; and then, with all eyes on him, he took out from beneath his cloak a sword, and raising it, he drove it deep into the tree-trunk, even to the hilt.

No one in the hall spoke or moved, and in the silence the stranger said, 'To him who can draw forth this sword I give it as a gift, and he shall find that never has he borne a better weapon.' And then, without another word, he turned and went from the hall, and there was no one there so bold as to prevent him.

When he was gone, a whisper went around the hall from one man to another. 'He had but one eye, did you mark it? Who knows but that it was Odin the Allfather himself? A sword from Odin would be a goodly gift indeed.' And immediately each man there wished that he might be the first to lay his hand upon the sword. But King Volsung ordered that his guests should be before any in trying to draw it forth, and with a smile King Siggeir grasped the hilt and pulled. But though he strove with all his might, the sword could not be moved. He hid his disappointment with crafty smiles, as, after him, in order of their rank, his nobles tried their strength; but they also failed, which gave him satisfaction, for he did not wish to be outdone by any of his followers.

Then came the turn of Volsung's chieftains, and of his sons, the eldest first. But they also failed, and not one inch could the sword be drawn from the tree-trunk until it came to the turn of Sigmund. He smiled. 'I shall not succeed where my brothers have failed,' he said. 'Yet it shall not be said of me that I did not try.' And he laid hold of the golden hilt of the sword. But with no more than the slightest effort he drew it from the tree-trunk, almost as though the sword had only been waiting for the touch of his hand to spring forth of itself.

Sigmund was as surprised as anyone there at his great good fortune, and he stood beside the Branstokk staring at the sword he held in his hands, and then slowly a smile of joy and pleasure spread across his face as he saw how splendid a weapon it was. He hardly heard the congratulations and the admiration of the others who crowded round. 'The Allfather has chosen you to be his own warrior, Sigmund. You will be a mighty man.' And of all present, only King Siggeir was silent, as he looked upon the sword with envious eyes.

Still holding the sword and thinking of nothing else, Sigmund returned to his place in the feasting, and flushed with joy and pride, sat down to drink the horn of ale which someone offered him. He felt a hand upon his arm and looked up to see Siggeir smiling there.

'It is a fine sword, Sigmund,' said Siggeir smoothly, 'but it is a weapon more fitted to one older than yourself, to a tried and proven warrior. I will give you three times its weight in gold, if you will let me have it.'

Sigmund stared up at the smiling face and the eyes that were too close together, astonished at Siggeir's words. He did not see a guest of his father, to whom it was fitting to be courteous, he saw only a man whom he did not like, and one who was taking from him the sister who had shared so much of his young life. 'If the sword had been for you,' he said, 'you could have taken it from the Branstokk, even as I did. But since it is mine, I would not let you have it for all the gold you own.'

The smile never left Siggeir's lips, but his eyes grew hard, and one hand clenched at his side. 'As you will, Sigmund,' he said, and returned to his place beside his host, But the boy's scornful words had bitten deep into his heart, and he swore to himself that one day the sword would be his, and he would be revenged on the Volsungs. And all the while he talked and laughed and drank at his wedding feast, he planned in his mind how this might come to pass.

The next day was fair and bright, with a fresh breeze, and Siggeir said to King Volsung, with his usual smile, 'The wind is favourable for a return to my own land, it would perhaps be best if I delayed no longer in your country, but set sail today, before the autumn gales are on us. For it will soon be ill voyaging upon the sea.'

Volsung and his sons were surprised by his words, for the feasting for the marriage should have lasted for several days yet; but they saw at once that Siggeir wished to depart, and being courteous, they did not seek to keep him with them against his will. 'It shall be as you consider best,' said Volsung, and ordered his thralls to pack up with no delay the gifts that he had made ready for his daughter's husband to take home with him.

'It grieves me that I should have to go so soon,' said Siggeir. 'To show that you do not consider me unfriendly, give me your word that you will come to my country, together with your sons and your noblest followers, to finish the wedding feast with me in my own house, when once the winter is past.'

Willingly, King Volsung agreed to this, both from friendship and because he was glad to think that he would see Signy once again so soon; and as he bade her farewell he said, 'Dry your tears, my child. The winter will soon be over and I and your brothers shall see you again.'

But Signy clung to him and whispered, 'Keep me here with you, father, and do not force me to go away with Siggeir. I do not love him and I never shall.'

Volsung stroked her golden hair. 'It is only because he is still a stranger to you that you think thus. It would be a great disgrace both to us and to him if this marriage were broken off without a cause, and it would bring hatred and enmity between our two lands. No, my child, you must go with your

husband. Remember that you are a Volsung and be brave.'
And he kissed her and led her to King Siggeir. 'Be kind to
her,' he said, 'for she is yet young, and she loves her old home
and her brothers.'

'She will be safe with me, I promise you,' smiled Siggeir,
as he took her on board his ship.

2

As soon as the dark days of winter were passed, and the
snow had melted from the lower-lying ground, King Volsung and his sons made ready three ships and called together
the noblest of their men, and one spring morning they set sail
from Gautland with a favourable wind, and after a swift
voyage reached the shores of King Siggeir's country late one
evening.

They disembarked and drew their ships up on to the beach
in the growing dusk, and King Volsung looked about him. 'It
is strange,' he said, 'that no one of all King Siggeir's men, nor
our host himself, is here to welcome us. Our ships must surely
have been sighted as we drew near the coast.'

And they waited by the ships in the grey twilight for the
sign of a welcome, yet no one came to them. But when it was
almost dark, a slight figure appeared, running across the
sands. 'It is a woman,' said Volsung's eldest son. 'Is this all the
escort our sister's husband can send to us?'

But Sigmund strained his eyes against the darkness. 'It is
Signy,' he exclaimed.

And Signy indeed it was, pale and fearful, and breathless
from her haste. She kissed her father and her brothers. 'He
was watching me in the house with his fox-eyes, or I should
have come sooner,' she said. 'But it is not yet too late. Oh, my
father, Siggeir has gathered together a mighty army and he

will fall upon you and kill you all for the sake of the sword that Sigmund would not give to him. I overheard him talking with his men last night when he thought I was not there. I beg of you, my father, and you, my brothers, sail away while there is time, call together our people, and then come back and kill him who would have broken the laws of hospitality and slain his invited guests.'

Many cried out in surprise and anger at her words, that any man could deal so basely with his wife's kinsfolk; but Volsung stood silent, thinking. At last he spoke. 'Long, long ago I swore an oath that never should I fly from sword or axe through fear. That oath have I always kept. Now that I am old, shall I break my word? And I would not have my sons a target for the scorn of maids and women, that they fled by night from an enemy. All men must die sometime. Though one may fly from other ills, when the day is come, from death there is no fleeing. Besides, I have fought in many battles, and sometimes the enemy was of lesser strength, and sometimes of greater, but always was the victory mine. Why should that not be so today?'

And in spite of Signy's tears and her entreaties, he was resolved, and only said, 'Go back now to your husband and remain with him, no matter what befall us. And remember always that you are of the Volsung race.' And weeping, Signy left them.

At dawn King Volsung and his sons and nobles put on their helmets and their byrnies, mailed corslets of brazen links, well wrought; and took their swords in their hands and waited for King Siggeir. They had not long to wait, for soon a mighty army, with Siggeir at its head, charged forward over the sand; and in the fierce battle which followed, King Volsung and all his men, save only his ten sons, were slain. And the ten young men were overcome by the great numbers of those who fought against them, and were disarmed and bound.

Siggeir himself took up the sword which Odin had given to Sigmund and carefully wiped its blade on a tussock of grass. He turned and smiled at Sigmund. 'You would have done better had you sold it to me when I asked for it,' he said. But Sigmund gave him no answer.

When Signy heard how things had gone in the battle, how her father and his men lay dead, and how her brothers were taken and to be slain by order of King Siggeir, she went to her husband and said, 'If I were to ask for the lives of my brothers, I know you would not hear me, yet this boon I beg of you, that you will not straightway kill them, but that you will permit them to remain alive in bonds until death comes to them of itself, whether in ten days or in twenty, since I would think of my brothers as being among the living for a little time longer.' For she thought that while her brothers yet lived, she might find a way to help them.

Siggeir laughed. 'You are out of your mind,' he said, 'that you deny to your brothers a quick and easy death. But I will do as you ask, for I care not how long or how grievously they suffer. Indeed, it pleases me well that they should learn to desire death earnestly before it comes to them to spare them further torments.' And he ordered that the ten brothers should be taken to the edge of the forest, and that there their feet should be set in stocks, so that they might remain thus, without food or drink or warmth, until they died. And it was done as he commanded.

In the king's house, Signy was watched carefully, that she did not go to help her brothers; and all day she paced her bower, thinking how she might save them, but no way could she find.

And all day the ten young men sat beneath the boughs of

the birch-trees, watching the fresh spring leaves turn from
gold to green and from green to grey as the sun sank lower in
the sky, until it was all darkness around them and they could
see no more. And at midnight a wolf came out from the forest
and killed and devoured the eldest brother, while the other
nine were helpless to protect him.

After a night of tears and apprehension, Signy sent out,
early in the morning, an old man who was the only servant
in Siggeir's house whom she could trust, to see how her
brothers fared. And when he brought back word that
her eldest brother was dead, her tears flowed faster and her
anxiety grew greater; but still she could think of no way to
save the others.

Later in the morning King Siggeir sent out his men to the
edge of the forest, and when he heard how the eldest Volsung had died, he smiled and mocked Signy. 'It was but a
poor boon you craved for your brother, that he might be
slain by a wolf and not by the sword.'

That night the wolf came again from the forest and killed
and devoured the second brother; and once again, in the
morning, Signy wept when she heard of his fate, and King
Siggeir smiled. 'A fine death indeed for a warrior,' he sneered,
'to be torn by the teeth of a hungry wolf.'

And so it was on the next night, and the next, and on until
only Sigmund was left alive; and all the while Signy had sat
in her husband's hall, or paced up and down her bower, trying to find a way of escape for the Volsungs, until it was too
late and all the Volsungs were dead save only Sigmund her
twin. And then suddenly, in her desperation, an idea came
to her, and she took a jar of honey and sent her trusted
servant with it, secretly, to Sigmund, telling him to smear
the honey on her brother's face. The old man did as she had
bidden him; and that night, when the wolf came out from

the forest, it smelt the honey and paused to lick the sweetness off Sigmund's face before it killed him. And Sigmund gripped the wolf's jaw with his teeth and hung on ever more firmly while the huge animal strove to free itself; until at last, with the mighty struggling of the two of them, the stocks were wrenched apart and Sigmund was able to break free.

And in the morning King Siggeir's men, finding no trace of Sigmund, told him how the last of the Volsungs had perished after a mighty battle with a wolf, and he smiled and said, 'So am I rid of them for all time,' and looked up at the sword which Odin had given to Sigmund, where it hung on the wall above his high seat.

But Signy's trusted servant went to the edge of the forest and talked with Sigmund where he was hidden among the trees, and brought word to his mistress that her brother was alive and would speak to her.

Now that she was watched no longer, and might leave Siggeir's house, Signy took a knife and a warm cloak for her brother and went to the edge of the forest to where Sigmund waited for her. Clinging together in the shadow of the pine-trees, the two who were all that remained of their family swore to avenge the treacherous deaths of their father and their brothers. 'Siggeir shall know that the Volsungs do not forget,' said Signy, as they parted. 'I shall send you a son of mine to help you avenge us.'

Signy went back to her husband's house, and Sigmund built for himself a home in a cave under the ground, where Signy sometimes went to him or sent him food or weapons by her servant. And from that moment she was no longer the gentle, kindly maiden she had once been, but became instead an icy-hearted woman whose only thought, carefully concealed, was to avenge the Volsungs.

Soon after, a son was born to Signy and King Siggeir, and Signy rejoiced, thinking, 'Here, maybe, is another Volsung to help Sigmund in his task.' And when, a year later, a second son was born, she thought, 'There are now two to choose from. Surely the Volsung blood will be strong in one of these boys.' And through the years which followed she watched her two children carefully, training them in hardiness and courage.

When the eldest boy was ten years old, Signy sent him out to the forest to Sigmund, bidding her brother test the child, to see whether he would prove a fitting companion for him in his great task.

Sigmund received the boy in his underground cave in the forest, and pointing to a bag of barley meal, said, 'I must go forth to fetch faggots for the fire. In that bag is flour, bake from it a loaf for our supper.'

When he returned carrying the wood, he found the boy sitting in the cave and the bread unmade. 'Why have you not baked a loaf?' asked Sigmund.

'I was afraid to open the bag,' said the boy, 'for I saw that there was something alive and moving in it.'

And Sigmund sighed, for he knew that this boy could offer him no help.

And when Signy came the next day to hear how her son had fared, Sigmund said to her, 'He is no Volsung, for he was afraid of a bag of meal.'

'He is too much his father's son,' said Signy bitterly, and returned to Siggeir's house.

A year later she sent her second son to Sigmund, and once again Sigmund left the boy to bake a loaf while he went to gather sticks. And once again, when he returned, the loaf was unmade. 'Something moved inside the bag, and I was afraid to open it,' said the child.

'He is no Volsung,' said Sigmund to his sister, 'for he feared a bag of meal.'

And Signy wept tears of sore disappointment, that her sons had both failed her.

A little time after this, another son was born to her, and she named him Sinfiotli. He was a handsome child, much like the Volsungs, and he grew tall and strong, and was bold from his earliest years. 'May the gods grant,' thought Signy, 'that here is a son who will not disgrace his mother's race.' And even before he was ten years old, she sent him into the forest to Sigmund.

Sigmund received him in his underground cave, as he had received his brothers, pointing to a bag of meal and saying, 'I must go forth into the forest to gather wood. Here is barley meal, bake from it a loaf for our supper.'

When he returned he found the supper prepared, and Sinfiotli waiting to break the bread. 'When you opened the bag, did you find anything in the meal?' asked Sigmund.

'When I first began to knead it, I thought that something moved in the flour. But whatever it may have been, I kneaded it in and baked it with the meal.'

Then Sigmund laughed in triumph and caught the boy to him. 'You have baked into that loaf a venomous serpent,' he said. 'You are indeed a kinsman after my own heart.'

But Sinfiotli only said, 'I am hungry. May I eat?'

'Not of that loaf,' answered Sigmund, 'for it will be poisoned by the venom of the serpent.' And he gave him other food to eat. But because the gods had given him the gift of being unharmed by all poison, Sigmund ate of the loaf himself.

And when Signy came to her brother in the morning, Sigmund said to her, 'He is a true Volsung, and a fit companion for me in my endeavour.'

And Signy rejoiced with all her heart and kissed her son. 'I will leave him here with you in the forest, that he may learn to be a warrior,' she said to Sigmund. 'And I will tell Siggeir some lie as to why he returns not home.' And she did even as she had said; and King Siggeir believed the boy to have been over venturesome and strayed and been lost.

3

So Sinfiotli lived in the forest with Sigmund, and learnt battle-craft and feats of arms; and in all things he showed himself brave and ruthless, and often spoke to Sigmund of how he longed for the day when he should be thought old enough to join with him in avenging the grandfather and the uncles of whom his mother had told him so much; so that Sigmund marvelled at it, that one so young should show such determination.

One day when Sigmund and Sinfiotli travelled through the forest together in search of adventure, they came upon a house in which two men lay sleeping, and beside each of them was a wolf-skin. 'They will be werewolves,' whispered Sigmund. 'So many days will they pass in the shape of men, and then will they put on their wolf-skins, and so many days will they live as wolves.'

'Let us put on the wolf-skins,' said Sinfiotli, 'it may be that we shall profit from it. Let us put on the skins and then go our separate ways, and when we meet again we shall see which of us has the best tale to tell of his adventures.'

And though Sigmund was unwilling, he agreed, for he did not wish to prevent young Sinfiotli from any bold design by which he might gain more cunning and more hardihood for the slaying of King Siggeir. 'We will put on the skins,' he said, 'and then each go his own way through the forest. But if either of us shall meet with more than seven men, he shall

THE STORY OF THE VOLSUNGS

call to the other in the voice of a wolf, and the other shall come to his aid. For however valiant we both may be, it is not to be thought that either of us should fight alone with more than seven men.'

Sinfiotli agreed to this; and immediately they put on the wolf-skins, but found that they could in no way take them off again. And thus they had to remain for five days. And at the end of that time they met again in their own shapes in Sigmund's cave, but neither had much to tell the other in the way of adventures, so it was agreed that they should once more fare forth in wolf guise.

The fourth day from then, before Sigmund had gone very far alone in the forest, he encountered a band of huntsmen, seven, and well armed. He sprang at the throat of the nearest of them and flung him to the ground; but seeing how the others closed in around him, he feared for his life, and howled aloud in his wolf voice to Sinfiotli, who hastened to his side. And in a very short while the seven men lay dead.

The next day Sinfiotli fell in with a number of huntsmen, and though there were eleven of them, he fought with them alone, and though sorely wounded by their spears, he killed them all. Then he lay down under a tree, weak and spent.

By and by Sigmund ran that way, and seeing Sinfiotli lying amidst the eleven men whom he had slain, he asked, 'Why did you not call to me, that I might have come to your aid?'

Sinfiotli raised his head and answered, 'Because you sought my help in the killing of but seven men. I am little more than a child, yet I would have you know that I slew eleven men without your aid.'

Sigmund was angered by this answer, and because of the wolf nature that was upon him, he leapt forward and bit Sinfiotli in the throat, so that he lay as dead. Immediately Sigmund repented of his anger, but he could in no way bring movement back into Sinfiotli's body. Cursing the ill fortune that had caused them to find the wolf-skins, and despairing because they might not come out of their wolf shapes until the following day, Sigmund dragged Sinfiotli back to their cave and watched over him all night, nuzzling Sinfiotli's head with his wolf jaws and licking his paws with his long wolf tongue. But Sinfiotli never stirred.

At dawn, hearing a noise as of some small beasts fighting, Sigmund went out from the cave, and in the entrance he saw two weasels struggling. One of them bit the other in the throat, so that it fell dead. Immediately the first weasel saw that the other did not rise again, it ran off into the wood and returned a few moments later, bearing in its mouth a leaf which it placed upon the throat of the other weasel, and at once the wounded beast sprang up, alive and well.

'If I could but find a leaf of such power as that,' thought Sigmund, 'I might yet save Sinfiotli.' And even as he wished for it, a raven flew down to him with a similar leaf in its beak, laid the leaf before him and was gone. 'That must surely have been one of Odin's own ravens, that it came to my aid so swiftly,' said Sigmund to himself; and he picked up the leaf between his teeth, and running back into the cave, laid it upon Sinfiotli's throat. Immediately Sinfiotli arose and stretched and shook himself. And at that moment the sun shone forth over the forest and a new day had begun, so that Sigmund and Sinfiotli were able to come out of the wolf-skins and take their own shapes once more.

Sigmund snatched up the wolf-skins. 'They are evil things,' he said. 'Let us not wear them again.'

'It were best we did not,' agreed Sinfiotli.

'Let us burn them, so that they can never harm another man who may chance to come upon them,' said Sigmund.

And together they piled high the fire with wood and laid

the wolf-skins on the flames, and waited until they were utterly burnt away.

When the last shred of wolf-skin was turned to ashes, Sinfiotli said to Sigmund, 'How think you, have you yet made full trial of me, and may we not be about avenging the Volsungs?'

And Sigmund looked at the boy's eager eyes with their unflinching gaze, and he said, 'We will go tomorrow to King Siggeir's house.'

And Sinfiotli laughed for gladness, and set to sharpening his sword.

In the evening of the next day they came to the house of King Siggeir, and unseen by anyone, they slipped into the porchway before the great hall and hid themselves behind some ale casks which stood there, waiting until they might send word to Signy that they were come.

In the great hall, King Siggeir sat and boasted to his nobles, drinking mead from a golden cup, and Signy sat silent by the wall with two of her women, spinning reddish-dyed wool, while their two youngest children played with a ball at the farther end of the hall, nearest to the door. Out in the porchway beyond, crouched behind the ale casks, Sigmund and Sinfiotli listened to the voices from the hall and planned how they would fall upon King Siggeir while he slept.

As they played, their ball rolled through the open doorway into the porch, and with laughter the two children ran to fetch it. 'It has rolled among the ale casks,' said one, and as he picked it up, he saw, half in the darkness, Sigmund and Sinfiotli. 'There are two men here,' he said. And then, running back into the hall, the children called out to their father, 'There are two men with swords and helmets hidden behind the ale casks in the porch. What are they doing there?'

Signy stopped her spinning and her heart beat very fast;

and Siggeir turned to his companions. 'Who can they be?' he asked. 'Who of you here would hide behind an ale cask with a sword?'

'They will be strangers, seeking admission,' replied one man.

'They will more likely be enemies who hope to fall upon you by night, lord,' said another.

Guessing something to be amiss, Signy's two women went and stood beside the men to hear what they were saying. Signy rose, and unnoticed by anyone, took her children, one by either hand, and went swiftly from the hall out to the porch. 'Sigmund, Sinfiotli,' she whispered, and they came from behind the casks. 'Take care,' she said, 'for Siggeir knows that you are here.'

Sigmund frowned, but Sinfiotli only said, 'Then shall we enjoy an even mightier battle than we had hoped for.'

Her face hard and her heart like ice, Signy thrust forward her two little boys. 'Kill for me these children of Siggeir,' she said, 'for they have betrayed you.'

'They are but little children,' said Sigmund. 'I would not kill a child.'

But young Sinfiotli, smiling grimly, stepped forward, and before they even knew what he was about, he had struck off the boys' heads. 'It is done, my mother,' he said.

In the hall, King Siggeir and his men took up weapons and shields and came towards the porch.

'Fly,' said Signy, 'and let us avenge the Volsungs another day.'

Sigmund shook his head and put her gently aside from the doorway. 'What has to be done we shall do tonight,' he said, 'or we shall perish.' And he and Sinfiotli held their swords firmly and strode together into the hall to meet their enemies. But lest she should at any time be needed to help her brother and her son, Signy slipped out into the darkness of the night through the house door, that her husband might not know her hand was against him. And Siggeir did not guess that she had been with the strangers.

Sigmund and Sinfiotli fought valiantly, and slew many men, but in the fighting King Siggeir kept well out of their way, and there were too many ranged against them for them to prevail; so that at the last, towards dawn, they were taken and bound fast.

Siggeir looked at them as they stood helpless before him, and he did not know them for his wife's brother and her lost son. He smiled, as was ever his way, and said, 'You two shall have the least pleasant death I can devise.' And after he had considered, he ordered a great barrow to be built, a burial mound where the two of them might be laid alive.

A pit was dug, and across it, from end to end, dividing it exactly, a stone was set, and on one side of the stone was laid Sigmund, and on the other, Sinfiotli, that they might speak to one another while they lay dying, but never come together for their comfort or to combine their strength in an attempt to escape. Over the pit was laid a roof of rock, and the barrow was piled high with stones and turf and wagon-loads of earth.

King Siggeir stood by, smiling, while the work was done, and Signy stood afar off, wringing her hands. And then suddenly she saw a last hope for her brother and her son, and turned and ran back into the house. It was empty, for all had gone to watch the living burial of the strangers, and Signy stood upon the king's high seat and took down Sigmund's sword from the wall above it. From the rafters of the kitchen she cut down a ham and into it she thrust the blade of the sword. Then she hastened out to the byre and wrapped the sword and the ham in straw, so that the ham-bone showed at one end, but the sword was quite hidden. Then, with the bundle beneath her cloak, she went down to where the barrow rose ever higher, and unnoticed by Siggeir or his friends, she held out the bundle to one of the thralls who was carrying stones to set upon the mound. 'I do pity those men,' she said, 'for all that they would have slain the king. It is a cruel death they die. There is food here. Of your mercy, drop it down to them.'

The thrall saw the ham-bone and did not guess there was a weapon in the straw. He hesitated. 'Do as I ask,' pleaded Signy.

'You have ever been kind to me, mistress,' said the man. 'I will do as you ask.' And he took the bundle, and going to the top of the barrow with his stones, he dropped it down through the only gap left uncovered, and it fell beside Sinfiotli.

And when the barrow was built and the last wagon-load of earth piled on it, King Siggeir returned to his house to feast his escape from death with his friends and his wife.

In the darkness Sigmund lay and wondered how Signy fared. 'There are now no Volsungs left, save only she,' he thought, 'and our father and our brothers, and Sinfiotli and I ourselves, will be unavenged.'

But on the other side of the stone Sinfiotli unfastened the straw bundle. 'Someone has sent us down some meat,' he said. 'I have no doubt it was my mother. From the smell, it is a good ham. I would that I could get some of it to you.' And then his fingers felt the cold metal, and he drew the sword out of the ham. 'She has sent us a sword,' he exclaimed.

'Small good will it be to you now,' sighed Sigmund, 'save to fall upon and end things quickly, hoping thereby to enter Valhall, welcome to Odin through a wound and spilt blood. But there is no warrior's death for me. I must lie here helpless, fretting against my fate, until I sink slowly down into the house of Hel.' And he sighed again and closed his eyes.

'It is a fine sword she has sent us,' called Sinfiotli. 'There are runes graven on the blade, runes of power and good fortune, and the hilt is patterned and set with gems. I do not doubt that such a handsome hilt is made of gold.'

Sigmund opened his eyes and sat up in the darkness. 'If your fingers have felt truly,' he said, 'that will be the sword that Odin gave to me. Siggeir stole it from me long ago.' His hands clenched. 'If it is my sword, it is the best sword in the world, and what can we not do with the Allfather's gift?' Excitedly he went on, 'Sinfiotli, try to thrust it through the stone to me.'

'No sword could go through rock,' said Sinfiotli. But nevertheless he thrust with all his might, and the blade passed through the thick stone, and Sigmund caught at the point in the darkness and pulled; and together they sawed through the dividing rock until they had made a gap wide enough for Sinfiotli to creep through, and then they stood together on the same side of the barrow.

Sigmund fingered his sword lovingly. 'It now only remains for us to cut our way through the mound to freedom beyond,' he said. 'And then for our vengeance upon King Siggeir. But we must wait until we are sure that it is night, for we must not be seen.'

While the wind drove dark clouds across the moon, they stole back to the house, and set straw and brushwood against the walls all around. Then they kindled fire and set light to the wood, and it blazed up fiercely, fanned by the cold night wind. They took burning brands and flung them upon the roof, which was built of turf and beams of oak. And above the roaring of the flames, Sinfiotli laughed. 'A mighty burning will King Siggeir have for his funeral pyre,' he said.

Then Sigmund took his sword and Sinfiotli snatched up a heavy branch to serve him as a club, and together they went to stand before the porch door, to drive back any who should seek to come out, that all his men might perish with the king; for there was but one entrance to the house. And with the crackling of the fire, the men sleeping in the hall awoke and found the great room filled with smoke; and the women who slept in the bower above the hall heard the sound of fire on the roof, and crying out, they hurried down the wooden steps into the smoke-misted hall. And with the wailing and the shouting, Siggeir awoke in the king's bed, where he lay with Signy by his side. 'What is amiss?' he asked.

'The house is burning,' said Signy, who had not slept all night for thinking of her brother and her son.

'How does it come to be burning?' asked Siggeir as he leapt up.

'No doubt someone has set fire to it,' said Signy calmly.

King Siggeir ran out into the great hall. 'Who has done this thing?' he cried. And his cry was taken up in smoke-stifled voices, 'Who has done this thing?' until the question reached the ears of the two men outside, and Sigmund lifted up his voice in answer. 'It is I, Sigmund the Volsung, who has done this thing, King Siggeir. I and Sinfiotli, my sister's son. Know by this that all the Volsungs are not dead.' And they drove back with sword and club the men who struggled to come out, two at a time, through the narrow doorway to the open air; calling as they did to Signy.

And Signy fought her way through the terror-stricken men and women until she reached the door, and came out to her brother and her son, her face grimy, her hair dishevelled and her eyes streaming from the smoke; but on her lips a smile of triumph, that the moment she had longed for was now come at last.

Sigmund caught her to him. 'When this deed is done, my sister,' he said, 'we will go home together, you and I and your son, and we will drive out whatever usurper sits in the hall of the Volsungs, and be great and powerful once more. Oh, Signy, we shall see our home again, the places which we loved and where we played as children, and the Branstokk.'

But she shook her head. 'You must go home, Sigmund, and take Sinfiotli with you, and you must win great glory for yourselves. But my life is over, now that all that I have lived for since our father and our brothers died has come to pass. And though unhappily I lived with Siggeir, happily enough shall I die with him, now that he pays for his crimes.'

And though they sought to prevent her, she kissed her brother and her son, and slipped back into the burning house, and would not come out again for all their entreaties. And there she died with King Siggeir and all his household.

4

When the Volsungs were avenged, Sigmund went back over the sea to his own country, and Sinfiotli went with him. They found, as they had expected, that a neighbouring king had usurped the land, and was living in the great house which King Volsung had built. But the people welcomed Sigmund home and rose against the usurper and killed him and drove away his followers; so Sigmund became king in his father's land, and he ruled well and mightily. He married a wife named Borghild, who was beautiful but crafty; though Sigmund, because he loved her, saw no more than her beauty, and thought her fit to be his queen.

Sigmund would have urged Sinfiotli to remain with him, that they might rule the land together, but the love of slaughter and of battle were too strong in the young man, and he gathered together a band of other men like to himself, and Sigmund fitted out a ship for them, and they went a-viking, all along the coasts, from one land to another, harrying and fighting, and winning great renown. Yet ever when the winter months made sailing dangerous, Sinfiotli would return home, and glad would Sigmund be to see him once again.

One day Sinfiotli met a maiden whom he wished to make his wife, but she was already wooed by the brother of Borghild, Sigmund's queen. At Sinfiotli's suggestion the two men fought for her, as to which of them should have the right to demand her in marriage; and Borghild's brother was slain.

The queen was very angry when she learnt of this, and spoke to Sigmund of it. But Sigmund made light of the matter because he loved Sinfiotli, saying, 'Young men have ever quarrelled over pretty maids, and your brother is not the first to have died thus. Besides, he was slain in fair fight.'

But when Sinfiotli returned home in the autumn, Borghild would not speak with him, nor even look at him, and ever she tried to persuade Sigmund to banish him from the land. But Sigmund said, 'I will not have him driven from his home, no matter how dearly you wish it. He shall pay you weregild for your brother's death.' And he gave Sinfiotli much gold, and Sinfiotli gave it, with more of his own that he had won a-viking, to Borghild, in atonement for her brother's killing. And though at first she would not, at the last Borghild accepted it, saying, 'Now is all well between you and me, Sinfiotli, and my brother is avenged and forgotten, if my husband will but hold a feast in his memory, as is fitting to do.'

So Sigmund gave a great feast in honour of the dead man, and at the feast Queen Borghild carried round the drink to the guests. And when they had drunk much, she brought once again the horn to Sinfiotli, saying, 'Drink, kinsman.'

Sinfiotli took the horn, but something in her voice made

him look up into her eyes, and he saw the hatred in them. Then he looked into the horn and said, 'There is that in the ale which should not be there, and it will do me no good.'

Sigmund heard his words, and to prevent a quarrel between the two of them before all his guests, he held out his hand for the horn. 'I will drink your ale.' And though there was poison in it, he was unhurt by it, for ever had he been able to taste of poison unharmed. And Borghild taunted Sinfiotli for a weakling who must have another man drink his ale for him.

Then a second time she brought him a poisoned drink, and he looked into the horn and said, 'There is treachery in this ale, I would be a fool to drink it.'

And again Sigmund held out his hand for the horn, saying, 'I will drink it for you.' And once again he drank unharmed. And Borghild laughed in mockery of Sinfiotli.

A third time she brought him the horn. 'If you have the courage of a true Volsung, you will drink,' she said. And he saw into the horn and said, 'There is poison in the ale,' and he looked towards Sigmund.

Now, the ale at that feasting was strong, and Sigmund had drunk deeply, both of his own and of Sinfiotli's, and he had grown sleepy, so that this time he did not hold out his hand, but said instead, 'Drain the horn when she is not looking,' meaning that Sinfiotli should pour the ale away. But Sinfiotli misunderstood his words, thinking them to mean that he was to drink himself; and so he drank, and instantly he fell dead from his chair to the ground. And so died, at the hands of a woman, Sinfiotli the warrior, who had never felt pity for another.

Sigmund's grief for Sinfiotli's death was great, and he took the young man's body up in his arms and carried it out from the house towards the woods, for he wished to be alone for one last night with Sinfiotli; to watch over his sister's son in the forest, even as he had so often watched over him as he slept, all those years before, when Sinfiotli had been but a boy, in King Siggeir's land.

To reach the forest he had to cross a stream, and as he made for the place where there was a ford, an old man in a grey cloak rowed to the bank in a little boat and offered to ferry him over. Sigmund laid Sinfiotli's body in the boat, but when he would have boarded her himself, the old man rowed away, saying, 'There is not room enough for two.' And in mid-stream the little boat vanished as though she had never been there.

And it was only then that Sigmund realized how he had once seen that boatman before; an old man in a wide-brimmed hat, an old man with but one eye, who had driven a sword deep into the Branstokk; and he knew that Odin himself had come to fetch the dead Volsung away.

After the murder of Sinfiotli, Sigmund sent Queen Borghild from his house, for he had not the heart to put her to death, since he had loved her once.

5

In his old age, Sigmund became a suitor for the hand of Hiordis, the fair young daughter of King Eylimi. She had another wooer, Lyngvi, the son of King Hunding, a young man from a rich and mighty kingdom. King Eylimi was hard put to it to choose between his daughter's suitors, and knowing her wisdom to be far beyond her years, he sent for her and asked her which of the two men she would marry.

Hiordis considered for a while and then she said, 'Hard indeed is it for a maiden to make such a choice, yet if you will truly allow me to have which of my wooers I please, then, good father, I would have King Sigmund. He is an old man, but he has been a great warrior in his youth, and the fame of his just dealing has spread far. No small honour would it be to be the wife of old King Sigmund.'

So Hiordis was betrothed to Sigmund, and the marriage was celebrated with much rejoicing, and Sigmund travelled back to his house with his young bride. But Prince Lyngvi was greatly angered that he had not won the maiden on whom he had set his heart, and he resolved to break for ever the power and the pride of the Volsungs. Therefore he called together all his brothers and their followers, and marched with a mighty army into Sigmund's land.

With no delay Sigmund summoned his men, and King Eylimi, hearing of the danger in which he stood, came with all his warriors to fight by the side of his daughter's husband. But even so was Sigmund's army poor compared with the great numbers led by Lyngvi and his brothers.

'Lest the day go ill with us, fair wife,' said Sigmund to Hiordis, 'take with you as much gold as you can carry, and hide in the woods. For if I and your father should be slain, it may well be that Lyngvi will carry you away to his own land, and there he may show you but little honour, since you have slighted him.'

So together with one trusted bondmaid, Hiordis left her husband's house and hid in the woods, taking with her a coffer of gold and jewels.

For all Prince Lyngvi's greater numbers, when the battle was joined, it seemed almost as though Sigmund's little army might prevail, so valiantly it fought. And Sigmund and King Eylimi were ever in the front of battle, encouraging their men and doing great deeds. And to the enemy as well as to his own men, it seemed as though no warrior had ever fought

KIDDELL-MONROE

a braver fight or slain more adversaries than did old Sigmund with the sword that Odin had once given him.

But when the day had advanced towards the afternoon, there came into the fighting a man in a grey cloak and a wide-brimmed hat, carrying a spear and having but one eye. He came up against Sigmund in the press of battle, and raising high his spear, struck with it Sigmund's sword, so that the sword broke in two pieces. And instantly the stranger vanished. Then Sigmund knew that Odin willed he should not prevail that day, and he knew also that the Allfather had come himself to choose him for Valhall.

After that, though they fought fiercely, things went against Sigmund and Eylimi, and by evening King Eylimi was dead, Sigmund was wounded even to death, and the greater number of their men were slain.

That night, when the moon rose over the battlefield where lay so many dead and dying men, Hiordis came out of the wood to seek her husband. She found him at last, lying beside his broken sword, very near to death. When he saw her he smiled a little, as though he would comfort her. 'The day is lost for us, fair wife, and tonight Lyngvi and his brothers sup in our house. But do not weep, for it is even as Odin willed it, and you, at least, have not been harmed.' And he told her of how the old man in the grey cloak had broken his sword, so that she saw there had been, from that moment, no hope of their success. 'But take the broken sword,' said Sigmund, 'for I know that a son will be born to us, though I shall see him not, and one day he shall bear a sword that is forged of these pieces, and he shall call it Gram and do great deeds with it. And not the least of these deeds will be the avenging of his father and good King Eylimi.'

Hiordis took the broken sword and laid it in the coffer which her bondmaid carried. Then she set Sigmund's head upon her knee and smoothed his grey hair with her gentle fingers, and thus they remained all night. And at day-dawning Sigmund died.

Hiordis laid his head softly upon the ground and covered his face with his cloak. 'Today he will feast with Odin in Valhall,' she said, 'so it is not right that I should weep for him.'

But her bondmaid looked out to where the sea lay before them and saw a score of ships making for the shore, and the foremost of them had already touched the beach and the men were leaping from her on to the sands. 'They will be strangers who have come a-viking,' she said. 'Oh, mistress, what will they do to us? There is no place where we can go to save ourselves, for Prince Lyngvi has taken all the land, and now can even the sea before us offer us no way of escape.'

'I would not that any harm should come to her who is to be the mother of Sigmund's son,' said Hiordis. 'For the boy will lack a father, and it is too hard on any child that he should also miss a mother's love. Besides, if I cannot urge him on to vengeance, Sigmund will never be avenged.' She turned to the servant. 'If you ever held King Sigmund in honour, change garments with me, so that these men may think you are the mistress and a queen, and I no more than your handmaid. For maybe they will do no harm to a poor serving-girl, whereas they might mistreat a queen.'

And because the girl was good and loved her mistress, she was glad to help her, and she took off her kirtle of rough homespun cloth and put on the queen's rich gown and her jewels.

By that time, the men on the shore had seen the women, and they were hurrying across the field towards them, marvelling as they came at the signs of the recent mighty battle that lay all around. Now, these vikings were led by young

Prince Alf, the son of King Hialprek from Denmark, over the sea, a valiant and a good young man. When he came to where the two women waited fearfully, he greeted them courteously and asked who they might be, and the bondmaid answered, 'I am Queen Hiordis, the wife of King Sigmund who lies here slain.' And she told him of the battle and its outcome.

'Then shall you sail with me to my father's land, across the sea, since here there is no longer a home for you,' said Alf, and he led her on board his ship. And Hiordis followed on behind, carrying the coffer wherein lay the broken sword.

In the house of King Hialprek the supposed queen and her servant were shown much honour and kindness; and after a little time Hialprek's wife, the mother of Prince Alf, marked how often her son would glance at the bondwoman, when he thought no one saw him. One day she spoke to him of it. 'It seems curious to me also,' she said, 'that of the two women who have found shelter in our home, it is the servant-girl who should be the fairer and the more quiet-spoken.' And she put it in her son's mind that he should test the two of them.

So on an evening after the feasting, when he saw that she sat alone, Alf went to her whom he thought to be Queen Hiordis, and talked to her for a while of one thing and another. And then he asked, 'How is it, good queen, that you know when the dawn is near, if from your bed you cannot see the moon or the stars or the first faint light of day?'

The bondwoman smiled. 'Why, that is easy for me,' she said at once, without thinking whether it would be wise or not to speak the truth, 'for when I was but a very young maiden it was ever my custom to rise at dawn to milk my father's cow, and since that time have I always woken early.'

'It is strange indeed that one who was later to wed with a king should ever have risen at dawn to milk her father's cow,' said Alf quietly. And the servant bit her lip and frowned, for she saw that her answer had been unwise.

Then Alf went to Hiordis, where she sat beside the fire, staring into the flames and wondering what the future held for her. He greeted her and sat down beside her and talked to her for a while. Then he asked her the same question that he had asked of the serving-woman.

'When I was a very little maid,' replied Hiordis, 'my father gave me a golden ring of such a kind that it grows cold at the approach of dawn. So by this can I tell that the night is over, for I have ever kept the ring.'

Alf smiled. 'There must indeed have been gold a-plenty in the place where you were born, that even the child of a thrall wore a golden ring.'

Hiordis blushed and looked away from him, for she feared that she had unwittingly betrayed herself.

'Queen Hiordis,' Alf said gently, 'why did you not tell me the truth? My father and I would never bring to harm the widow of good King Sigmund. There was no need for you to fear us.'

'I could not know that,' said Hiordis. 'You might have been even such a man as Lyngvi, who slew my father and my husband, and who shall, in his turn, one day be slain by Sigmund's son.' Then she turned to him and smiled. 'I am glad that you know the truth,' she said, 'for it has grieved me to deceive so long one who has offered me such kindness.' And she gave him her hand in friendship.

Soon after, a child was born to Hiordis, King Sigmund's son, who was to avenge his father; and though she rejoiced in his birth, she wept a little as she looked at him, and thought that his father would never see how fine a son he had. She called him Sigurd, and King Hialprek and Prince Alf loved him as though he had been their own kin, and gave him all honour in their house.

And after a time, a great love grew between Hiordis and Alf, and they were married.

6

From a fair child, Sigurd grew into a youth of much beauty. His hair was golden and his eyes a keen, bright blue, and from his earliest years he showed great strength and skill in all games and feats of arms. But in spite of all his might and the respect men offered him, he was ever courteous and gentle and good-tempered, and was much loved by little children.

In King Hialprek's house there lived a certain man named Reginn, who had come there so many years before that no one remembered when; and no one knew whence he had come, though it was whispered that he was kin to the dwarfs. Besides being a most skilful smith, he had many other accomplishments, and Sigurd was given into his care, that he might be taught all those things which the son of a king should know. And much did Sigurd learn from Reginn.

One day, as they played at chess together, Reginn said to Sigurd, 'It is sad indeed that you, a king, should have to live in another's house where your word is of no account.'

Surprised, Sigurd replied, 'But in King Hialprek's house am I always shown honour, nor am I ever made to feel myself a stranger who has no right here. Why, Reginn, everything I want they give me, the good king and his son, my mother's husband, and there is at all times a place in their councils for me.'

'Then why have they never given you a horse?' asked Reginn quietly, with a little twisted smile.

But Sigurd could give him no answer save, 'Because I have never asked them for a horse.' Then he considered a while and said, 'Since you have put the thought into my mind, I will go to the king and ask for a horse that I may call my own.'

So Sigurd went to King Hialprek and asked that he might have a horse, and willingly the king granted his request. 'Go to the field where the young horses run free by the river, and choose which you will for yourself,' he said.

And Sigurd thanked him and went out of the house to the stables for a halter, and then along to the field. And as he stood watching the horses, wondering which he should choose, he was suddenly aware of an old man who stood beside him, wearing a cloak and a wide-brimmed hat. He had a long white beard and but one eye. 'Drive the horses into the river, Sigurd, and then see what will happen,' he said.

So Sigurd drove the horses into the river, and half-way across, where the water was deep, they all turned and swam back to the safety of the bank again; all save one, a grey colt who did not turn back, but reached the other side. Yet then, finding the grazing not to his liking on the opposite bank, he went of his own accord into the water and swam back to his familiar field.

'Choose the grey colt, Sigurd, for he is of the race of Sleipnir, who is Odin's horse,' said the old man. So Sigurd went and put his bridle on the horse that had swam twice across the stream; but when he would have led him back to where the old man had stood, he saw that the stranger had vanished, as though he had never been there. With awe, Sigurd thought, 'That must indeed have been the Allfather himself who chose my horse for me.' And he called the colt Grani, and no one but he ever rode him.

On another day, as they sat together near the fire one

winter's evening, Reginn said to Sigurd, 'Hard must it be for you, who were born a king, to have no gold or treasure of your own save one coffer which your mother brought across the sea with her.'

'I am young,' answered Sigurd, 'and I have as yet no need of treasure. I do not doubt but that, when the time comes, good King Hialprek and my mother's husband will give me all the gold I require.'

Reginn played with the fringed ends of his tunic, plaiting them together as though he cared more for such sport than for the words he spoke. 'But would you not rather have gold of your own, than ask it of however kindly a king?'

Sigurd laughed. 'Where should I find gold, Reginn? It does not grow on trees.'

Reginn looked at the woollen strands between his fingers as he twisted them, and spoke lightly. 'On Gnita Heath, away in the northlands, lives the dragon Fafnir in a cave, and that cave is full of treasure which he guards. Such treasure would last you a lifetime though you gave generously of it. Take Fafnir's treasure, Sigurd, and you would never want for gold.'

'I have heard men speak of Fafnir the dragon, and how great and fierce he is,' said Sigurd, thoughtfully.

Reginn's cool voice mocked him. 'And I have heard men speak of the Volsungs, that they were brave. But I think that you cannot resemble them, if you fear to face a dragon and win great treasure for yourself.'

Sigurd laughed, unangered by Reginn's words. 'I am yet young, Reginn. When I am older there will be time to talk of dragon-slaying. And I do not think that when the day comes, I shall be afraid.'

Reginn's hands grew suddenly still, and when he spoke his voice was strange. 'Then one day you will kill him, Sigurd?'

For the first time he looked up, and the boy was surprised at the burning eagerness in his dark eyes.

'Good Reginn, why should you desire this thing so much?'

'Listen,' said Reginn, 'and I will tell you. It is a long tale and so one well fitted to a winter's evening.' He let the fringes fall from his fingers and drew his stool closer to Sigurd's. 'There was once a man named Hreidmar. Who he was and what he was is the concern of none, but he had three sons, Fafnir, Otter, and Reginn. Yes,' he said, in reply to the question which he did not give Sigurd time to ask, 'it was I, Reginn. I was the weakest and the least in all things of the three, but then, as now, I had great skill in all a smith's craft, and I wrought many things for my pleasure. Otter was a cunning fisherman, and he knew moreover the secret of changing his shape, and all day he would spend down by the river in the guise of an otter, whence he gained his name. Fafnir was the eldest of us. He was great and grim, and ever he wished that all things might be for him, with never anything to spare for Otter or myself. But because he was a tall and mighty man, there was little that we could do, save bear it. One day, as my brother Otter fished close by the waterfall that was named Andvari's Fall, after the dwarf who lived there in the shape of a pike, Odin the Allfather, with bright Hönir his brother, and Loki the god of fire, passed that way and saw Otter, in his beast shape, eating on the river's bank the fish he had caught. Now, my brother did not see them approach, since he ever ate with his eyes closed, for he was greedy and cared not to watch the food disappearing in his very sight. Thinking him to be an otter, Loki, ever mischievous, for his sport took up a stone and flung it so skilfully that my brother fell dead beside the stream. Then Loki flayed off the otter's skin, and together the gods went on their way; and that evening they came to my father's house and asked shelter for the night. My father, Fafnir and I at once knew that the skin they carried was Otter's, and my father demanded that the gods should pay weregild for my brother's slaying, or else that Loki should forfeit his life. The three gods agreed that this was just, and when Loki said how he knew that Andvari the dwarf had a hoard of gold, Odin and Hönir sent him to fetch it, while they remained in my father's house as hostages. "When the otter's skin shall be all covered with gold, so that not a single hair shows through, then may you go free," my father said. Loki went to Ran, the goddess of the ocean, and borrowed from her the net with which she catches the hapless sailors when the seas are wild; and, returning to Andvari's Fall, he cast the net into the pool, and the pike was caught in it. Then Loki threatened to kill Andvari unless he swore to give him all his store of gold. Terrified and angry, Andvari took his own shape as a dwarf, and going to the hollow rock where he kept his treasure, he gave it all to Loki, save one arm-ring of fine workmanship, called Andvaranaut, which he would have kept for himself. But even this Loki forced him to give up, saying, "Odin shall wear this ring." And Andvari flung down the ring, crying in his rage, "Since my gold may no longer be mine, may it bring ill fortune to all who possess it." But Loki only laughed and carried the treasure back to my father's house, gave Andvaranaut to Odin, and covered the otter-skin with the rest. But when all the gold was laid out, there was still one whisker left uncovered, and my father demanded that it also should be hidden. So Odin took from his arm the ring Andvaranaut and laid it upon the pile so that even the last whisker was covered and my father was satisfied. But Loki only laughed and said, "A high price it is that has been paid for my life, yet small gain will come of it to any of you." Then the three gods went their ways, and we saw them no more. My father hid the gold away in two chests and seemed not to think of it again; but Fafnir thought of nothing else, and often would he urge my father to bring the treasure out and divide it; but my father would not. And then there came a day when Fafnir struck down our father and killed him, for the sake of this same gold that he desired. But he would give me no share of it, and took the two chests to a cave on Gnita Heath, where night and day he watched over his hoard, suffering no man to approach him, nor even spending his wealth for himself. And in time he became so savage and so merciless that he changed into a monster. And there on Gnita Heath he lives to this day, watching over his treasure, Fafnir the dragon. But I, cheated of all share in my brother's weregild and my own heritage, I came to Denmark to the house which is now King Hialprek's, where I have since lived as a smith.'

When Reginn had done speaking, Sigurd was silent for a while, then he said, 'Truly, your trouble has been great, good Reginn. Yet I will avenge you and kill the dragon, if you will but make me a sword, as well you know how, that has no equal in the world. Do this, and Fafnir dies and the gold is yours.'

Reginn shook his head. 'The gold will be yours, I want it not. But I will make you a sword which shall be the best I ever made, and great deeds shall you do with it.' He smiled his twisted smile. 'And not the least of them will be the slaying of the dragon.'

So Reginn wrought in his smithy and he fashioned a sword for Sigurd, and it was keen and bright. He called Sigurd into the forge and gave the sword into his hands. 'See, here is the sword I have made for you, with which you shall kill Fafnir.'

Sigurd took the sword, and to test it, he struck with it upon the anvil with all his might; and so powerful was the blow that the sword was broken. Sigurd laughed. 'I shall need a better sword than that, if I am to fight with a dragon, Reginn,' he said.

Reginn made him another sword, and it was keener and brighter than the first; but when Sigurd tested it, it too was shattered against the anvil. 'Come, Reginn, would you have me slain by the dragon Fafnir?' Sigurd asked with a smile. But Reginn was angry and flung down his tools.

Then Sigurd went to his mother, Hiordis, and said, 'Good mother, you have often told me how, as he lay dying, my father gave to you the broken pieces of the sword that Odin had once given him, so that, when the time came, there might be fashioned from them a sword for his son. I think that the time has now come, dear mother, for that sword to be made.'

Hiordis rejoiced when she heard his words, that he was ready to avenge his father, and she gave him the broken sword from her coffer and bade him take it to Reginn. 'But mind,' she said, 'that when the sword is made, the first deed you do with it shall be to seek out King Lyngvi and show him that though many years have passed since Sigmund died, the Volsungs do not forget a wrong.'

And Sigurd gave her his promise to slay Lyngvi and all his brothers, and she kissed him joyfully.

Sigurd took the broken sword to Reginn and bade him fashion another from the pieces; but Reginn was still angered with him and would not speak with him nor suffer him to watch while he worked. But nevertheless he fashioned a sword, and when it was made he sent for Sigurd. 'I am no craftsman if this sword breaks,' he said.

Sigurd looked at the sword with its edge so keen that it might have been aflame, and he raised it high and smote upon the anvil, and the anvil was cleft in two. 'It is the best sword in the world,' he exclaimed joyously.

But Reginn only said drily, with his twisted smile, 'Now

that we have seen how strong your arms are, young Sigurd, it is time for us to see how sharp is the sword which I have made.' And he gave Sigurd a tuft of wool and told him to take it down to the river and cast it in against the current, and hold the sword in its path. This Sigurd did, and the wool was cut in two. He ran back to the forge in triumph to tell Reginn of the keenness of the sword.

Reginn smiled and asked him, 'Now that I have made you a sword, will you go to Gnita Heath and kill Fafnir for me?'

But Sigurd answered, 'I have promised that first I shall avenge my father. When that is done, I will kill Fafnir for you.' And though he was ill content, Reginn was forced to wait.

And thus gained Sigurd his sword Gram, which was the best in all the world.

7

A short while after, Sigurd went to King Hialprek and told him that the time had come for him to be avenged upon King Lyngvi and his brothers, and besought him that he would give him men to fight with him and a ship to sail to Lyngvi's country. 'Willingly shall I give you all that you need for your enterprise,' said the king; and he gave Sigurd as many men as he could wish for, all hardy fighters and strong, and not one ship, but as many as were needed to carry the warriors, and arms and much clothing besides. And on a fine spring morning, watched from the shore by his mother and Prince Alf and good King Hialprek, Sigurd sailed away for Lyngvi's land.

They sailed with a favouring wind, and in but a few days they had landed on the enemy's shores, even before he knew that they had come; and as they advanced across the country and laid it waste, King Lyngvi gathered together his men and came out to meet them, with his brothers at his side. There was one great and terrible battle in which Sigurd fought mightily with his good sword Gram, and proved himself a great and daring warrior, for all his youth. And he himself it was who slew King Lyngvi and all his brothers, the sons of dead King Hunding, so that at last Sigmund was avenged.

Then with great booty Sigurd and his men sailed home, that he might tell the glad tidings to his mother; and joyful indeed was Hiordis to see him come, unwounded and with such renown.

'I have done the first deed, which was my duty,' said Sigurd to her, 'and now must I do more great deeds which will make my name and yours honoured for evermore.'

Hiordis smiled at his youthful eagerness. 'The summer is nearly over,' she said, 'wait here with me until the spring, and then go forth again.'

But Sigurd would not, for ever beside him was Reginn, reminding him of his promise to kill Fafnir the dragon; so he remained in King Hialprek's house but a brief time after his return, and one early autumn morning he kissed his mother good-bye and bade farewell to his stepfather and to King Hialprek, saying, 'I shall be back before winter.' And, alone with Reginn, taking their two horses, he set sail in a ship that was bound for the northlands. And there, their voyage over, they mounted their horses and rode to Gnita Heath.

The moor stretched pale and wide, strewn with mighty boulders, and here and there small groups of trees, old pines and silver birches whose leaves were turning yellow, and sometimes an oak or a linden. Sigurd rode first, on Grani, and after him came Reginn on a black horse, watching carefully from side to side for a sight of his brother, and every now and then Sigurd would turn Grani's head and ride back to his

companion, to ask the way that they should go to find Fafnir's cave. He laughed and jested, 'If your horse were not so
slow, or rather, had you more heart for meeting with a
dragon, we might ride abreast and so reach our destination
sooner.'

But Reginn only said, 'I have never been a warrior, I leave
that to the Volsungs and such others. Besides, I know Fafnir
of old, and he was mighty and evil, even as a man.'

At last they reached a little stream that wound its way
down from the hills, and there, leading to a certain spot on the
bank, they found the track made by the dragon when he came
from his cave to the water to drink. The path was smooth and
wide that had been worn by his feet and the coils of his scaly
tail, and the grass on either side had been scorched by his
poisonous breath. Sigurd saw it with astonishment. 'Fafnir is
indeed a great dragon,' he said.

'Dig a pit,' said Reginn, 'right in the middle of the path,
and cover it with branches and heather, and hide in it, and
when he comes by, lift up your sword and pierce him through
the heart.'

So Sigurd set to digging a pit; but Reginn rode away to
wait at a distance, for he was afraid of Fafnir, and he took
Grani with him, at Sigurd's wish. Sigurd dug beneath the
overhanging branches of a linden-tree, for he thought that
the shadow it cast might help to conceal the pit below. When
the pit was dug, he made to leap into it, but he was suddenly
surprised to see, standing close by and watching him, an old
man in a cloak, with a wide-brimmed hat.

'What are you doing, Sigurd?' asked the old man. And
when Sigurd had told him, he said, 'Have you not considered
how, when your sword pierces the dragon's heart, his blood
will gush forth and fill the pit, and thus you will be drowned?'

'Indeed,' said Sigurd, 'I had not considered it.' He looked

at his pit. 'Tell me, old stranger, how can I avoid such a fate?'

'From each side of the pit, dig a narrow trench, so that along these channels the blood may drain away. But do not seek, Sigurd, to avoid the dragon's blood, for whoever bathes in the blood of Fafnir, while it is yet warm, shall become proof against all weapons. No sword or spear may pierce his skin, once it has been bathed in Fafnir's blood.' And before Sigurd could question him further, or even utter his astonishment, the old man had vanished, as though Sigurd had dreamed his presence. And Sigurd marvelled, thinking, 'Once again have I seen Odin. The Allfather himself came from Asgard to give me his good advice.' And he set to work to dig trenches leading from the pit, as he had been bidden.

When the task was completed, he jumped into the pit and waited, and after a time he could feel how the earth began to tremble with the dragon's mighty footfalls as he came slowly along the track towards the stream. Nearer and nearer Fafnir came, an immense and hideous monster, breathing forth poison and fire. And Sigurd waited with his good sword Gram, ready to strike. When Fafnir's huge length came above the pit, Sigurd thrust upward with Gram, and the sword went right into the monster's heart and his blood poured out, all over Sigurd, soaking through his clothes, so that from head to foot he was bathed in Fafnir's blood, save only in one spot between his shoulder-blades where a leaf had dropped on his back from the linden-tree; for it was early autumn, and the leaves were falling.

In the agony of his death, Fafnir thrashed his tail from side to side of the path, so that bushes and rocks were torn from the earth, and the ground echoed with his groaning. But when he knew that he must die and that all struggles were hopeless, he lay still upon the pathway, his great scaly sides heaving with his last breaths. Then Sigurd left the pit and approached carefully, and Fafnir saw him and asked, 'Who are you, youth? For many years I have been the terror of all, and no man has dared approach me to do me harm. Yet now are you come with your boldness and your beauty, and I must die. Tell me who it is that has killed me.'

'I am Sigurd, and Sigmund was my father.'

Fafnir's once mighty voice was little more than a sigh. 'If you are wise, Sigurd whose father was Sigmund, you will run from this place, and quickly, and never stop to look behind you until you are back whence you came. For very often a slaying is avenged upon the slayer.'

'Who is there to avenge Fafnir, whom all men hated?' asked Sigurd. 'I shall not ride home unless I have your gold with me.'

'Small good will it bring to you, Andvari's accursed gold,' whispered Fafnir. 'Small good did it bring to my father, and small good has it brought to me. Think not, young Sigurd, that it will serve you better than us.'

'If giving up all thought of your gold would make me live for ever, then might I ride home without it. But all men die some day, whether for the sake of their gold or for some other cause. You will not make me fear, Fafnir.'

But Fafnir did not hear his words, for the great dragon was dead.

Sigurd walked to where Reginn hid with the horses beside an overhanging rock. 'Fafnir is dead, Reginn,' he called.

Seeing him so covered with the dragon's blood, Reginn asked anxiously, 'Are you wounded, Sigurd?'

Sigurd smiled. 'I have not even a scratch, Reginn, yet I am all but drowned with dragon's blood. But that need not be accounted a misfortune.' And he sat down upon the heather and told Reginn of the old stranger whom he believed to be

Odin himself, how he had bidden him dig trenches for the blood to be drained away, and how he had said that Fafnir's blood would be a sure protection against all weapons. And Reginn marvelled at it all, and marvelling, remembered how he had once heard it said that whoever ate of Fafnir's heart should understand the speech of the birds, though he did not know if it were true or not. But of this he said nothing to Sigurd, and only pondered it in silence.

'Why do you not smile and rejoice more, Reginn?' asked Sigurd. 'Fafnir is dead at last.'

'It is my brother you have killed, Sigurd.'

Sigurd laughed. 'Surely you will not demand weregild for a slaying you urged me to?'

Reginn said nothing for a while, and then, his mind made up, he said, 'Go back to the place where you slew him, and cut out Fafnir's heart for me, and cook it that I may eat it.'

Sigurd watched Reginn thoughtfully and after a time he said quietly, 'How you must have hated your brother, Reginn.' And he reached out for Gram and rose and went back to where the dragon lay, and found him still and cold. He cut out the monster's heart and carried it back to Reginn, and fetching faggots, he made a fire and spitted the heart over the flames. 'It will not be cooked yet awhile,' he said to the silent Reginn. 'There will be time for me to go to the stream and wash off the blood.'

Sigurd went to the little stream, and untying the lacings of his reindeer-hide shoes which were bound crosswise about his legs, he took off his woollen tunic and his leggings and washed both himself and his clothes free of the dragon's blood.

Reginn brought his own cloak to the bank and waited. 'Wear this until your clothes are dry,' he said. And then it was that he noticed that there had been a linden leaf lying between Sigurd's shoulder-blades, and the underside of the leaf, where it had lain next his skin, was clean and dry and free from blood. 'There is one spot on your body which was not bathed in Fafnir's blood,' he said. 'Here, on your back.' And he touched the spot with his finger.

Sigurd smiled over his shoulder at him. 'So there is still one place where a weapon can harm me,' he said. 'I must take care to tell of it to no one save a friend like yourself.' He laughed, untroubled. 'You must protect my secret well, Reginn.' He took the cloak which Reginn held out to him, and together they went back to the fire and Sigurd spread out his clothes to dry and sat with Reginn beside the blaze. 'Later,' he said, 'I shall go up to Fafnir's cave and bring away the gold.' His eyes shone eagerly. 'I shall do great things with it, Reginn, great things indeed.' He laid his hand impulsively on Reginn's arm. 'Never forget, if you should change your mind and wish for any of the treasure, you have only to ask me for it.'

But Reginn moved his arm away, almost roughly. 'I want none of the gold,' he said; and rising, walked from the fire.

Sigurd watched after him, thinking, 'How strange that he should not be more happy, now that I have done as he has so often asked.' And then he reflected, 'Fafnir was his own brother, however evil he may have been, so perchance it is for the boy that he played with and perhaps once loved that he sorrows now, and not for the man who cheated him of his heritage, or the dragon who was the terror of Gnita Heath.'

But Reginn went and sat at a distance, for his mind was full of thoughts. 'The gold is mine, as Hreidmar's son and Fafnir's brother, why should young Sigurd have it?' Then he hid his face in his hands. 'He loves me well, and has ever been as a foster-son to me. How can I think such thoughts?' But because there was Andvari's curse upon the gold, however hard he struggled with himself, Reginn could not cast out from his mind his desire for the treasure which he had given so lightly to Sigurd while it was yet the dragon's. And the longer he sat alone, the stronger grew the workings of the dwarf's curse; and the longer he pondered, the blacker grew his thoughts.

In the warmth of the fire and the brightness of the afternoon sunshine, Sigurd's clothes dried, and he put them on again, folding Reginn's cloak carefully and laying it on the heather; moving so gently that he did not even scare away the birds which twittered on a tree close by. Then he sat down again to watch the dragon's heart as it roasted over the flames. 'Surely it must be cooked,' he thought, and forgetting how hot it would be, he touched it with one finger, and was burnt. With a half-annoyed, half-amused exclamation at his own stupidity, Sigurd put his finger in his mouth to take away the smart, and instantly found that he could understand what the birds in the tree were saying.

'Foolish, foolish Sigurd,' sang one of them. 'He sits there roasting the dragon's heart for Reginn, when he might eat of it himself.'

'And what does Reginn do?' chattered another. 'He sits out of sight, he sits out of sight and he plots, and he plots.'

'Oh, foolish, foolish Sigurd,' sang the first bird. 'Foolish, foolish Sigurd.'

Sigurd took the heart from off the spit and cut a portion of it and laid it aside to cool. When it had cooled he ate it, and immediately the voices of the birds came louder and clearer than before.

'If Sigurd only knew what Reginn was thinking, over there, out of sight, he would know that Fafnir's brother is no better than Fafnir was.'

'No better than Fafnir, no better than Fafnir,' piped a little brown bird.

'Oh, foolish, foolish Sigurd,' sang the first bird that he had understood.

'It must be my imagining,' thought Sigurd, 'that I should think they warn me against Reginn.' But he thought on it further and said to himself, 'Yet he must have known that to eat of the heart of the dragon would give him knowledge of the speech of the birds, or else he would not have bidden me cook it for him. For I see now that it was not hatred of Fafnir that urged him to act thus. But because he bade me cook it, does it follow that he alone would have eaten of it, and would not have shared his new power with me? When he comes, I will tell him, and we both will laugh over it.' He thought yet further, and grew doubtful, 'Or perhaps we shall not laugh.' And round and round in his puzzled mind the thoughts chased themselves until he grew confused. He lay down beside the now dying fire. 'I will try to sleep,' he said. 'I am tired and my mind runs on wildly. Reginn is ever my good friend.'

A little while later Reginn rose and walked back to the spot where he had left Sigurd, and as he approached, he saw him lying as though asleep, face downwards on the ground. He stopped and stood for a moment. 'I alone,' he thought, 'in all the world, know how he may still be killed.' And in that moment his mind was made up. 'There will be no pain for him, for he will not awake. One quick stab and the gold will be mine.' Reginn drew the knife from his belt and stepped carefully closer.

'Wake up, wake up, wake up, Sigurd,' sang the birds.

Sigurd sighed. 'Will they never let me rest,' he thought. 'It were better by far that I had never learnt their speech.'

'Take care, foolish, foolish Sigurd. Take care. See where

the knife is raised to strike, see the knife above you,' sang the
first of the birds.

The birds fluttered along the branches of the tree, and
some of them flew down low, close to Reginn's head. 'Sigurd,
Sigurd, Sigurd, look at the knife, where it shines in the sun.
Sigurd, wake up and look at the knife.'

Sigurd opened his eyes on to the heather and raised his head a
little, enough to see that a shadow had fallen between him and
the sun, and in one quick movement he rolled aside, over on
to his back; and the knife was buried to its hilt in the ground.

Sigurd sat up. 'Reginn! Are you out of your mind?'

Reginn snatched the knife out of the earth and flung himself at Sigurd. But he was no warrior, and Sigurd was too
quick for him and was again out of his reach. And before
Reginn could strike once more, Sigurd had stretched out
his hand for Gram, and kneeling on the ground, even as
Reginn struck at him yet again, he ran him through the heart
with the sword he himself had made.

For a long time Sigurd stared at Reginn lying there, until
his sword fell from his numbed fingers, and he leant forward
to touch Reginn's hand. 'Reginn, wake up, it was only a
nightmare. Reginn, wake up.' He shook his arm a little.
'Reginn, Reginn, wake up.' And then suddenly he covered
his face with his hands and began to weep like a child. And
save for the sound of his weeping, it was silent everywhere,
for it was evening and the birds were all flown. And darkness dropped like a cloak over Gnita Heath.

8

At dawn the birds returned and their songs began once
more. 'Foolish, foolish Sigurd,' sang the foremost of them,
'to sit here weeping for false Reginn while Brynhild waits at
the top of the hill. Oh, foolish, foolish Sigurd.'

Sigurd raised his head to hear them. 'At the top of the hill that is called Hinda-fell, beyond the encircling fire, there waits Brynhild, sleeping. Go and wake her, go and wake her, Sigurd.'

And Sigurd thought, 'I heeded their warnings yesterday, and my life was saved. Perchance this advice is also good.' He looked down at Reginn, lying dead and pale. 'Since I have killed my good friend, I cannot return to King Hial-prek's house, so I may as well ride to Hinda-fell and see this Brynhild, whoever she is.' And he wrapped Reginn's cloak gently around his cold body and laid it in a cleft between two rocks and covered it with branches and fallen leaves, that the carrion birds might not find it.

He saw then that Reginn's black horse had wandered away in the night, but Grani was waiting patiently for his master beneath a tree. Sigurd saddled him, and mounting, rode away, with a last look back at the spot where Reginn lay. And all the birds broke into their loudest singing to speed him on his venture.

He rode first up to Fafnir's cave, and there he found And-vari's gold, hidden away in two chests, glittering like a million prisoned sunbeams in the darkness of the cave. And on the very top of the hoard lay Andvaranaut, the ring. Sigurd took it and put it on his arm, and then closed the chests, and roping them securely, tied them one each side of Grani, and they were almost a greater weight than any horse could bear. But when Sigurd took hold of the bridle and made to lead Grani from that place, the grey horse would not stir, for all his master's coaxing; until at last Sigurd knew what Grani wanted him to do, and he leapt into the saddle, and in a moment, with no urging, Grani galloped away down the hill-side, as though he carried no more than his master.

Sigurd rode right across Gnita Heath towards the hill

KIDDELL-MONROE

that was called Hinda-fell, and after several days' journey through bleak and barren country where only a few birch-trees stood, he saw the hill before him, and it was the highest peak of a dark and forbidding line of mountains, with pines and fir-trees growing on their slopes, and waterfalls which seemed to drop from the sky, like silver streaks amongst the black rocks. And at the very crest of the peak that was Hinda-fell there was a brightness as of fire.

He rode up the mountain side and he rode up the steep sides of the peak, and there at the very top stood a tower built of stone, with one great door; and encircling the tower, a wide ring of fire with flames as tall as trees.

'If the birds spoke truly,' he thought, 'within that tower lies Brynhild, whoever she may be. Having come so far to look at her, shall I be daunted by a ring of flames?' He urged Grani on into the fire, and the brave horse never faltered but leapt straight through the flames. There was a great roaring about Sigurd's ears, lightning flashed before his eyes, and the earth trembled as though it would crack apart; but Grani galloped on and paused only before the tower door.

Sigurd dismounted, and when he tried the door, he found to his surprise that it was open. He entered the tower and saw how its single room was empty save for where, in the very centre, upon a heap of furs and fleeces, as on a couch, there lay a young man sleeping. He seemed no more than a youth, and he wore a byrnie made of links of gold, and a wondrously wrought golden helmet. Sigurd stood beside the couch and looked down at the sleeper and thought that he had never seen a face more fair; then gently he took off the young man's helmet and a shower of red-gold hair tumbled about the sleeper's head, and Sigurd saw that it was a woman who lay there.

'This will be Brynhild, of whom the birds told me,' he

thought. And he touched her cheek with his fingers, and she awoke and opened her eyes and sat up and looked at him. 'Who are you?' she asked, and her voice was low and quiet and very beautiful.

'I am Sigurd, son of Sigmund, of the Volsung race.'

She watched him keenly. 'You look a likely warrior, Sigurd, son of Sigmund. Have you any worthy deeds to tell me of?'

'Little enough so far,' said Sigurd, 'for I am young. Yet in the years that I have lived, I have had vengeance upon those who killed my father, and I have slain Fafnir, the dragon who dwelt on Gnita Heath. Little enough indeed, but one day there will be more to tell you of.' Brynhild smiled as though she were pleased, and Sigurd asked, 'Your name I know to be Brynhild, for I heard the birds sing of you, but that is all I know. I have spoken of myself, most lovely maiden, will you not now tell me your story?'

Brynhild moved, so that he could sit down beside her on the couch, but for a time she did not speak; and then at last she sighed and said, in her deep, quiet voice, 'As you have been told, I am Brynhild, but if you know no more than that, you will not know that I am—or rather, that I was once—a Valkyr, one of Odin's warrior-maidens. It was all so long ago, and I must have slept here a great time, but once in a battle I disobeyed the Allfather when he would have given the victory to an old and mighty warrior named Hialmgunnar. But I pitied Agnar, the brave young man who fought against him, and in the battle I struck down Hialmgunnar and carried him to Valhall across my saddle-bow, and Agnar had the victory. And Odin was very wrathful with me, that his much-loved warrior would fight no more battles on earth, and he cast me forth from Asgard, saying that I must henceforth be no more than a mortal maiden, to wed with a man and be the mother of children, and at the last to die and go down to the house of Hel. But I begged Odin for one favour, that he would not let me be the wife of a coward, and he heard my pleading and set me here in this tower, ringed round by fire, to sleep the years away until a man came who dared the flames to wake me and win me for his bride.' She was silent for a while, and then she said, 'If you love me, Sigurd, then I am yours, but if you care not to have me for your wife, then go away from here and leave me to my sleeping until another comes who is as brave as you.'

But Sigurd took her in his arms and kissed her, and swore that he would never love another woman, not though he lived a thousand years. He took off Andvaranaut and put it on Brynhild's white arm, saying, 'This ring which I won from the dragon's hoard, let it be a pledge between us, that we love each other truly, and that none but you are my bride.'

And for many days Sigurd stayed with Brynhild in the stone tower, in love and joy, and much wisdom did she tell him of the things which she remembered from the time when she was one of Odin's warrior-maidens; and there was no happiness in all the world like theirs.

But Sigurd felt that his deeds were not yet enough to be offered to the woman he loved, as a gift worthy of one who had been a Valkyr, so there came a day when he said to Brynhild that he must leave her for a little space, to fare forth in search of new and mightier adventures; that when he felt himself to be truly a great warrior, he could return to her and offer her her rightful share in the honour men would pay to him. 'It will not be so long that I am gone,' he said, 'for I shall ever be spurred on to warrior's deeds by the thought that you are waiting for me, and in a very little time I shall be back to fetch you, and together we shall go and live among men, and no one in all the world shall be prouder of his wife than I of you.'

And though Brynhild was loath to see him go, she shed no tears nor sought to keep him with her, but sent him forth with smiles and with encouragement, only bidding him return to her soon and never forget her. 'I shall be waiting for you,' she said, 'in my tower ringed with flame, and though other men may ride this way and try to woo me, I have no doubt that the next man to pass through the fire and reach my doorway will once again be you, for there is no other man so daring or so brave in all the world.'

Sigurd kissed her and leapt on Grani's back, and the flames died down to the ground for him as he rode away, turning once to see Brynhild standing beside the tower, before the flames rose high again and shut her from his sight. Then he galloped down Hinda-fell, eagerly seeking adventure, and longing for the day when he should ride that way again.

But Brynhild sighed, though she did not weep, and returning into the tower, closed the door and began her weary waiting. And in time a child was born to her, a little girl with hair as fair as Sigurd's, and Brynhild called her Aslaug, and was glad that when Sigurd returned she would have their daughter to show him. But since a flame-girdled tower was no place to rear a child, she wrapped the babe in warm fleeces and carried her out from that place, through the flames which divided for her and down the hill to the valley. There Brynhild sought out the house of a good man named Heimir, and besought him to stand foster-father to Sigurd's child, and willingly Heimir undertook the task until such time as Sigurd should return to fetch his wife. And with a last long look at the babe, Brynhild returned to the tower to wait once more for Sigurd, lying in sleep upon the couch, clad in her golden helmet and her byrnie, as she had been when he first saw her and took her to be a youth.

9

Sigurd rode southwards for many days and crossed the sea once more, having but few adventures and meeting few men of note, until, south of the River Rhine, he came to the kingdom of the Giukungs. Here Gunnar ruled, who was the eldest son of King Giuki, who was dead; and with Gunnar ruled his two brothers, Hogni and young Gotthorm. Hogni was a doughty warrior and Gotthorm was little more than a boy; but Gunnar was famed for his skill on the harp, and for his lovely voice which surpassed that of all other men. Gunnar and his brothers were as yet unwed, and all women's matters in Gunnar's house were managed by his mother, Grimhild, whom men whispered to be a witch. And indeed, she had no little skill in magic arts, some of which she had taught to her eldest son, though he cared but little for them and only accepted her teaching through courtesy, because she was his mother. The young Giukungs had one sister, Gudrun, and she was the loveliest maiden in all their land.

To the house of Gunnar Sigurd came one evening, and the brothers welcomed him kindly. As they all sat at the feasting together, Queen Grimhild looked long at Sigurd without being observed of any, and to her it seemed as though she saw before her at last a man who was worthy to wed with her daughter, the lovely Gudrun, so she bade Gudrun go to pour out ale for their guest. Gudrun filled Sigurd's drinking horn for him, and he thanked her with courtesy and smiled, but never even glanced at her face, for his mind was too full of his memories of Brynhild for him to look with gladness on any other maiden.

And Grimhild, watching, saw how Sigurd never looked at Gudrun and she thought, 'Perchance he cares not for women and thinks only of battles and swords, or perchance he loves already. But Gudrun is very beautiful, and given time, he will surely look on her, and having looked on her, how could he fail to love her as other lesser men have done in vain?' And she spoke aside to Gunnar and bade him ask Sigurd to remain in the house for longer than one night. 'For,' she said, 'he seems a noble man and a brave one, and he may well be a good friend to you.'

'Glad are we to have you among us, Sigurd,' said Gunnar. 'Let my house be as your own for so long as you care to stay in it.'

And Sigurd was pleased, for in the few brief hours he had spent in their company, he had grown to like Gunnar and Hogni; though Gotthorm, the youngest of the three brothers, seemed to him to be a silent, sullen youth, with little to recommend him.

That evening, when Gunnar played his harp and sang, Sigurd, hearing him for the first time, was astonished. 'Truly,' he said, 'I think that Gunnar's harp and voice would charm even the beasts of the forest, and lull to sleep the snakes that dwell among the rocks.' And Gunnar smiled, glad at his praise.

In the days that followed, Sigurd and the two elder Giu-kungs were ever together, hunting, riding, and talking, and there sprang up between them a deep friendship which they believed nothing might ever break. And one day the three of them took the oath of blood-brotherhood, digging up a turf from the ground and mingling their blood in the earth; a vow which bound them always to serve each other and to share all things.

And every evening, as they sat at the feasting, Grimhild

would send Gudrun to pour out Sigurd's ale, but never once did he show the lovely Giukung maiden more than the courtesy he would have shown to any woman; and it was as though, to him only, out of all other men, she seemed not beautiful. And in her heart Gudrun sorrowed at his indifference, for she had loved him since that first evening she had seen him.

And Grimhild, always watching, thought, 'It must be that he loves another.' And she sought to find from him by careful questioning if it were so. But Sigurd would not speak to her of Brynhild; nor did he mention her even to Gunnar and Hogni, for Brynhild, his bride, was his own secret, to be shared with no one else; though willingly enough had he told the two brothers even of the linden leaf that had lain between his shoulder-blades on the day he had slain Fafnir.

But Grimhild knew that she had guessed aright, for all Sigurd's silence, and with her sorceries she prepared a drink which would cause the drinker, for a certain length of days, to forget utterly the one whom he loved. This potion she poured into a horn of ale, and carried it herself to Sigurd, saying, 'May you ever prosper, Sigurd, our good friend.'

He took the horn and drank, and straightway he forgot Brynhild, as though he had never seen her or even heard her name.

'Come, Gudrun,' Grimhild called, 'bring more ale for Sigurd.'

Gudrun hurried forward to refill the horn, and when Sigurd turned to thank her for the drink, he saw that she was beautiful, and was surprised that he had never noticed it before. And when she had left him and returned to sit beside her mother, Sigurd glanced across the hall to her once or twice, thinking that, with her soft brown hair and her grey eyes, she was easily the fairest maiden he had ever seen. And behind her long white fingers, Queen Grimhild hid a triumphant smile.

The next day Grimhild sent for Gunnar, and when he came to her where she waited in the women's bower, she bade him sit and drink with her wine made of cranberries and honey; and while he drank she asked him, 'Sigurd is your good friend, is he not?'

Gunnar smiled. 'I think I hold him above all other men. Not even my brother Hogni is more dear to me.'

Grimhild folded her hands on her lap. 'That is well, my son, for thus it would please you should he marry with your sister.'

Gunnar was surprised. 'But Sigurd pays no heed to Gudrun,' he said. 'He never speaks to her, and indeed he does not love her, though sometimes of late I have feared that she loves him.'

Grimhild smiled at her son. 'It needs a woman's eye to see these things, Gunnar,' she said. 'And I have seen how often Sigurd watches Gudrun when he thinks that no one looks at him. Offer her to him as a wife, and I think that they will both be happy.'

So Gunnar, with great joyfulness, asked Sigurd if he would marry Gudrun, and after a brief hesitation which he himself could not have explained, Sigurd said, 'The bonds which join us, Gunnar, could not be stronger than they are, yet if anything might strengthen them, it would be this marriage. Gladly will I take your sister as my wife, if she herself is willing.'

'Go to her and ask her,' said Gunnar.

Sigurd went to where Gudrun sat spinning with her mother, and the queen greeted him and bade him stay a while and talk with them. But after a short time, Grimhild rose and said that she must be about her household duties, seeing that the servants were not idling, and she bade Gudrun entertain their guest.

Sigurd sat on a stool and watched Gudrun spinning and wondered why he did not say what he had come to say; and Gudrun looked only at the fine white wool she spun and wished that Sigurd would go away, for she feared he might guess that she loved him though he cared not for her, and considered she would thus be shamed in his eyes.

But Sigurd thought, 'I have no reason for not speaking, Gunnar and Hogni are my good friends, and Gudrun is lovely and gracious.' And so he said aloud, 'Gudrun, your brothers and your mother have all given their consent, there remains but yourself to ask. Would you be willing to marry me?'

Gudrun was so startled that she dropped her spindle, and a length of the woollen thread upon it was unwound; and she was so confused that she could not answer him. Sigurd handed her back the spindle. 'The thread is tangled,' he said. 'I fear that it will need unravelling.'

She took it, murmuring, 'Thank you,' and with eyes downcast began to rewind the wool with fingers that all of a sudden felt clumsy and trembled.

'You have given me no answer, Gudrun,' said Sigurd. 'Will you marry me?'

'If that is as my brothers and my mother wish it,' she whispered, 'I will marry you.' And when she looked shyly up at him, Sigurd saw that her eyes were full of tears.

'You are weeping,' he said. 'This talk of marriage is not pleasing to you. You are not happy in this matter.'

But Gudrun shook her head. 'It is because I am so happy that I weep.' She laughed a little, and in a voice which shook, she said, 'You have made me very happy, Sigurd, far happier than I dared to hope.'

And Sigurd laughed and said, 'Truly, the way of maidens is strange, that they weep when they are happy.'

And thus was Sigurd pledged to Gudrun; and though he did not love her, he honoured her and thought her beautiful, for by reason of the magic draught he had forgotten utterly the red-gold hair and flashing eyes of Brynhild.

The marriage was celebrated with much rejoicing, and no bride could have been happier than Gudrun who had won her heart's desire, for little did she dream of the sorrow that would come of it. And seeing her so lovely and so loving and so happy, Sigurd thought, 'Truly, I am fortunate, and no man could have a better wife.' And he was glad, and believed himself at last in love with her.

10

When Sigurd's marriage was two years old, one evening, laying by his harp, Gunnar said to him, 'Seeing you so content with my sister, I feel that I too should take a wife, that there may be a young queen in my house.'

'That is well thought of, my son,' said Grimhild, who was sitting close by. 'I have long wished to see you wed.'

'Only such another as my Gudrun would be a queen fit for you,' said Sigurd, laying his hand with affection upon Gunnar's arm. 'And where will you find her in all the world?'

'Where indeed?' asked Hogni. 'For there could be no other like Gudrun, however long one searched for her.'

Gunnar laughed, 'It seems then,' he said, 'that I must remain unwed, in spite of my good mother's wishes.'

'There are maidens enough in the world,' said young Gotthorm, who spoke seldom, 'and many of them fit to be queens.' But no one heeded his words.

Grimhild rose and stood behind Gunnar's chair with one of her white hands lying upon each of his shoulders. 'I have heard,' she said, 'of a Valkyr, one of Odin's battle-maidens, who lies sleeping in a tower ringed by flame, far away to the north. They say she awaits the coming of a warrior who is bold enough to seek her, and that she is destined to be the wife of him who rides through the flames to win her. Might not such a wife be worthy of my eldest son?'

Hogni turned to Sigurd, 'As you travelled from the north, did you hear tell of this tower and this maiden?'

Sigurd shook his head. 'Never.' Yet even as he said the word, it seemed to him that he did not speak the truth; but on considering it, there was no reason that he could remember why it should be untrue.

'How is she called?' asked Gunnar, and Grimhild answered him, 'Her name is Brynhild.'

'Brynhild,' Sigurd repeated the name. 'Brynhild.' He placed his hand across his eyes as if to think the better.

'You have heard of her?' asked Hogni.

Sigurd took his hand from before his eyes and shook his head. 'The name seemed familiar when Queen Grimhild spoke it, but I was mistaken, for I have never heard of her. Yet she sounds a likely wife for Gunnar.'

Grimhild ran her fingers lightly through Gunnar's hair. 'What do you think, my son?' she said softly.

'It would be an adventure worthy of a Giukung, to win a wife no other man might attain,' said Gotthorm.

'Well, Gunnar, what of it?' smiled Sigurd.

Gunnar jumped to his feet. 'I will go tomorrow to search for this Brynhild—yes, and to win her—if you will ride with me, Sigurd, and give me your company on the way.'

'I will go with you,' said Sigurd. 'I have been idle at home too long.' And his eyes were alight with eagerness at the thought of new adventures.

The next day Sigurd and Gunnar set off; and after asking

often on their way of the maiden who slept in a tower ringed with fire, they crossed the sea to the northlands and came at last to the hill that was called Hinda-fell. And it was to Sigurd as though he had never seen the place before.

They rode up as far as the ring of flames, and there they dismounted and Gunnar embraced Sigurd, saying, 'Wait here for me and I will come back through the flames with my bride. But if by the time that three nights are past, I have not returned to you, then go home and tell my mother and my brothers how I perished wooing Brynhild.' Then he leapt upon the back of his horse Goti, and urged him on into the fire. But Goti trembled and would not face the flames, so that Gunnar was forced to desist.

'Take Grani,' said Sigurd, 'for he will pass through fire.'

'How can you be sure of that?' asked Gunnar, who had thought his horse as good as Sigurd's.

And the question puzzled Sigurd, how he should be so certain of what he had said, so that he frowned, thinking. And then he smiled, as though he had found the answer, and patted Grani's neck, 'Because he is the best horse in the world, and of the race of Odin's Sleipnir, that is why,' he said.

So Gunnar mounted upon Grani's back, but the grey horse would bear no other man than Sigurd, and for all the spurring and the coaxing he did but stand like a rock. Gunnar sighed. 'It seems,' he said, 'as though the gods are all against me, and do not think me worthy of so famed a bride.'

'I would that I might ride through the flames and win her for you,' said Sigurd. 'For there is nothing that I would not do for so dear a friend.'

'My mother Grimhild once taught me how to change shapes with another, both being willing. If I can remember the spells—and I fear that I paid but little heed to them—will you go in my stead?'

'Most gladly,' replied Sigurd. And Gunnar set himself to recollect the spells he had been taught, and he succeeded; and in a little space, he stood there on the hill-side in the likeness of Sigurd, while with Gunnar's stature, Gunnar's brown hair and grey eyes, and Gunnar's voice, Sigurd mounted Grani and rode into the flames.

There was a great roaring about his ears as though of thunder, lightning flashed, and the earth trembled as if it would crack apart; and then Sigurd was before the door of the tower, and dismounting. It did not seem strange to him that, when he tried it, the door should be open; but when, a little later, he stood beside the couch of furs and fleeces, he did not remember ever having done so before. He looked down at the sleeper and thought, 'So this is the far-famed Brynhild. How fair she is!' And he touched her hand where it lay on her breast, and immediately Brynhild awoke, thinking, 'It is Sigurd come back.' But when she opened her eyes and sat up, she saw a stranger before her, and the joy died from her heart. 'Who are you that have come through the wall of fire?' she asked.

'I am Gunnar, the son of King Giuki,' replied Sigurd, 'and I have travelled many miles from the south to woo you, Brynhild.'

She rose and looked at him. 'Did you come through the flames alone and unaided?' she asked.

'I came alone and unaided save by my horse.'

'You are not the one I expected,' she said.

Sigurd smiled. 'It grieves me that you are disappointed, fair Brynhild. Yet men have called Gunnar brave and handsome enough.' Glad to praise his friend, he smiled again, but met no answering smile.

Brynhild turned away from him and paced across the tower room, back and forth, while he watched her, remembering nothing of the days he had once spent there. At last she stood before him and looked him in the eyes. 'Since it is as Odin wills, that I must wed with the man who comes through the fire to claim me, I have no choice, Gunnar, son of Giuki, but to go with you wherever you choose to take me. But this one thing I ask of you, that you will allow me one year's delay before you lead me from this place.'

'That I cannot do,' said Sigurd, 'unwilling though I am to refuse you.'

'Give me but one month,' said Brynhild.

Sigurd shook his head. 'I cannot.' Then he remembered what Gunnar had said to him before attempting to ride into the flames, and he thought, 'He will wait three nights for me, even as I would have waited for him. I may grant her that short space of time. And aloud he said to her, 'I will stay three nights longer in your tower, but no more.'

And Brynhild said to herself, 'I have waited three years for Sigurd, and three nights are but a short time, yet even in three nights, he may come for me.'

So for three days and three nights Sigurd and Brynhild waited together in the tower, he for the moment when he could tell his friend how well he had served him in winning him so fair a bride, and she for the husband she loved, that he might save her from this stranger. And because she was to be Gunnar's wife, in all the time they were together, Sigurd spoke no word of love to Brynhild, nor asked her for a single kiss, though he thought her far more beautiful than Gudrun.

Before dawn on the fourth day, Sigurd said to Brynhild, 'I will go now and wait for you beyond the ring of flame. At dawn, come to me, and we will ride together to my home in the south.'

And Brynhild thought, 'For three years and three days I

have waited, and still Sigurd has not come. Surely he has met with some harm, or he has forgotten me.' And because she had no power to evade the fate laid on her by Odin, she said, 'I will come to you at dawn.'

Then, thinking to please Gunnar by bearing him a gift from his bride, Sigurd asked, 'Will you not give me some token of your love that I may always cherish? That ring upon your arm, perhaps?'

'No,' said Brynhild, 'not that. Take anything but that.'

Wondering at her reluctance, he looked more closely at the golden ring, and at once a strange feeling came over him that he had seen it somewhere before. But though he puzzled over it, he could in no way say where or when, and knew only that he must have the ring, yet not for Gunnar, but for himself. He held out his hand and smiled, 'Come, give it to me.'

'No.' Brynhild's eyes were burning, but he never looked at them, only at Andvaranaut upon her arm.

'Why do you refuse me?'

But she would not answer him, for she did not wish to speak of Sigurd, lest harm should come to him from it.

'Give me your ring, Brynhild. I will give you all my other jewels in return.'

She put her hand over her arm, covering the gold, and turned and walked away from him. Her voice was very angry when she spoke. 'I will never give you my ring. If you dare to, come and take it from me.'

And because to Sigurd, at that moment, there was nothing else that mattered save that he must possess the ring, he went to her and took it from her arm and left the tower without another word. He leapt upon Grani's back and rode into the flames and they parted for him; and Gunnar started up from a rock on which he had been sitting and ran to meet him. 'You are safe, Sigurd,' he cried joyfully. 'How did you fare?'

'Your bride is won, Gunnar, and shortly Brynhild will be here. Let us change shapes quickly, and I will ride home before you to prepare for your coming.'

So Gunnar spoke the spell his mother had taught him, and in a moment he was himself once more, and Sigurd too had his own form again.

'I will go immediately,' said Sigurd, 'so that Brynhild does not see me, for it would be best if she thought that you had come a-wooing all alone.'

'Is she as beautiful as she is said to be?' asked Gunnar eagerly.

'She is the most beautiful woman that has ever lived,' answered Sigurd.

'And will she love me?'

'She will love you,' said Sigurd; and for a moment he almost gave Andvaranaut to his friend, but then, because of the strange compulsion that was on him, unnoticed by Gunnar, he knotted the ring in a corner of his cloak and rode down the hill.

And at dawn Brynhild came slowly out of the tower for the last time and walked into the flames, and they died down for her into a ring of ashes, never to flare up again; and slowly she walked towards Gunnar, her eyes hard and cold, and her heart aching. And Gunnar saw that it was even as Sigurd had said, and there was no lovelier woman; and joyfully he set her on his horse before him and rode southwards to the sea.

11

As swiftly as Grani could carry him, Sigurd returned to Gunnar's house where Gudrun met him in the courtyard, held Grani's bridle, and took her husband's cloak from him.

Then Sigurd told to all the welcome news that the king had won his bride and was even then on his way home with her. But only to Hogni, his sworn brother, did he tell how he and Gunnar had changed shapes because of Grani, for he did not think it was a thing which Gunnar would care to have others know.

Overjoyed by the tidings of her son's successful wooing, Grimhild saw to the preparations for the marriage feast, and everywhere in Gunnar's house was bustle and excitement, with much bringing-out of festive clothes and unlocking of jewel coffers.

As she laid it by, her husband's journey being done, knotted in a corner of his travelling cloak, Gudrun found Andvaranaut and held it up. 'Where did you come by this?' she asked. 'It is of most incomparable workmanship.'

'I had it from Brynhild,' Sigurd answered, the old problem gnawing at his mind once more as to why it was familiar to him.

'Why should Gunnar's bride give you a ring?' demanded Gudrun.

And because Sigurd feared that here might be cause for women's jealousy, he smiled, saying, 'Because she thought me to be Gunnar.' And he told her the truth, swearing her to secrecy.

'I am indeed glad that you were able to help Gunnar,' she said, 'and I shall ever keep the secret. But, dear Sigurd, it is a lovely ring, will you not give it to me?' She slipped her hand in his and smiled at him.

He hesitated, but she coaxed and pleaded, until at last he said, 'It is yours on the condition that you neither wear it nor show it to anyone, for it would be an ill thing for your brother's wife to see how her love-gift had reached the wrong hands. Besides, Brynhild, above all others, must never know it was not Gunnar who rode through the fire to her.'

And with many promises, Gudrun kissed Sigurd and hid Andvaranaut away at the very bottom of her jewel casket.

As soon as he reached his home, Gunnar handed his bride into the care of his mother, and well pleased by Brynhild's beauty and bearing, Grimhild led her up to the women's bower which was built above the great hall; a long, low room, higher by far in the middle than at the sides, by reason of the slope of the roof. Here Gudrun received her with smiles and a kiss, while the women of the household stared curiously at their master's strange bride, and whispered about her beauty and her silence which was not as the merry chattering of other maidens.

Gudrun herself decked Brynhild for the marriage feast, bidding her sit while she combed her hair. 'Truly, dear sister, I have never seen hair the colour of yours, nor so smooth and so long. You are fortunate indeed, and I envy you.' She brought her own jewel casket and bade Brynhild choose from it. 'My brother Gunnar will give you jewels of your own, but for today, take what you will of mine, for the wife of a king should wear rich gems, it is only fitting.'

Brynhild picked out one brooch, the first that she saw, without caring. Gudrun pinned it at her shoulder for her, surprised. 'Is that all you will wear, good Brynhild? Yet perhaps you are right. With your hair you have gold in plenty, and will look a fair enough queen unadorned. How strange it must have been for you,' she went on, 'to live all alone on the top of a hill, wearing a helmet and a byrnie. Tell me, did you not find a byrnie uncomfortable wearing, and was the helmet heavy?'

'Had it been as heavy as Hinda-fell,' thought Brynhild, 'it would not have been heavier than my heart is today.' But aloud she only answered Gudrun, 'I found it not so.'

When all was ready, Gudrun bade Brynhild stand where the light was best that she might see her well. She smiled in pleasure. 'Truly, sister, you are a bride that might please any king.' Impulsively she pressed Brynhild's cold hands in hers. 'I wish you all joy of your marriage, good Brynhild. May your wedded days be as happy as mine.'

And in reply to such kindly words, Brynhild felt she could do no less than smile a little and ask, with courtesy, though she cared nothing for the answer, 'You are wedded then, Gudrun?'

Gudrun's happiness glowed in her smile. 'I have been a wife for almost three years. My Sigurd dwells here in my brother's house.'

'Sigurd, he is called?' Brynhild's white face went whiter, and her eyes burnt dark.

'Sigurd, the son of King Sigmund, of the Volsung family. A great prince he is, and a fine warrior, and he slew the dragon Fafnir. He is tall and handsome, and his hair is even fairer than yours.' She stopped. 'Why Brynhild, what ails you that you have grown so pale? Are you sick?' She called out to one of the women to bring a stool, that Brynhild might sit.

'There is nothing amiss,' said Brynhild.

'You will be tired after your journey,' said Gudrun. 'Sit, and I will fetch my mother. She is skilled in simples and has a remedy for every ill. She will bring a drink to give you strength.'

'I have strength enough,' said Brynhild. But Gudrun was already gone, calling to Grimhild to come.

But when Grimhild came with a cup of wine in which healthful herbs had been steeped, and bade Brynhild drink, saying, 'This will bring some colour into your cheeks, my child,' Brynhild firmly put the cup aside. 'I need no wine, nor any healing drinks.' She rose and moved away from them. 'I thank you for your kindness, yet if you could but leave me for a little while, I should count it as a favour, for I would like to be alone.' And so they left her.

'This Brynhild,' said Gudrun to Sigurd, a little later, 'I fear that she is proud and haughty. She is pale and silent and speaks not. Thinking her to be shy among strangers on the first day in her new home, I chattered like a starling, but she gave me no word in reply. I offered her my jewels, but she did not even thank me. I do indeed fear that she is proud and haughty.' Gudrun sighed. 'May she soon mend her ways, for she will be ill to live with otherwise.'

Sigurd laughed. 'She will not have spoken to many, living in a flame-girdled tower. She is likely to talk little at first, and be unaccustomed to our ways. But I do not doubt that she will soon prove to talk as much as any other woman.'

A while after, when the guests were all gathered, Gunnar sent for Brynhild, saying, 'Go, Gudrun, fetch Brynhild that she may join us at the feasting, which is in her honour, as my bride.' And as Gudrun went to the bower, a strange feeling came over Sigurd at hearing Gunnar's words, and he frowned. 'Why should Gunnar send for Brynhild?' he thought. 'She is not his to send for. She is my bride, to sit at my side and to smile for me alone.' And then, as suddenly as it had come, the mood was over, and he was wondering how such a thought had ever come into his mind. 'It must be because I won her for Gunnar,' he comforted himself. 'It is nothing more than that.' And he looked towards the steps that led down from the women's bower into the great hall and saw Gudrun and Brynhild descending together. Gudrun smiling and adorned with gold and holding Brynhild's hand, and Brynhild in a white kirtle with but a single brooch, her face as pale and unmoving as though it were carved in ice, and her red-gold hair unbound.

And in that instant the magic draught that had numbed his mind for all but three years lost its power, even as the snow melts in the springtime, causing the rivers to flood, and Sigurd knew Brynhild and remembered all that had passed between them since that day he had first entered the stone tower and woken her out of her charmed sleep, swearing to love her for ever. With horror in his heart he turned to Gunnar, to tell his friend of the terrible mistake, but Gunnar, his face alight with joy and pride, was already hurrying along the length of the hall to greet his bride. He took her by the hand and led her to Sigurd, saying, 'This is my good friend Sigurd, son of King Sigmund. I hope that in the days to come you will learn to hold him very dear, even as I do.'

And Brynhild, who had schooled herself to meet this moment, looked at Sigurd as though he were a stranger, and said, 'I trust that in the days to come I shall hold dear all your friends, King Gunnar.' And Sigurd, confused, bewildered, and distressed, could find no words to offer her before she turned away from him to answer Hogni's greeting and to speak with young Gotthorm.

At the feasting which followed, Brynhild, staring before her in cold silence, left her food untasted; but it was not heeded, for a strange bride, at a wedding feast in a house she had never seen before, was expected to be nervous. But Hogni marked how Sigurd neither ate nor spoke, and questioned him; and like a man in a nightmare, Sigurd gave him an answer, though, a moment later, had he been asked, he could not have remembered what it had been.

Later in the feasting, when, as befitted the wife of the king, Brynhild carried round the ale to Gunnar's most favoured guests, Sigurd tried to whisper to her as she filled his drinking horn. But she never looked at him or gave any sign that she had heard. And Sigurd thought, 'How can she believe otherwise than that I have ceased to love her and have forgotten the promises I made? How could a thing be plain to her which even I cannot understand? That for almost three years I should have forgotten her so utterly that even seeing her and speaking with her on Hinda-fell could not make me know her, must surely be due to sorcery and to nothing else.'

And as he lay awake that night, living over in his mind everything that had befallen him since he had come to Gunnar's house, trying to find the moment when it was that he had first forgotten Brynhild, he remembered an evening when Grimhild herself had handed him a horn of ale, saying, 'May you ever prosper, Sigurd, our good friend,' and he had drunk from it.

'And it was upon the day which followed that Gudrun was betrothed to me,' he thought. And then, at once, it was all quite clear to him how he had been tricked into a marriage with the Giukung maiden. And for an angry moment he almost roused Gudrun from her sleep, to demand that she told him the truth. But immediately he regretted his suspicions of one who loved him so sincerely, remembering her joy on the day he had asked for her hand, and he thought, 'She, at least, is innocent, and knows nothing of this.' And then at once he fell to thinking of Gunnar and Hogni. 'They too are innocent, for they are my good friends, and however greatly they might have desired this marriage, they would not stoop to sorcery to gain their ends.' That left only Grimhild, soft-speaking Grimhild with the long white fingers, who was said to be a witch. 'It was sorcery that she taught to Gunnar so that he was able to change shapes with me upon Hinda-fell,' he thought. 'How simple would it be for a witch so skilled to prepare a potion that could make a man forget the woman he loved, even for three years.'

And thus the truth came clear to Sigurd; though not what he should do about it.

But in the days which followed, Brynhild spoke to Sigurd only when she had to and looked coldly upon him at all other times; and though he longed to justify himself to her by telling her the truth, for the sake of Gunnar who was his friend, and for Gudrun who was a loving wife to him, he held his peace and watched in silent unhappiness the woman he loved take her place as Gunnar's queen. And to Brynhild, who believed herself to have been forsaken by the man she loved, the only comfort was that Gunnar, for whom she cared nothing, was as good a man as Sigurd, for had he not ridden through the flames to win her?

12

And so things went on in the house of the Giukungs for almost a year, until one summer's morning when Gudrun and Brynhild went together to bathe in the river. The air was mild and the sun shone kindly, and the birds sang merrily in the trees, as the two women walked knee-deep through the pollen-hung grass and fragrant meadow-sweet. They did not talk, for in the days that had passed since Gunnar's marriage, Gudrun had found that it was but wasted time to try to persuade Brynhild to idle chatter and harmless gossiping such as the other women delighted in.

As they went, Gudrun gathered and laid in a basket the aromatic camomile which, from the whiteness of its flowers, was known as Balder's brow, that her mother might prepare from it her remedies and medicines.

For a while they sat on the bank of the river in the warm sunshine, and Gudrun sorted her camomile neatly in her basket, the yellow-eyed white flower-heads on one side, and the leaves on the other. But Brynhild moodily plucked a stalk of Tyr's helmet, the poisonous purple aconite that grew at the river's edge, and twisting it into a crown, flung it into the water and watched it as it was carried away down the stream, out of sight.

Her task finished, Gudrun placed her basket in the shade and stood up to take off her kirtle and fasten her hair on the top of her head. She smiled down at Brynhild. 'Are you coming?' she asked. And without a word Brynhild rose. Gudrun folded her kirtle neatly and laid it on the grass, but Brynhild dropped hers down impatiently and knotted up her red-gold hair. Watching her from the corner of her eye, Gudrun thought, 'How beautiful she is. Why can she not be better company?' And she sighed a little as she stepped carefully down the river's bank at a spot where it sloped gently, treading underfoot the little forget-me-nots which grew thickly down to the water's edge. From the water she turned and called back to Brynhild, 'It is so cool and pleasant, Brynhild. Hurry and join me.'

Brynhild walked to the edge and stood there, a little way downstream of where Gudrun, waist-deep in the river, poured water from her cupped hands over her shoulders, or splashed it into her face with shut eyes.

'Are you coming?' Gudrun called. She opened her eyes and saw how Brynhild, after reflection, deliberately turned and walked up the bank to a place where it sloped more steeply and was less convenient for entering the water. From there she was obliged to jump into the river, which, though she did it with great grace, caused her hair to tumble about her shoulders so that it was wet. Gudrun laughed. 'Why did you do that?' she asked, amused.

Brynhild stood in the water higher up the stream than Gudrun and once more knotted her hair. Then she turned and looked at Gudrun before she answered her. She saw the smiling face below the piled-up brown curls and thought, 'That is Gudrun whom my Sigurd loves, now that he cares for me no longer.' And in that moment she hated her. 'Because I would not bathe in water that has flowed past your body,' she said, and turned away to wade farther out into the river.

Gudrun stared at her in surprise. 'But why?' she asked.

Brynhild paused to look back at her. 'Because I am a nobler and a greater woman than you.'

The carefully smothered resentment of months broke out in Gudrun, and she forgot all kindliness before Brynhild's discourtesy. 'A nobler and a greater woman than I!' she exclaimed. 'How can a woman be nobler who spurns all well-meant offers of friendship with contempt and silence? And how can a woman be greater who cannot bake a single loaf or weave one strip of even the coarsest cloth?'

'I did not ask for your friendship,' said Brynhild quietly. 'I only wanted that you should leave me alone, you and your mother Grimhild, that you should leave me alone and in peace.' Her lovely voice grew louder. 'And as for the rest, you prattle of loaves and weaving and your petty women's crafts to one who has ridden through the clouds above the clang of battle, and borne the slain warriors to the feasting in Valhall, and been daily in the presence of the Allfather himself. What can you know of greatness, little Gudrun?'

Gudrun heard her in astonishment, but had no words to answer her, save only, 'What you or I can do alone is of no consequence, for a woman is but a woman, and she is noble and great only by reason of the glory of her husband, which she reflects as in a mirror.'

Brynhild laughed. 'It is unwise of you to speak of husbands, for mine is a king and rules over his land, while yours is but a guest in his house.'

Gudrun flushed and forgot all loyalty to her brother. 'My Sigurd is a mightier warrior by far than Gunnar. He avenged his father's death with great slaughter when he was but a youth. And has Gunnar ever killed a dragon? Besides, the gold that Sigurd won from Fafnir is more than Gunnar will own in all his life. My husband is far greater than yours, Brynhild.'

Brynhild smiled in scorn. 'You disparage your brother skilfully, Gudrun, but you forget how he rode through the flames to win me, and all else is as nothing to that.' She flung back her head proudly, and a red-gold lock fell down her cheek and lay across her shoulder.

'He did not ride through the flames to win you,' cried Gudrun. 'Sigurd alone could do that.'

'Shall I then not believe my own eyes,' asked Brynhild, 'when I awoke from my charmed sleep in the tower and saw Gunnar at my side? Think of a more likely lie, little Gudrun.'

Gudrun's voice rose shrilly. 'I am not lying. It was Sigurd who rode through the flames to win you.'

Brynhild stood, still as a white statue, one hand half-way to the fallen lock of hair, and when she spoke her voice was very quiet. 'What do you know of Sigurd's riding through the flames? Answer me that.'

'Gunnar was not man enough to do it for himself. For all he is my brother I tell you this so that your pride may be humbled at last. For I am weary of your haughtiness and your contempt, and I have borne them long enough. Gunnar dared not go through the flames to win you, and so he changed shapes with Sigurd as our mother had once taught him, and Sigurd went in his stead. It was Sigurd who rode through the flames to win you, Brynhild, yet not as a bride for himself, but for Gunnar.' Gudrun paused for breath, her face flushed and her hands clenched.

Brynhild's arm sank slowly to her side, down to the surface of the water. 'That is a lie, Gudrun.'

'It is no lie.'

'Then how did you learn it?'

'Sigurd himself told me. How else do you think I should know?'

'You cannot prove it,' challenged Brynhild.

'I can, for I have the arm-ring which you gave as a love token to Sigurd, believing him to be Gunnar.'

'I gave no love token to him, he took it from me against my will. Yet how should it come to your hands?'

'I asked Sigurd for it and he gave it to me. What other way should I have it? Do you think Gunnar would give me a gift he had received from his bride?'

'Show me the ring, that I may know you are not lying.'

'It is in my jewel casket, I will show it to you when we are home.'

Brynhild waded downstream past Gudrun to where the river's bank sloped shallow, and leaving the water, she stood on the grass above her. 'Show it to me now, for I cannot wait to know the truth.'

Looking up at her, seeing the anger in her eyes, Gudrun suddenly felt afraid, realizing what she had done; how she had broken her promises to Sigurd and betrayed Gunnar's secret which he did not even know she had been told; and she shivered at the coldness of the water which had seemed so refreshing but a little while before.

'Hurry,' said Brynhild, 'for I will not wait.' And she put on her kirtle and unknotted her hair.

Gudrun climbed out on to the bank, and with hands which trembled, reached for her gown.

'If you all have tricked me into a marriage with a coward,' said Brynhild, 'no one of you will ever forget my wrath.'

'It was not I,' said Gudrun. 'I knew nothing of it until it was done. And Gunnar is no coward. It was his horse that was afraid. Gunnar would have gone through the flames himself, if Sigurd's horse would have carried him. Oh, Brynhild, they meant no harm.'

'Hurry,' demanded Brynhild, 'and do not talk so much.' And she started off across the field. Gudrun caught up her girdle, which her cold fingers could not tie, and followed her. After a few paces Brynhild turned. 'You have forgotten your basket,' she said. And almost in tears, Gudrun ran back for it, while Brynhild waited for her scornfully, as though for a servant.

Back in the house, Gudrun opened her jewel casket and spilt out all her jewels: necklaces, brooches, and rings, cunningly wrought and set with gems; and at the very bottom of the box was Andvaranaut. 'There is your ring,' she said.

Brynhild took it up and looked well at it, and knew that Gudrun had not been lying. 'How they must have laughed at me together, the two of them, when he gave her this,' she thought.

'Do you believe me now?' asked Gudrun.

Brynhild looked at her with hatred, and then without a word, turned and made to leave her, still holding the ring. But Gudrun, thinking, 'What will Sigurd say, should he find it is gone?' held out her hand. 'Give me back the ring.'

Brynhild stopped. 'It is my ring.'

'It is no longer yours. Sigurd had it from you, but he gave it to me. Give it back to me, Brynhild.'

'It is my ring,' repeated Brynhild. And then she thought how it had once been Sigurd's gift to her, Sigurd who no longer loved her, and she said, 'It has lain among your trinkets too long, I care for it no more. Take it.' And she flung it on the floor at Gudrun's feet and went.

In apprehension, Gudrun called out after her, 'Brynhild, I beg of you that you will speak of this to no one.' But if Brynhild heard, she gave no answer. Stooping to pick up the ring, Gudrun broke into weeping; and crouched on the floor, holding Andvaranaut to her heart, she wept for the sorrow that must surely come from her rash words, spoken in her thoughtless anger.

13

Brynhild went to the queen's bower and lay down upon her bed; and she would neither eat nor drink, nor speak with anyone.

'What ails you, Brynhild?' asked Gunnar. 'You will surely die if you do not stir, and how could you bring such grief on me?'

But she only turned her head away from him in silence, and to all his entreaties she would give no reply. And at last Gunnar left her. 'Perhaps she is angered with me for some cause I know not of,' he said to Hogni. 'Go you to her and see if you may move her to speak of what is amiss.'

'How shall I have power to move her where you have failed?' asked Hogni. But he went to her and pleaded, 'Fair sister, tell me what ails you, that it may be put aright.' But she would not even look at him, and he fared no better than his brother. 'It is useless,' he said to Gunnar, 'she will not heed me.'

Then Gunnar went to Sigurd and begged him, 'Go you to Brynhild, perhaps Hogni too has angered her, yet she may speak with you and tell you what is amiss.'

And though Sigurd was unwilling, for Gunnar's sake he did as he was asked, and went in to Brynhild and spoke cheerfully to her. 'The sun is shining, Brynhild, and the birds are

262

singing. This is no time for lying abed. Come, rise up and smile.'

And at the sound of his voice Brynhild turned her head and looked at him. And then, for the first time, she spoke. 'This is the vilest insult of all that they have put on me, that they have sent you, of all men, to bid me be merry.'

Sigurd looked into her eyes. 'But I am your friend, Brynhild, and I ever wish you well.'

She sat up in her bed and spoke bitterly. 'Cease lying, Sigurd, for Gudrun has told me the truth, how you rode through the flames to win me for Gunnar. Knowing all that I know, should I believe that you are my friend, you who once swore to love me for ever?'

'That promise have I kept, Brynhild,' said Sigurd quietly. But Brynhild laughed at him in scorn. 'You do me wrong,' he said, and told her of Grimhild's magic draught, and of how he had forgotten her until he saw her as Gunnar's bride at Gunnar's marriage feast. 'But I love you still, Brynhild, and I shall for all my life.'

'But what of Gudrun?' she demanded. 'Gudrun who is your wife?'

'She is good and kind, and I honour her, but it is you whom I love.'

Brynhild thought deeply on all that he had said, and then she sighed and asked, 'What are we to do in this matter?'

'What can we do,' said Sigurd, 'save keep silence lest the others guess, and live as we have been living for the year past?'

Brynhild heard him with astonishment. 'If you truly loved me, as you say you do, you would go out now to the stables and saddle Grani, and I would come to you in the courtyard and we would ride away from here together and forget in each other's company all the sorrow that has been.'

'Brynhild, we cannot do that. Gunnar is my good friend, and you are Gunnar's wife.'

'I was your wife before ever I saw Gunnar,' she said. 'We have a daughter, Sigurd. That is something which you do not know.'

Startled, he stared at her. 'But where is the child? Is she safe? Is she well cared for?'

'She is safe enough, and well cared for, I do not doubt.'

'Tell me where she is, Brynhild, that I may bring her here.'

Brynhild's words rose in bitter mockery. 'That you may bring her here and give her to Gudrun for fostering? I would rather see her dead.' Her voice softened a little. 'Take me away from here, Sigurd, and we will fetch little Aslaug and make a home for her and for ourselves in another land.'

But Sigurd, with a breaking heart, could only repeat, 'Gunnar is my friend, and you are his wife, and Gudrun loves me above all else. Shall I betray them both?'

Brynhild's voice rang out in scorn. 'You set your love for Gunnar above your love for me, and you honour Gudrun more highly than you have ever honoured me. You will not take me away from here and call me your wife before all the world, and I will not live any longer as I have lived for twelve months past. I will not have two kings in one house, Sigurd. Now leave me, for I have nothing more to say to you.'

And because he saw that all further speech was useless, he turned away and left her.

Outside the chamber Gunnar and Hogni were waiting for him. They laid hold of him. 'Did she speak with you?' asked Gunnar eagerly.

'She spoke with me,' said Sigurd.

'What did she say?' asked Hogni.

'Did she give you any reason for her anger with me?' said Gunnar.

But Sigurd broke away from them and fled their company, so that they were amazed.

And in her anger, Brynhild rose from her bed and put on her kirtle and her jewels and braided her hair, and went out to Gunnar and Hogni. In mockery she spoke to Gunnar her husband, saying, 'Fine folly was it, Gunnar, to send Sigurd in to me. And fine folly is it to reckon him your friend.'

'What has Sigurd done?' they asked.

'He told me, Gunnar, that he loved me, and that he would that I were his wife and not yours.'

Gunnar frowned, and then the frown was gone and he said gently, 'You are beautiful, my Brynhild, above all other women, and it is no marvel to me that all men should love you and wish you for their wife, even Sigurd who is my friend. If he loves you, he loves you, and there is no shame to him from it, though it was wrong for him to have spoken of it to you.'

'You are blind, Gunnar, and over-trusting. Sigurd will not rest until I am his wife.'

'You are angry with him, Brynhild, but try to forgive him. This thing will be no more than the madness of a moment, it is Gudrun, our sister, whom he truly loves.' And Gunnar smiled and took her hand.

But angrily she moved away from him. 'You call it but the madness of a moment, yet it has lasted long enough. Sigurd loved me, Gunnar, before ever you saw me.'

'How could that be?' asked Gunnar, puzzled.

And in her wrath, Brynhild believed herself to hate Sigurd, so that she lied to his hurt. 'I have but now learnt what I did not know before, that it was Sigurd in your shape who won me on Hinda-fell. And in your shape he wooed me those three days and nights we were together in my tower. He told me that he loved me, he embraced me and called me his only joy, and I saw no wrong in it, never doubting him to be you.' She paused and saw the look on Gunnar's face, and knew that he believed her. 'He will not rest, Gunnar, until you lie dead, and I, your widow, am his queen.'

Gunnar hid his head in his hands. 'To think that all these months I have trusted him and held him dear, and all the while he has wished to be rid of me. What now should I do?'

'For shame, Gunnar,' Brynhild taunted him, 'does it need a woman to tell you what you should do? Surely it is plain that Sigurd can live no longer?'

'I have sworn oaths of brotherhood with him, how can I break those oaths?'

'I care not how many oaths you break,' cried Brynhild, 'so long as it is done. And on my part, I swear an oath to you, Gunnar, that I will leave this house and you shall never see me more, if you take no vengeance on Sigurd in this matter.' And without another word she left them.

'Hogni, what shall we do?' Gunnar's voice was flat and tired, and he stared at the floor, thinking, 'I cannot lose my Brynhild, whatever else befall.'

'There is but one thing to be done,' said Hogni.

Gunnar looked up, a sudden faint hope in his glance. 'I could speak with Sigurd,' he said. 'Perchance there is some explanation.' He rose. 'I must find Sigurd,' he said.

Hogni laid a hand on his arm. 'No, Gunnar, what must be done had best be done quickly, and words will only make it harder. Besides, you saw how Sigurd hastened away when we would have spoken to him as he came from Brynhild's bower. It could have been for no other reason than that he dared not face the man whom he wished dead.'

Gunnar sat down again, wearily. 'You are right,' he said. 'But I will not kill him, for he was my friend, and I have sworn oaths on his behalf which nothing can make me break.'

'And I also have sworn oaths with Sigurd,' said Hogni. 'I will not kill him either. Yet he must die.'

After a time Gunnar looked at his brother. 'There is young Gotthorm,' he said. 'He has sworn no oaths.'

'It is Gotthorm who must kill Sigurd,' said Hogni, and he sent for him.

When they told him what he must do, Gotthorm said nothing, as was his way; but he thought deeply on it for a while and then at last he spoke. 'There can be no slaying Sigurd in fair fight, for Sigurd has bathed in the blood of the dragon, and he is proof against all weapons. How can I kill him, my brothers?'

Gunnar and Hogni looked at each other, both wondering which of them would betray their friend. Then Hogni said, 'Brynhild is your wife, Gunnar, not mine,' and walked to the other side of the hall. And in a voice which was strangely unlike his own, without looking at Gotthorm, Gunnar said, 'When Sigurd bathed in Fafnir's blood, there was a linden leaf that lay on his back between his shoulder-blades. There only, the blood did not touch.'

'When is it to be?' asked Gotthorm.

'It had best be soon,' said Gunnar, 'before I weaken. For I cannot bear the thought of it.'

Hogni returned to the others. 'And it had best be out of the house,' he said. 'We could go hunting tomorrow, perhaps.'

For a time no one of them spoke, and then Gotthorm rose. 'If you have no more to say to me,' he said, 'then I will go sharpen my hunting spear.'

On the morrow the four of them rode out to the forest; and such was Sigurd's sorrow for all that had passed between him and Brynhild the day before, that he never marked how his companions avoided his eyes, and spoke in strained, unlikely voices.

In the forest they killed a deer, and Sigurd's spirits rose a little, for his had been the well-timed arrow that had slain it. Out in the woods, mounted on Grani, with Gram at his side, he could in a certain measure forget his grief, and his doubts for the future troubled him less.

At midday they dismounted beside a stream to drink. Sigurd smiled at Gunnar. 'You are the king among us all, Gunnar,' he said. 'You shall drink first.' And Gunnar knelt down by the stream and drank from his cupped hands; but the water tasted bitter to him, even as his bitter thought, 'It must be now, or it will be never.' He rose and gestured with one hand towards the stream. 'Drink, Sigurd,' he said, and the two words could hardly be spoken.

Sigurd unfastened his baldric and dropped Gram on to the grass, and, as Gunnar had done, knelt down by the stream and bent low over the water. And Gunnar glanced at Hogni, who nodded, and they both looked at Gotthorm; and Gotthorm took up his hunting spear and stepped forward.

A little brown bird from a tree close by sang out a shrill warning, 'Sigurd, Sigurd, beware!' But Sigurd never heard, for he was thirsty, and the stream was tinkling over its stones, bidding him hear no other sound.

Gotthorm raised the spear in both his hands and poised it over a spot between Sigurd's shoulder-blades. He took a deep breath, while Hogni watched in horror; but Gunnar turned away and covered his face with his hands.

With all his might, Gotthorm brought the spear down, straight through Sigurd's back, and drew it out again, so that the blood gushed forth, soaking into the grass and staining the pure water of the stream. With a groan, Sigurd turned over on his side, and supporting himself with one hand, he took hold of Gram with the other, and with his last strength struck out at Gotthorm, who was standing like one dazed, not thinking to move aside; so that the youth fell dead.

Sigurd tried to rise, but he sank back again. Hogni never stirred, seeming to have no power left to move, but Gunnar turned around, and came and knelt by Sigurd who looked up at him. 'Oh, Gunnar,' he said, 'this was not well done.' And he died.

And after a time, Hogni said, 'He should have had a warrior's death and been welcomed in Valhall, and not been slain like a thrall.' But Gunnar said nothing.

They bore the bodies of Sigurd and Gotthorm back to Gunnar's house, and Sigurd's body they gave to Gudrun. When she saw it, she neither cried out nor wept, but stared in stricken silence as though she did not understand. And when the women of the household came with tears to wash the body and deck it in fine linen and a byrnie, she sat upon a stool and watched, dry-eyed and unspeaking.

But Brynhild demanded of Gunnar, 'Is it done?'

'It is done,' he answered her, 'and Gotthorm, our brother, lies dead.'

And Brynhild gave one wild laugh and no more, so that Gunnar turned from her, shuddering.

But still Gudrun sat and neither spoke nor wept, until they said, 'Unless she weeps, she will surely go out of her mind.' And her women sought to bring her to a knowledge of her loss by the recital of their own sorrows. One old woman told how, of all her children, none remained alive. 'I have outlived my brethren,' she said, 'and the sons and daughters who should have comforted my old age are all of them dead, but I am yet here to mourn them. What a cruel fate is that!' But Gudrun answered not a word, nor wept.

Another woman, who had once been a queen, told of her husband slain in battle along with her seven sons. 'My father and my mother and my four brothers also, did I lose, on the ever-hungry sea. And there was no one to defend me from my foes, so that I was taken for a thrall, and every day I had to kneel before the wife of him who had killed my husband, and a harsher mistress no serving-woman could have found.' But still Gudrun answered not a word, nor did she weep.

And so could not any of their sorrows lure her tears, nor could Grimhild's ministering comfort her.

But a young maiden came forward saying, 'Sad as were your woes, you other women, they are not as the woes of Gudrun, the young widow.' And she drew away from Sigurd's face the cloth which covered it. 'Look upon your beloved husband once more, Gudrun. Kiss him as though he still lived.'

And Gudrun gave but one last look and fell to weeping. 'Of all men,' she said, 'my Sigurd was the best, and there was no other like him. My brothers have slain him, but sorely will they miss him when they next go out to battle and see Sigurd neither to the right nor to the left of them. This is Brynhild's doing, would that she had never come to Gunnar's house, that evil woman.'

And from where she stood at the other end of the hall, in the shadows, leaning against the farthest pillar, Brynhild heard her and laughed. 'Those are ill words, Gudrun,' she said. And slowly she came forward to look on Sigurd. The other women drew aside, as though from something vile, or turned their backs on her, for all she was their queen; all of them save Gudrun, and her tears were flowing too fast for her to be aware of anything, but only her great sorrow.

Brynhild stood for a little space, looking down on Sigurd; and then she turned away and left the hall, and no one, watching her, could tell what she was thinking.

Gunnar ordered a great pyre to be built, heaped high with

logs of oak and fragrant pine, that Sigurd, laid about with gold and goodly arms, might be burnt as befitted a king.

In Gunnar's house, where the other women, mourning for Sigurd, went with dishevelled hair, caring not for clothes or jewels, Brynhild sent for her tiring-maids and bade them comb her hair and bind it with a gold-embroidered fillet. In her finest kirtle of linen dyed with red madder, adorned with rings and a necklace of gold, she stood in her bower, arrayed as for a marriage feast. Then from her jewel casket she took out a little dagger and lay down upon her bed; and before anyone had understood what she was about, calmly and with deliberation, she had stabbed herself. Her women crowded round, but she gestured them aside. 'Go, fetch me Gunnar the king,' she said. And someone ran to do her bidding.

Gunnar came, and with him, Hogni, and the serving-women moved aside to let them reach the bed. When Gunnar saw the blood that flowed from Brynhild's wound, soaking into the white linen of the pillows, he laid his arms about her, beseeching her not to die.

But Hogni turned away, saying, 'Let her die, Gunnar, for naught but ill has she done for us since the day you brought her home.'

Yet Gunnar pleaded, 'Live, Brynhild, to give me joy, and never will I reproach you that you urged me to the killing of my friend.'

'Be silent, Gunnar,' she said, 'and let me speak, for I have much to tell you, and there is but little time. I lied to you, Gunnar, for Sigurd was guiltless of all wrong. Believe this, for I would not have you remember him as one who wished your death. That he loved me before ever you did, is true enough, but this is how it happened.' And, unfaltering, she told Gunnar of Sigurd's first ride through the flames, of Grimhild's magic potion and of the forgetfulness it brought.

RIDELL-MONROE

'But he was ever your true friend, Gunnar, and never did he wish that you should die.' She paused, and then went on, 'In a very little time, like Sigurd, I too shall be dead. Because of me he did not have a warrior's death, and so will the gates of Valhall always be shut to him. But I shall be treading close upon his heels on the long road down to the house of Hel. Never have I asked you for a favour, Gunnar, yet I ask one of you now. Lay me upon the bale-fire with Sigurd, for he rode through the flames to win me, and he was my husband, before ever I met you.' Her voice fell to a whisper. 'Farewell, Gunnar, I am leaving you now, for I would not that the doors of the house of Hel should shut behind Sigurd, leaving me outside.' And her proud head dropped to one side on the pillows, and she was dead.

When the pyre was built, it was spread with woven cloths, and gold and jewels and all manner of arms were laid on it, and on the top of all, a bearskin. Then Sigurd's body was carried from the house, and Gudrun herself went to the stables and led Grani forth in a last farewell to his master. She spoke to him as though he were a man, telling him that Sigurd was dead; and as though he had been a man, the grey horse understood, and bent to the ground and died, as if his heart were broken. For no other man might be the master of Sigurd's horse which had been chosen for Sigurd by Odin himself.

Sigurd's body was laid upon the bearskin, with Gram close by; and in her richest gown and decked with gems, her red-gold hair unbound, they set beside him Brynhild, his first and only true love. Grani also they laid upon the pyre, and the body of young Gotthorm, who had died avenging an imagined wrong. Together Gunnar and Hogni fired the pile, and so in the flames of the bale-fire ended Sigurd the Volsung and Brynhild who had been a Valkyr.

14

From that time onward, there was but little joy in Gunnar's house, with Gunnar ever grieving for the loss of Brynhild and for the slaying of his friend; and Gudrun silent and unforgiving, ever a reminder to her brothers of the sorrow that had been. Gunnar's harp and voice were heard no longer in his hall, and even the marriage of Hogni brought little rejoicing, though Kostbera, his bride, was comely, and skilled above all women in the reading and writing of runes.

When Sigurd had been dead three years and more, King Atli of Hunland, who was rich and powerful, but ever greedy of gold, thought how Gudrun would be the mistress of Sigurd's treasure that he had won from Fafnir, and how she would be likely to take it as a dowry to any husband that she wed. And he smiled, thinking of all the wealth that might be his if he took Gudrun as his wife. So he sent to the Giukungs, asking for her hand; and Grimhild was glad, saying, 'She has mourned long enough for Sigurd. Great shame it is that a fair young woman should be without a husband.'

But Gunnar said, 'Much sorrow has Gudrun had from me already. If this marriage is not pleasing to her, it shall not be.'

And when Gudrun was told of the matter, she said, 'One who has been the wife of Sigurd could never want another lord.'

Yet Grimhild sought to persuade her to the marriage, holding out to her great hopes of power and wealth in the country of King Atli. 'For he is a rich and mighty king, and also, he is no longer young and there is no man to help him rule his land, so, as his queen, much power would be yours.'

But Gudrun only answered, 'If I wed with King Atli, it will be not for power or wealth, for they mean naught to me, but only that I may leave this house where I have seen too much sorrow, and that I may be spared the sight of my brothers which ever reminds me of the ill they did.'

And at the last, half willingly and half unwillingly, Gudrun agreed to marry Atli. With an escort of horsemen and all her women, and with carved, four-wheeled wooden wagons piled high with rich stuffs and jewels, Gudrun was sent into Hunland. But the treasure that Sigurd had won from Fafnir she left in Gunnar's house, though Gunnar would have given it to her. 'If it were Sigurd's self,' she said, 'no man on earth should part me from him. But what is Sigurd's treasure without Sigurd? I have no use for gold.' So Atli of Hunland had his bride, but without the gold he coveted; and the thought of Sigurd's treasure grew bitter in his heart, and he desired it more each time that it came into his mind.

Now, Atli was crafty and cunning, and he was an old man who had had many years in which to practise guile, so it was not long before he had thought of a means by which he might possess the gold. He said one day to Gudrun, 'I am ageing, and there is no man of my kin to help me rule my land. I would that your two brothers might come and govern all things for me, for my nobles have grown too powerful and out of hand.' But Gudrun did not answer him, for she had no wish to see Hogni and Gunnar again.

Atli sent for Vingi, who was his trusted man, and for long the two of them sat together, laying their plans. 'If I can but get the Giukungs into my power,' said Atli, 'here, far from their own land, when they see death before their eyes, they will willingly pay me all Sigurd's gold as a ransom for their lives.'

But in the time that she had been wedded to him, Gudrun had learnt much of Atli's guile, and she marked how he and Vingi spoke apart with many smiles, and how Atli rubbed

his thin hands together and pursed his lips, as though he had
some secret which pleased him well, and she guessed that it
meant no good to her brothers. 'It would be no more than
they deserve,' she thought, 'for they slew my Sigurd, and
that will I never forgive. Yet they are my brothers, and I
cannot stand by and see them come to harm. Besides, King
Atli has grown hateful to me, and I would not see him
triumph over the Giukungs.'

So Gudrun took a slip of wood and on it she wrote runes,
warning Gunnar and Hogni against coming into Atli's land;
and she took a ring from her finger and around it she wound
the hair of a wolf. Then the wood and the ring she wrapped
in a cloth, and learning that Vingi was to be her husband's
messenger, she gave them into his hands, bidding him bear
her brothers her greeting and a gift from her. And this Vingi
promised to do. But before he and his men reached the Giukungs' land, Vingi unwrapped the cloth and read the runes
that were graven on the slip of wood. And when he had read
them, he smiled. Then he took his knife and altered the runes
skilfully, so that it appeared that Gudrun was bidding her
brothers come to her. Then he wrapped the wood and the
ring once again in the cloth, and went on his way.

Vingi and his men were welcomed with kindness in Gunnar's house, and a feast was prepared for them with much ale
and roasted meats; and Vingi gave to Gunnar and Hogni his
master's message. 'Good King Atli bids me tell you,' he said,
'that he is grown old and has no man of his kin to help him
rule his land. And he would that you were willing to come
for a time into his kingdom to govern it for him. He would
count it as the highest favour, and promises much gold and
horses and goodly apparel to both of you.'

'I have gold in plenty, and horses and goodly apparel,' said
Gunnar, 'and I am loath to leave my own land, even to help

King Atli. No, Vingi, I must refuse your master, though with all courtesy.'

'He will indeed be grieved,' said Vingi smoothly. 'So too will his lovely queen, your noble sister, who gave me gifts to bear to you, with her greeting.' And he held out to Gunnar the ring and the slip of wood.

Gunnar unwrapped the cloth and saw the ring and read the runes, and smiled. 'See, Hogni,' he said joyfully, 'how our sister bids us come to her. She has forgiven us at last, it seems.'

'Never will I believe that Gudrun has forgiven us, until she tells me so herself,' said Hogni. And he looked closely at the runes, but could find no fault with them.

'Willingly,' said Gunnar, 'would I go even into Atli's kingdom for a smile from Gudrun.' He turned to Vingi. 'I will go with you to Hunland,' he said, 'and may much good come of it both to King Atli and to me.'

'Much good, I know, will come of it,' answered Vingi, smiling.

But Hogni laid his hand on Gunnar's arm and spoke secretly, 'See here, my brother, where Gudrun has tied a wolf's hair around the ring she sent us. What think you that it means unless that Atli is disposed to us even as a savage wolf?'

Gunnar stared long at the ring before he spoke, but all he said was, 'I have given my word, Hogni, to go into Atli's land, I cannot break it now.'

'And though I like it not, Gunnar, I will go with you, whatever may befall,' promised Hogni.

The feasting continued late into the night; but when at last the hosts and guests alike were sleeping, Kostbera, Hogni's wife, took the slip of wood upon which the lying runes were graven, and crouching low over the fire, she set all her skill to read them truly; and little by little, she read at last Gudrun's warning to her brothers. Then silently and thoughtfully, she went to bed.

In the morning, when Hogni awoke, Kostbera said to him, 'While you slept last night I read the runes which Gudrun sent, and I think she did not mean that you should go to Atli's land. Beneath the runes of welcome, there are other runes of warning, and it were best you heeded those.'

And though in his heart he agreed with her, because Gunnar had given his word which might not be broken, Hogni said, 'I doubt that, in spite of all your skill, you have read the runes aright, for surely they mean what Gunnar and I have read them to mean.'

'In the night,' said Kostbera, 'I lay long awake, troubling my mind over this journey, but when at last I slept, I dreamt an evil dream. In my sleep I saw how your cloak caught fire, Hogni, and from the flames spread a great burning over all the house, so that it was utterly destroyed. Surely that is an omen not to be ignored?'

But Hogni made light of it. 'See, here is my new cloak that you have dyed for me yourself with bright and flaming dyes. I shall be wearing it upon the journey and its colours will show forth bravely. That is all your dream signifies.'

'I trust not this Atli, my husband. Do not go into his land.'

And though Hogni thought likewise, he answered her, 'You women are ever the same, always ready to mistrust and to suspect where a man sees only friendship. Gunnar has given his word, so we both go to Hunland, whatever befall.'

But Hogni went to Gunnar and told him of how Kostbera had read the runes, and because they both trusted her skill in such matters, they much doubted Atli's friendship to them.

'Yet why should he wish us ill?' asked Gunnar.

'Perhaps it is for Sigurd's gold which Gudrun did not take with her,' replied Hogni. 'Men have envied us for that, and it is said that Atli is ever greedy for gold.'

'It may be for Sigurd's gold,' said Gunnar, 'or it may be for another cause which we cannot guess. But if it is the gold, Hogni, whatever may become of us, it shall not fall into Atli's hands. Let us rather carry it to the river, my brother, and cast it in. Better that the waters of the Rhine should have Sigurd's gold, than that the king of Hunland should count it over and gloat upon it.'

So secretly, unknown to any other, Gunnar and Hogni rode down to the river, carrying each one of the great chests in which Fafnir had kept his hoard. And into the deep waters of the Rhine they cast them, so that never man saw again the disaster-bringing treasure upon which Andvari had laid his curse.

When the day came, Gunnar and Hogni and their men who were to go with them made ready to leave their home and travel with Vingi into Hunland. 'Bring your harp with you, Gunnar,' said Hogni, 'that we may have merry music on the way, for it may be the last journey we shall make.' So Gunnar fetched his harp, that had been silent for so long, and slung it across his shoulder.

Weeping, Kostbera clung to Hogni, and as he bade her farewell and put her gently from him, he thought how he was likely never to see her again. 'Be happy,' he said, 'whatever may come.'

'They will be home again,' said Vingi. 'It is not for ever that they will be gone.' But Kostbera could not believe this. 'It is the truth,' swore Vingi. 'May I perish if I lie.'

Yet it was with many tears that those who remained in Gunnar's house saw the Giukungs ride forth.

On the journey Gunnar sang and played his harp, and found comfort in it, so that as they neared the house of Atli his spirits had a little revived, and he thought it even possible that Atli meant no treachery; and he was glad at the thought of seeing Gudrun once again. But Hogni kept a watchful eye ever about him, lest at any time they should be taken unawares.

As they rode towards the house of Atli, armed men came running out to meet them; and as they rode through the high open gates, they saw how the courtyard was astir with warriors crowding about the house door.

'What means this?' asked Hogni, his hand tightening on his battle-axe.

Vingi laughed. 'It means,' he answered, 'that you have walked into the trap. There is nothing left now for you but to die.'

'Then shall you die first,' cried Hogni, and he swung his axe high and felled Vingi to the ground.

Then the Giukungs drew up their men at the gates and saw that they were outnumbered easily by the king's men who stood before the house. 'Well would it have been had we heeded Kostbera's warning,' said Hogni. 'But since we are here, and the trap is sprung, there is no help for it.'

King Atli came forth from his house and called out, 'You have slain my good friend Vingi, King Gunnar, but for all that shall you be welcome here if you have brought with you the gold that was Sigurd's and now is the portion of Gudrun.'

'We have brought no gold with us,' said Gunnar, 'and if we had, it would not be for you. But we have brought swords and spears with us, and our goodly shields. And I think that you will not find gifts wanting, King Atli, when our arrows begin to fly, for there will be one apiece for you and all your men.' And he turned to speak cheering words to those few who had come with him from his land, bidding them fight bravely and not count the cost. 'If Sigurd were beside us now,' he said to Hogni, 'we should have less reason to fear the outcome of this day.'

Word was brought to Gudrun in her bower that the Giukungs were come to Atli's house, and she said to herself, 'Fools that they were not to heed my warning. But why should I sorrow for those who killed my Sigurd? Let them now taste treachery, even such treachery as they dealt to him.' And she went on with her spinning.

But she had found no happiness in Atli's house, and the longing was on her to look again upon the brothers whom she had once loved, so she laid aside her distaff and went to the doorway of the house. And when she saw how many were the men of Atli, and how few were her own fellow countrymen, drawn up bravely at the gates, she knew that there was no hope, and that Gunnar and Hogni and all their warriors would be dead before the day was over. She went to King Atli and asked him, 'Is your mind set upon this thing, my lord? Is there no other way by which you may be appeased? Must my brothers fight and die?'

And Atli answered her, 'Unless I have Sigurd's gold, I will have their blood.'

'Then give me but leave to speak once more with my brothers, before the battle begins.'

Atli laughed. 'Go, bid them farewell, my Gudrun, for you will not speak with them again.'

She walked across the courtyard to them, and when Gunnar and Hogni took her in their arms and kissed her, as though there had been no quarrel between them, her determination to greet them with the coldness which she had felt for them since Sigurd's death, broke and was gone, and with tears she clung to them. 'Why did you come, my brothers? I bade you keep away.'

'We were tricked from the first,' said Gunnar, 'and we fell into the trap.'

'Small joy have I had of Atli, since I came into his house,' said Gudrun bitterly. 'But now that he has done this thing, small joy shall he have of me.'

'Have you forgiven us, Gudrun? We shall fight the better for knowing,' asked Hogni.

And though her love for Sigurd was no less than it had ever been, in that last moment Gudrun knew she had forgiven them. 'I have forgiven you,' she said.

Atli called to her across the courtyard, 'Gudrun, make haste.'

'You had best go,' said Gunnar. 'In a moment the arrows will start to fly, and a battleground is no place for a woman.'

She kissed them for the last time, and though the tears were streaming down her cheeks and her voice shook, her words were firm and angry. 'Remember,' she said, 'if you are slain today, Atli shall die for it. I promise that to you.' Then she tore herself away from them and went back to where Atli, with a sneer on his thin lips, waited to raise his red shield and give the signal for the battle to begin.

The battle was fierce, but it did not last long; and though Gunnar's men fought as they had never fought before, by midday they were all slain; though their numbers were exceeded by far by the numbers of Atli's dead. But now there remained only Gunnar and Hogni, who fought back to back against an ever-increasing horde, until at last they were cast down, disarmed, and taken captive before the king. And he ordered them to be laid in fetters in separate places, Hogni in the courtyard, and Gunnar in his hall.

And when this was done, he went to Gunnar and said, 'If you will tell me where you have hidden Sigurd's treasure, I will give you your life.'

Gunnar looked into Atli's cruel eyes and looked away again, and he thought for a while. 'When he learns the truth,' he said to himself, 'he will be angered, and likely enough he will cause us to die in torments, Hogni and I. And I would not that Hogni should suffer more than he has suffered already, whatever happens to me. In any case, he is like to die, sooner or later. What difference can it make, so long as the death is quick?' And he looked again at Atli and said, 'Bring me the heart of my brother Hogni, and I will tell you what you want to know.'

But Atli was crafty and cunning, and he spoke apart with his men, bidding them kill a thrall named Hialli, who kept the king's pigs, and cut out his heart.

The men went with drawn swords to the courtyard where Hogni lay in chains, but when Hialli saw them approaching, he guessed what they had come to do, and he ran screaming from them. Hearing the cries, Hogni looked up and asked what was amiss, and one of the men laughed and told him.

'If he loves his life, then give it to him,' said Hogni. 'And by all means cut out my heart, if only to spare me his screams.'

Yet they did as Atli had ordered and cut out Hialli's heart; and Atli took it to Gunnar and said, 'Here is your brother's heart.'

But Gunnar looked at it and said, 'That is not the heart of Hogni, for it flutters and trembles in death, even as it must have fluttered and trembled in life, and the heart of Hogni is steadfast and brave.'

Angry that his trick had failed, Atli sent his men to kill Hogni and to cut out his heart. They went to the courtyard, and when Hogni saw them coming, their sharp swords in their hands, he mocked them, saying, 'So in the end, it was my heart that you needed. Fools, did you think that the heart of a thrall would suffice?' And he laughed as he died, so that his courage was long spoken of by Atli's men.

When Gunnar saw Hogni's heart, he said, 'That indeed is the brave heart of Hogni, for it faints not nor trembles in death, but is steadfast even as it was while he lived. Now, Atli, will I tell you what you wish to know, for only on me can your anger fall, now that Hogni is dead. Sigurd's gold shall never be for you nor for any man, since it lies deep in the Rhine, whence no man shall raise it up.'

Then, in his rage, Atli had Gunnar cast, with bound wrists, into a pit of snakes, there to lie until they killed him. When Gudrun saw what was done, she covered her face with her hands and cried aloud in her anguish; until suddenly there came into her mind the words spoken by Sigurd long before, 'I think that Gunnar's harp and voice would charm even the beasts of the forest, and lull to sleep the snakes that dwell among the rocks.' And she ran to find Gunnar's harp, where it lay fallen in the courtyard, and she flung it down to him in the pit.

But since his hands were bound, Gunnar might only play the harp with his feet; yet such was his art, and so skilfully did he strike the strings with his toes, that all who heard him marvelled, reckoning no other man to have played better even with his hands. And so Gunnar played his harp and sang his last songs, and lulled the snakes to sleep, even as Sigurd had said; all save one viper that was larger and more venomous than the rest, and that viper crawled ever closer, until at last it bit him, so that he died.

And Atli in his hall drank deeply and taunted Gudrun. 'Your brothers are dead, and it is I who have killed them. What think you of that?'

And Gudrun remembered her promise to Gunnar and Hogni, that if they were slain, Atli should die for the deed, and she fought back her tears and held her head high and answered him, 'Why should I grieve for my brothers, for was it not they who killed by treachery my first husband, even brave Sigurd?'

Then Gudrun sought to rival Atli's cunning with her own, meeting craft with craft. She spoke lovingly to him and poured out ale that he might drink; and he trusted her and was beguiled.

And that night, when Atli lay asleep, Gudrun rose from the bed and fetched his sword. She raised it in both her hands, and it seemed heavy to her, for it had been wrought for a man's wielding. Three times she raised it, and three times she lowered it again, for she could not bring herself to do the deed. She sought to strengthen her purpose by thinking, 'There is no one left but I to avenge the Giukungs. It must be I, for there is no one else.' But it was all to no avail, and her tender heart shrank from killing even Atli, whom she hated. Then she taunted her own weakness, thinking, 'Were I Brynhild, I would not hesitate. There was a woman to do such a deed. Come, shall Gudrun be weaker than Brynhild?' And she raised the sword again and plunged it into Atli's breast.

And Atli awoke with the pain of his wound and saw Gudrun standing there, pale and fearful. 'Who has done this thing?' he asked.

'It was I who did it,' she answered. 'Even as I had sworn to do.'

'Ill was this marriage of ours,' said Atli. 'Ill was it while it lasted, and ill is its ending. But I have been a mighty king, Gudrun. Give me a fitting bale-fire.'

'I will give you a fitting bale-fire, Atli, no other king shall ever have the like.'

'May never another man have such a wife as you,' said Atli, and so he died.

And Gudrun laid his body straight upon the bed, and placed his jewels and his weapons around him. Then she put straw and kindling all about the room, and set light to it, so that the whole house was burnt. Such was Atli's bale-fire, and no other king had ever the like.

Then Gudrun fled away down to the seashore, as dawn came and the sun rose over the water. And she thought, 'My brothers are dead and their deaths are avenged, and my Sigurd died long ago. Now have I nothing left to live for.' And she flung off her cloak and waded into the sea and set to swimming. And she swam ever onwards, away from the shore; praying that Ran, cruel goddess of the oceans, might take her in her dread net.

IV

The Two Wives of Ragnar Lodbrok

I

THERE was in the northlands a rich and mighty jarl, a chieftain who ruled over much land and many men. His name was Herraud and he had one daughter whom he loved above all else. She was called Thora and she surpassed every other maiden in beauty and in all pleasant accomplishments. Her father built for her a fair bower beside his house, and here she would pass her days in happiness and content.

Each day Jarl Herraud would send a gift to Thora for her pleasure and entertainment. One day it might be a golden ring, another day a hound, and yet another day it would be a bright-dyed new kirtle; and all of his gifts she welcomed and prized. Once, while he was hunting, he found, hidden beneath a stone, a tiny dragon, green and scaly. He thought how it would be a pretty toy for his daughter, and one such as he had never given her before, so he took it home with him and sent it to Thora in her bower.

Thora had never seen such a thing as the little green dragon before and she was greatly pleased with the gift, calling it her pet and her plaything and finding it a cosy nest in the wooden chest where she kept the gold her father sent her.

But the little dragon grew quickly, and soon there was not room for it in the chest, so it climbed out and lay instead beside it. And in time it grew large enough to coil its length all around the chest of gold, and there it lay, with its head touching its tail, and its bright eyes watching. And Thora laughed to see it and clapped her hands in joy and said, 'How quickly my dragon is growing!'

But in time the dragon grew too long to coil around the chest, so it moved and lay against the walls of the room instead. And there it grew so fast, that almost before anyone had noticed, it was lying all around the room with its head touching its tail, so that it was difficult for anyone to pass in or out through the door.

Jarl Herraud considered it doubtfully. 'Are you sure,' he asked his daughter, 'that you still wish to keep your dragon?'

And Thora smiled happily and answered, 'If you will allow me, father, I will keep it if I may, for I am certain that no other maiden in all the world has a dragon in her bower.'

But one day the dragon had grown too long to lie around the room in comfort, so it slipped out through the door and lay instead against the outside wall of the bower. And there it grew so fast that, almost before anyone had noticed, it was lying all around the bower with its head touching its tail. And by now it had grown so large and so strong, that no one might leave or come into the bower, save with the dragon's permission. And before very long it would let no one by but the man who brought it its meat.

So then Jarl Herraud might not send his daughter a gift, nor go himself to see her, nor might she leave her bower to walk in the courtyard beyond. And soon there came a day when no one would go to Jarl Herraud's house for fear of his daughter's dragon.

The jarl was at his wits' end to know how he might free Thora, but with every day that he pondered, the dragon grew larger, until it was eating a whole ox at each meal, and the jarl's herds were greatly diminished.

At last Jarl Herraud swore an oath, before all his fellow jarls, bidding them make his oath known through all the country, that he would give his daughter in marriage, with much gold for her dowry, to the man, whoever he might be, who would kill the dragon and rescue her. But for a long time no one dared to try his luck, and the dragon grew larger each day, until Jarl Herraud was in despair.

Now, at that time there lived a young man named Ragnar who was a mighty fighter, and very brave, and when he heard of the dragon that lived by Thora's bower, he made up his mind to kill it. To this end he made himself a coat and breeches of shaggy fur, and these he boiled in pitch, so that when they were dry, they were so stiff and stout that no knife might cut them. When his companions saw him wearing his strange garments, they laughed at him and gave him the name of Lodbrok, Hairy-Breeks, but he paid no heed to their mirth and only sharpened his spear and loosened the nail which held the head to the shaft.

Then he set sail from his home and came to Jarl Herraud's land, and very early one morning, leaving his ship and his men in a sheltered bay, while it was yet dark, he set off for the jarl's house, arriving at the gates before anyone there had woken. He walked straight to the bower where the dragon was, and so silent and swift was he, that he had struck a blow at the monster before it was aware of him. It gnashed its teeth and blew its poisonous breath at him, but he was well protected by his stout clothing, and was unharmed. Again he struck at the dragon, a mighty stroke that reached the monster's heart; and because of the nail that he had taken from the shaft, the head of his spear broke loose and remained in the dragon's body.

The noise made by the dragon in the agony of its death was so great that all those who slept in Herraud's house were awakened and came running forth, but they were too late to see who had slain the monster. Yet Thora, peeping out of her bower, had caught sight of a handsome young man, tall, and clad in strange garments, and carrying a spear shaft, running away from her father's house; and she wondered greatly who he might be.

Jarl Herraud was much pleased that the dragon had been killed, but though he was ready, as he had promised, to give his daughter in marriage to the man who had done the deed, he had no way of telling who, of all men, it might be. Yet he had the spear-head that he had taken from the dragon's death-wound, and he sent out a call to every man near to come to a Thing, a gathering where chieftains and their warriors might discuss matters of note.

On the appointed day they came together, and Ragnar, whose ship was still drawn up in the bay, went ashore and walked to the Thing, where he stood a little apart from the rest.

Jarl Herraud stood up before all the men and told them of the slaying of the dragon. 'And now,' he said, 'there but remains for the man who did this mighty deed to claim his just reward. He left his spear-head in the dragon's wound, and I have it here, so if there is any man at this Thing who says that it was he who freed my daughter from the dragon, then let him show me the shaft of the spear.' And each man there handled the spear-head, but no one of them all had a shaft to fit it.

And when all present had tried, Ragnar stepped forward and begged that, though a stranger, he might be allowed to see the spear-head, and it was given to him; and immediately he fitted it on to the shaft he carried with him, so that it was plain to all that he had killed the dragon and his must be the reward.

With great rejoicing Ragnar Lodbrok married Thora, and took her home to his own land, and for many years they lived there in much happiness. But on a sad day, Thora fell sick and died, and so grieved was Ragnar that he left his lands for others to rule, and took to the sea, where he spent his days a-viking; and thus he won much booty for himself, and great fame for his mighty deeds.

2

Soon after the deaths of Sigurd and Brynhild, good Heimir, to whom Brynhild had given the fostering of her little daughter Aslaug, fell upon hard times and was forced to flee from his home in order that his life might be safe from his enemies. He took Aslaug with him, and as many of his jewels as he could carry, and he caused a harp to be made that was great enough for Aslaug and the jewels to be hidden in it. Carrying this harp, he journeyed from place to place, only opening it and bringing Aslaug out when he was far from the eyes of other men. She was a good and patient child, and bore well the discomfort of her life, carried all about the land within a harp; and whenever she grew fretful and wept, which was but rarely, old Heimir would play on the harp for her, and at once she would smile.

One day he came to a place named Spangar Heath, and here, in a little house, dwelt a peasant called Aki, with his wife Grima. Heimir knocked on the door of the house and Grima opened to him, her husband being out gathering wood in the forest. Heimir asked for shelter for the night, and the woman said he was welcome.

While they sat beside the fire together, the woman's prying eyes caught the gleam of a golden arm-ring beneath the rags he wore. And she was curious, also, over the harp, which seemed so great and fine a one for a tattered old beggar. 'You had best sleep outside in the shed where we store the barley, stranger,' she said, 'for my husband and I talk late at nights over all the happenings of the day, and we would not wish to disturb your rest.'

Heimir thanked her and took up the harp, and she led him out to the shed and left him there, with wishes for his good rest.

When Aki came home he was in an ill temper, for he had had a hard search and found but little firewood that had not needed much labour to cut; besides, owing to her curiosity about the stranger, his wife had done nothing but think since she had left Heimir to sleep in the shed.

'I wish I were a woman,' grumbled Aki, 'to sit all day in comfort by the fire with no work to do. Have I not had a hard enough time today, without coming home to no supper?'

'Do not be angry,' said Grima, 'for I think that in but a short time we shall own much riches.'

'How can that be?' asked her husband.

And Grima told him of the stranger, and of the gold ring she was sure she had seen beneath his rags. 'And he carries a harp,' she said, 'the like of which no man has ever seen before, so great and fine it is. I am certain that there are many jewels and much gold hidden inside that harp.'

'Of what profit is that to us?' said Aki.

The woman smiled. 'We may kill the old man and take the gold,' she said.

'Few enough men travel this way and ask us for shelter,' said Aki. 'It seems to me churlish to betray this man.'

But Grima poured scorn upon him for a coward and a fool; and though at first he protested, at the last he let her have her way, and taking the axe she put into his hands, he went out to the shed. There he found Heimir sleeping, with his harp beside him. In spite of his terror, Aki raised the axe and struck a great blow, and Heimir died at once. Then Grima came running out from the house to take up the harp and carry it indoors, that she might open it and see the treasure it held.

But when she opened it, she found inside, not only gold and jewels, but a little girl of some four years old. 'It would have been better had I never heeded your advice,' said Aki. 'Now shall we have a child to keep.'

They questioned Aslaug and asked her who she was, but never a word did she answer in reply, and it was even as though she were dumb.

So the two peasants kept her in their house and gave out that she was their daughter, and they called her Kraka, which had been Grima's mother's name. And because she was fair and beautiful and unlike her supposed parents, they hid her hair beneath a cloth and stained her skin with dark juices and gave her only rags to wear, and thus no one supposed that she was more than a peasant girl. The man and his wife spent the gold that had been hidden in the harp and bought themselves a fine herd of cattle, but never a piece of gold did they spare for the unhappy Aslaug.

And so the years passed, and when she was older, Aslaug was given all the hardest work to do while Grima idled her time away, and her only friend in the world was Aki's mongrel dog. And because she never answered them or spoke at all to them, Aki and Grima fancied that she could not speak; yet when she was alone, far from the house, she would talk to the dog.

One day, in the course of his roving, Ragnar Lodbrok touched land at the shore near Spangar Heath and sent his cook-lads ashore to bake bread. Seeing the little house near by, they said, 'Maybe the goodwife of that place will let us use her oven,' and they went and knocked on the door. Now, Aki was gathering wood and Aslaug had gone out with the cattle to the fields and only Grima was at home. She welcomed the men and bade them bake their bread in her oven. 'Were my hands not so old and stiff,' she said, 'I would help you in your baking. But I have a daughter, when she comes home she shall help you.' So Grima spoke, for she had grown lazy in all the years that she had done no work.

From the field where she watched the cattle, Aslaug saw Ragnar's great ship in the bay, and she saw the men come ashore and go to Aki's house. 'Perchance there will be one among them who might wish me for his wife,' she thought, 'and so might I escape for ever from this hated life of mine.' And she ran to a little stream and washed off, as she had been forbidden to do, all the dark juices with which her white skin had been stained. Then she took off the rags which hid her hair and let it down, and it was bright golden and reached even to her knees. There was little that she could do about her tattered kirtle or her bare feet, but when she looked at her reflection in the stream, she thought that she was fair enough.

Then she went back to the house and stood close to the

cook-lads and watched them kneading their bread. And they looked up at her and thought how beautiful she was, and they asked Grima, 'Is this lovely maiden your daughter?'

And Grima hid her anger at Aslaug's disobedience, smiled as well as she could for rage, and said, 'That is indeed Kraka, my daughter.'

'She has not her mother's looks,' laughed one of the men.

And Grima said quickly, with a toss of her head, 'When I was younger, I would have you know, I was not ill-favoured myself.'

And at that they all laughed. But Aslaug helped them, and set the loaves in the oven for them to watch. Yet they stared so much at her as she went about her other tasks in the house, that before they were aware of it, the bread had burnt; and because they had no more barley meal with them, they had to take the burnt loaves back to the ship.

Ragnar was angry at having to eat blackened bread, and he demanded from the cook-lads the reason why the loaves were spoilt, and they said to him, 'It is because in the kitchen of the house where we went to bake the bread, there was a young maiden more beautiful than any woman in the world, and watching her, we forgot to watch the loaves.'

'She could not have been more beautiful than my dear dead Thora was,' said Ragnar.

But they swore to him that never could there have been a lovelier maiden than she whom they had seen that day. By this time Ragnar was curious to see this maid of whom his men spoke, and he said, 'I will look at her, and if she is indeed as fair as you say, then shall you be forgiven for spoiling the bread. But if she is no fairer than any other maiden, then will your punishment be heavy indeed.' And he sent others of his men to bid her come to him on his ship. 'And to test whether she is as clever as she is beautiful, bid her come to me neither naked nor clad, neither fasting nor having eaten, and not alone, yet unaccompanied by any man,' he said.

The men went to the house and gave their message, and Aslaug thought much on the terms of her meeting with Ragnar.

'There is no way that you may be naked and yet clad, fasting and yet fed, alone and yet accompanied,' said Grima. 'Truly, that Ragnar is out of his mind.'

But Aslaug only thought the harder. 'Tell your leader,' she said, 'that I will come to him in the morning.' And Aki and Grima were astonished to hear her speak.

In the morning Aslaug arose, and pulling up a leek from the garden, she bit into it, but swallowed no morsel of it. 'So shall I be not fasting nor yet shall I have eaten,' she thought. Then she took off her rags and wrapped herself in one of Aki's fishing nets and shook out her golden hair like a cloak around her. 'So I shall be neither naked nor clad,' she said to herself. Then calling the old mongrel dog to come with her, thinking, 'So shall I be neither alone nor accompanied by any man,' she left the house and walked down to the shore, and the men took her on board the ship and brought her before Ragnar.

He laughed mightily when he saw how cleverly she had obeyed his commands, and was no less moved by her beauty than by her wit. 'I thought,' he said, 'that when my dear wife Thora died, no other woman could ever win my heart. But then I had not dreamt that in the world there lived such a one as you. I cannot believe that you are the child of two peasants.'

So Aslaug told him how she was the daughter of Sigurd and Brynhild, and how the peasants had slain good Heimir and treated her harshly since childhood on, and Ragnar marvelled at it all. Then he said, 'When my Thora died, I never guessed that the thought of a marriage with any other woman could be anything but hateful to me. Yet if you will be my wife, I think that I could be happy once again, as I was before she died.'

And Aslaug laid her hand in his and said, 'I will marry you, good Ragnar.'

And so they were married, and very happy they were together for many years.

V

The Tale of Nornagest

THE Norsemen believed that at the birth of a child who
was to become a man of note, the three Norns who lived
beside the spring which flowed by that root of the ash-tree
Yggdrasill which was in Asgard, would come down to Midgard, the earth, to give him their blessing. The three Norns
were Urd the ancient, who was the past; Verdandi the fear-
less, who was the present; and Skuld the veiled, who was the
future; and they dwelt beside the fountain called Urd where
swam the two holy swans from which are descended all the
swans that have ever lived on earth.

One day, in the northlands, a son was born to a nobleman
and his young wife. It was their first child, so the rejoicing
in their house was great. Many guests from far and near were

bidden to a feast; much ale was brewed for them, and much good meat roasted for their enjoyment.

But three unbidden guests set out from Asgard to take part in the feasting, Urd, Verdandi, and Skuld. When they reached the house they found it filled with a great crowd of people, and more arriving in the courtyard every moment; so that no one paid any attention to the three women or guessed whom they might be.

They went at once to where the young mother sat by the fire, holding her babe in her arms and answering the questions of the admiring friends who stood around. And when she looked up and saw them there, she alone, of all those in the room, knew them for the Norns, and she was filled with pride that it was her son who should have been honoured by their visit.

Urd, the wrinkled old crone, thrust her way through the crowd, and laying her gnarled hand upon the child's head, she smiled and said, 'This child shall be as handsome as any man could wish to be, and as brave as any warrior could desire.'

Then bright-eyed Verdandi, with head held high, advanced, and touching the babe's tiny hands and laying one of her fingers upon his lips, she said, 'This child shall be a great skald, a poet whose singing and harping all men shall admire and respect.'

It should then have been the turn of Skuld to step forward with her blessing, but when she came to do so, she found herself roughly pushed aside by a too eager late-comer who had not yet seen the child, and who came hurrying with her congratulations. Angered, Skuld frowned behind her veil, and going to a pillar on which a taper burnt in a socket to give light to the room, she snatched up the taper, and holding it above her head, she cried out in a terrible voice, 'The child shall live only so long as this taper is unburnt. I, Skuld, have spoken.' Then she dropped the taper back into the socket and was gone.

A great fear came upon the mother, for the taper was more than half burnt and would not last but an hour, or barely an hour, and she clasped her child to her breast and wept. But old Urd stepped forward, and taking up the taper, blew it out and gave it to the young woman saying, 'I may not alter what my sister has decreed, for she is the future and I am the past. Yet there is no need for the taper to burn. Keep it carefully and never light it again, and your son shall live so long as it lasts.' Then she and Verdandi also vanished.

The little boy was called Nornagest, in honour of the three Norns, and so long as he was a child, his mother kept the taper safe. But as soon as he had reached an age at which he might be told the truth, she gave the taper into his keeping, telling him of the prophecy of Skuld, and the comforting words of Urd, and bidding him ever take care of the taper, for it was his life.

As Verdandi had promised, Nornagest became a great skald, and his playing on the harp and his singing were unequalled in the world. He travelled from land to land, and from house to house, singing his songs and making sweet music wherever he went; and his precious taper he kept carefully hidden in the frame of his harp. And because he never lighted it, he lived on and on, until he had lived in one place or another for 300 years, and still he appeared young and was gifted.

In all the 300 years of his life and travels, Nornagest had seen great changes come to the northlands, and the greatest of them was the new faith that was spreading from the south and causing the Norsemen to forget Odin and the old gods.

It happened in the reign of King Olaf Tryggvason that

Nornagest came to his court in Norway, and there he sang and played for the king the stories of the old heroes, many of whom he had known. He told of Sigurd who had slain the dragon, and of the grief of Gudrun, and of Gunnar's brave death in the snake pit; and his singing and playing were applauded by all.

Now, King Olaf was a follower of the new faith, and worshipped the White Christ, as he was called by the Norsemen; and in the short time since Olaf had become king in Norway, he had sought to turn all men to his way of belief. But he was a follower of the White Christ only in name, for he was cruel and merciless, and all who would not be baptized he put to death; so that by burnings and torments, and by the sword, he had converted the greater part of Norway.

In the silence that followed Nornagest's singing, King Olaf asked him if he were a Christian. 'I hold to the old gods, even as I have ever done,' replied Nornagest quietly.

And after that King Olaf could not rest until the famed and beloved singer was converted, and at last with threats he forced him to accept baptism. And then, since everyone had heard the story of Nornagest's taper, King Olaf thought how it would be a fine thing for his faith, and prove its power over the old gods, if he made Nornagest set light to his taper and let it burn out, and still go on living afterwards.

So although Nornagest was unwilling, King Olaf called together a great crowd of people, and there, before that vast gathering in the house of the king, Nornagest had to light his taper. It burnt lower and lower as all eyes watched it, while King Olaf sat smiling and Nornagest stood holding his harp close in his arms. An hour passed, or barely an hour, and the taper flickered and went out; and a great sigh, like the wind, rippled through the people there.

'See,' said King Olaf with triumph, 'the taper has burnt

out, and you are yet alive.' And he turned to Nornagest, and saw him sink slowly to the ground, dying. And a low cry rose up from all the people; while King Olaf sat silent and pale, staring at the dead man.

And that is the tale of Nornagest, as it was told by those who were still true to Odin and the old gods. But those who followed the White Christ told it differently.

An Alphabetical List of Names Mentioned in the Stories

AEGIR: the god of the deep ocean.

AESIR: the gods who cared for mankind.

AGNAR: brother of Geirröd; protected by Frigg.

AGNAR: a young warrior to whom Brynhild gave victory, thus angering Odin.

AKI: a peasant; Aslaug's foster-father.

ALF: son of King Hialprek of Denmark; second husband of Hiordis, Sigurd's mother.

ALFHEIM: the home of the light elves, between earth and sky.

ALLFATHER: Odin, the king of the gods.

ANDVARANAUT: Andvari's arm-ring which Sigurd gave to Brynhild.

ANDVARI: a dwarf, forced by Loki to give up his gold.

ANGRBODA: Loki's giant-wife.

ASGARD: the home of the gods.

ASK: the first man.

ASLAUG: daughter of Sigurd and Brynhild.

ATLI: king of Hunland; Gudrun's second husband.

AUDUMLA: the cow whose milk was drunk by the giant Ymir, in the very beginning of things.

BALDER: the sun-god, son of Odin and Frigg.

BARREY: the forest where Gerd met Frey.

BAUGI: a giant, son of Gilling and brother of Suttung.

BERGELMIR: a giant; with his wife he was the only survivor when the other giants were drowned in Ymir's blood.

BESTLA: a giant-woman, Odin's mother.

BIFROST: the rainbow bridge between Asgard and Midgard.

BLODUGHOFI: Frey's horse.

BODVILD: daughter of King Nidud.

BOLVERK: the name taken by Odin when he worked for the giant Baugi.

BORGHILD: Sigmund's first wife.

BORR: Odin's father.

BRAGI: the god of poetry, son of Odin and Gunnlod.

BRANSTOKK: the great tree around which Volsung built his house.

BRISINGA-MEN: Freyia's necklace.

BROKK: a dwarf who made a wager with Loki on the skill of his brother Sindri.

BRUNNAK: the home of Idunn and Bragi.

BRYNHILD: a one-time Valkyr, beloved by Sigurd.

BURI: the first god.

DRAUPNIR: Odin's arm-ring, made by the dwarf Sindri.

DROMI: the second fetter with which the gods bound Fenris-Wolf.

EGILL: brother of Völund.
EIR: the goddess of healing.
ELDIR: Aegir's serving-man.
ELLI: old age, the lord of Utgard's nurse.
EMBLA: the first woman.
EYLIMI: father of Hiordis.

FAFNIR: the dragon killed by Sigurd; son of Hreidmar and brother of Otter and Reginn.
FENRIS-WOLF: a huge wolf, son of Loki and Angrboda.
FENSALIR: Frigg's palace in Asgard.
FIALAR: a dwarf; together with Galar he killed Kvasir.
FIOLSVID: a giant, guardian of Menglod's house.
FOLKVANGAR: the place where Sessrumnir, Freyia's palace, stood.
FREY: the god of nature who ruled over the light elves; son of Niord.
FREYIA: the goddess of love and beauty; daughter of Niord.
FRIGG: the chief of the goddesses; Odin's queen.
FULLA: Frigg's handmaiden.

GALAR: a dwarf; together with Fialar he killed Kvasir.
GARM: the hound of Hel, the queen of the dead.
GAUTLAND: a province in Sweden, ruled by the Volsungs.
GEIRRÖD: brother of Agnar; protected by Odin.
GERD: a giant-maiden, beloved by Frey.
GILLING: a giant, father of Suttung and Baugi.
GINNUNGAGAP: the vast chasm in the beginning of things.
GIOLL: the bridge into Niflheim.
GIUKI: a king who ruled a land south of the Rhine; father of the Giukungs.
GIUKUNGS: the children of Giuki: Gunnar, Hogni, Gotthorm, and Gudrun.
GLEIPNIR: the chain forged by the dwarfs with which Fenris-Wolf was bound.
GNA: Frigg's messenger.
GNITA HEATH: the moor where Fafnir the dragon lived.
GOTHS: the people ruled by King Siggeir.
GOTI: Gunnar's horse.
GOTTHORM: younger brother of Gunnar, Hogni, and Gudrun; slayer of Sigurd.
GRAM: Sigurd's sword.
GRANI: Sigurd's horse.
GRIMA: a peasant-woman; Aslaug's foster-mother.
GRIMHILD: wife of King Giuki; mother of Gunnar, Hogni, Gotthorm, and Gudrun.
GRIMNIR: the name taken by Odin when he went to King Geirröd's house.
GROA: wife of King Solbiart; mother of Svipdag.
GUDRUN: Sigurd's wife; sister of Gunnar, Hogni, and Gotthorm.
GULLFAXI: the horse of the giant Hrungnir.
GULLINBURSTI: Frey's golden boar.

GUNGNIR: Odin's spear.

GUNNAR: eldest son of King Giuki; brother of Hogni, Gotthorm, and Gudrun.

GUNNLOD: daughter of the giant Suttung; mother of Bragi.

GYMIR: a giant, father of Gerd.

HATI: the wolf who pursued the moon.

HEIDRUN: the goat who gave mead for the gods to drink.

HEIMDALL: the watchman of the gods.

HEIMIR: Aslaug's first foster-father, killed by Aki and Grima.

HEL: the queen of the dead; daughter of Loki and Angrboda.

HERMOD: the messenger of the gods.

HERRAUD: a chieftain; father of Thora, Ragnar Lodbrok's first wife.

HERVOR: a Valkyr, wife of Völund.

HIALLI: King Atli's swineherd.

HIALMGUNNAR: a favourite warrior of Odin, slain in battle by Brynhild.

HIALPREK: king of Denmark; father of Alf.

HINDA-FELL: the hill where Brynhild slept, surrounded by a ring of flame.

HIORDIS: second wife of Sigmund; mother of Sigurd.

HLADGUD: a Valkyr, wife of Slagfid.

HLIDSKIALF: Odin's throne and watch-tower in Asgard.

HLIN: a goddess who served Frigg.

HÖD: the blind god of darkness; son of Odin and Frigg; twin brother and slayer of Balder.

HOFVARPNIR: Gna's horse.

HOGNI: brother of Gunnar, Gotthorm, and Gudrun.

HÖNIR: the bright god; Odin's brother.

HRAUDUNG: a king, father of Geirröd and Agnar.

HREIDMAR: father of Fafnir, Otter, and Reginn.

HRINGHORNI: Balder's ship.

HRUNGNIR: the strongest of the giants; slain by Thor.

HUGI: thought, a youth in the lord of Utgard's house.

HUNDING: a king; father of Lyngvi, Sigmund's enemy.

HUNLAND: the land ruled by King Atli, Gudrun's second husband.

HVERGELMIR: the sacred spring that flowed in Niflheim by the root of Yggdrasill.

HYMIR: a giant, owner of a large brewing-cauldron.

HYRROKKIN: the giant-woman who launched Balder's funeral ship.

IDUNN: daughter of Ivaldi the dwarf; wife of Bragi.

IORMUNGAND: the Midgard-Serpent; child of Loki and Angrboda.

IOTUNHEIM: the home of the giant-people.

IVALDI: a dwarf, father of Idunn.

KOSTBERA: Hogni's wife.

KRAKA: the name given to Aslaug by Aki and Grima.

KVASIR: a wise man; killed by Fialar and Galar.

LAEDING: the first fetter with which the gods bound Fenris-Wolf.

LIF: the only woman to be saved alive at the end of all things.

LIFTHRASIR: the only man to be saved alive at the end of all things; from him and Lif a new race was to be born.

LOGI: wild-fire, a servant of the lord of Utgard.

LOKI: the god of fire.

LYFIABERG: the hill on which Menglod's house was built.

LYNGVI: son of King Hunding; Sigmund's enemy.

MAGNI: Thor's son.

MENGLOD: the maiden wooed by Svipdag.

MIDGARD: the world of men.

MIDGARD-SERPENT: Iormungand, monster-child of Loki and Angrboda.

MIMIR: the giant who guarded the spring that flowed in Midgard by the root of Yggdrasill.

MIOLLNIR: Thor's battle-hammer.

MODGUD: the maiden who guarded Gioll, the bridge into Niflheim.

MUSPELLHEIM: the land of flaming fire.

NANNA: a goddess, Balder's wife.

NIDUD: a king who took Völund prisoner.

NIFLHEIM: the land of mist where Hel ruled over the spirits of the dead.

NIORD: the king of the Vanir; god of the shore and shallow sea.

NOATUN: Niord's palace.

NORNAGEST: a skald who lived for 300 years.

NORNS: the three fates: Urd, Verdandi, and Skuld.

NORSEMEN: the people who came originally from the countries now called Scandinavia, and who later settled in many parts of Europe.

NORTHLANDS: in this book, the lands now called Norway and Sweden.

OD: a god, Freyia's husband.

ODIN: the Allfather, king of the gods.

OLAF TRYGGVASON: historical king of Norway; he lived from about A.D. 969 to 1000.

OLRUN: a Valkyr, wife of Egill.

OTTER: son of Hreidmar; brother of Fafnir and Reginn.

RAGNAR LODBROK: a favourite Norse hero of whom many tales are told.

RAN: the goddess of the deep sea; wife of Aegir.

REGINN: Sigurd's instructor; son of Hreidmar; brother of Fafnir and Otter.

RERIR: king of Gautland; father of Volsung.

RIND: the mother of Vali.

SAEHRIMNIR: a boar in Asgard; slain and eaten each day, it came to life again each night.

SAEVARSTAD: the island where Völund was imprisoned.

SESSRUMNIR: Freyia's palace.

SIF: a goddess; Thor's wife.

SIGGEIR: king of the Goths; husband of Signy.
SIGMUND: son of Volsung; father of Sigurd.
SIGNY: twin sister of Sigmund.
SIGURD: son of Sigmund and Hiordis.
SIGYN: a goddess, Loki's wife.
SINDRI: a dwarf, a skilled smith; brother of Brokk.
SINFIOTLI: son of Signy.
SINMORA: a giant-woman mentioned in the tale of Svipdag and Menglod.
SKADI: daughter of Thiazi the storm-giant; wife of Niord.
SKIDBLADNIR: Frey's ship which could be folded up and carried in a wallet.
SKIRNIR: Frey's servant and friend.
SKOLL: the wolf who pursued the sun.
SKRYMIR: the name taken by the giant lord of Utgard when he met Thor
and Loki on their travels.
SKULD: the future; one of the three Norns.
SLAGFID: Völund's brother.
SLEIPNIR: Odin's eight-legged horse.
SOLBIART: Svipdag's father.
SPANGAR HEATH: the place where Aki and Grima lived.
SURT: the giant from Muspellheim with the flaming sword.
SUTTUNG: a giant, father of Gunnlod.
SVADILFARI: the black stallion owned by the giant stone-mason who built
the gods' citadel.
SVARTALFHEIM: the home of the dwarfs below the earth.
SVIPDAG: Menglod's suitor.
SYN: Frigg's doorkeeper in Fensalir.

THIALFI: Thor's servant.
THIAZI: the storm-giant; father of Skadi.
THÖKK: a giant-woman who would not weep for Balder; thought to be
Loki in giant shape.
THOR: the god of thunder.
THORA: first wife of Ragnar Lodbrok.
THRUDGELMIR: a six-headed giant.
THRUDHEIM: Thor's home in Asgard.
THRYM: the king of the frost-giants who stole Thor's hammer.
THRYMHEIM: the home of Thiazi the storm-giant.
TYR: the god of war.

URD: the past; one of the three Norns.
URD: the spring, guarded by the Norns, that flowed in Asgard by the root
of Yggdrasill.
UTGARD: a fortress in Iotunheim.

VALHALL: the hall of the slain where the dead warriors feasted in Asgard.
VALI: son of Odin and Rind; he avenged Balder's death.
VALKYRS: Odin's warrior-maidens who carried the slain to Valhall.

VANIR: the gods of nature; Niord was their king.
VERDANDI: the present; one of the three Norns.
VIDAR: the silent god; Odin's son.
VINGI: King Atli's messenger.
VOLSUNG: king of Gautland; Rerir's son.
VOLSUNGS: the descendants of Volsung.
VÖLUND: a most skilful smith; Slagfid and Egill were his brothers.

YGGDRASILL: the great ash-tree of the universe.
YMIR: the first giant.

A Note on Pronunciation

No one is absolutely certain of the pronunciation of the Old Norse language, but the following rules give an approximate pronunciation which should be close enough to the original for the average reader.

VOWELS

a (short): as in 'hat'.
a (long): as in 'father'.
e (short): as in 'men'.
e (long): as *a* in 'fate'.
i (short): as in 'is'.
i (long): as in 'machine'.
o (short): as in 'on'.
o (long): as in 'old'.
ö: as *ö* or *oe* in German 'schön' and 'Goethe'; the nearest equivalent sound in English is *er* in 'her'.
u (short): as in 'put'.
u (long): as *oo* in 'droop'.
y (short): as *i* in 'is'.
y (long): as *i* in 'machine'.

As a very rough indication of the length of a vowel, it may be taken that vowels are short (marked ˘ in example) when they are followed by a doubled consonant (e.g. Gŭnnar) or two different consonants (e.g. Rĭnd); and long (marked ¯ in example) when followed by a single consonant (e.g. Vāli), although there are very many exceptions to this.

DIPHTHONGS

ae: as in Scots 'brae' or as *ay* in English 'day'.
ai: as *i* in 'fine'.
au: as *ou* in 'out'.
ei, ey: as *ey* in 'they'.

CONSONANTS

The consonants may be pronounced as in English, but the following points should be noted.

G is always hard as in 'get', never soft as in 'gem'. When G comes before N at the beginning of a word (e.g. Gnita Heath) both letters should be sounded.

H before another consonant at the beginning of a word (e.g. Hreidmar) may be simply indicated by an initial breathing.

Y is used as if it were a vowel. See the note above.